TIMOTHY DALTON

A Complete Guide to His Film, Television, Stage and Voice Work

MARGARIDA ARAYA

First published 2016

This edition first published 2020

All rights reserved. No part of this book may be reproduced or utilised in any form or by any means, electronic or mechanical, including photocopying, recording or by any information storage and retrieval system, without permission in writing from the author.

Every effort has been made to trace the copyright holders of material quoted in this book. If application is made in writing to the author, any omissions will be included in future editions.

Text copyright and cover photo © Margarida Araya, 2016

td.fishers@gmail.com

Illustrations © Pat Carbajal

http://patart-pat.blogspot.com.es/

ISBN-10: 1539171388

ISBN-13: 978-1539171386

"Don't ask me about my career – I've forgotten most of it."

Timothy Dalton

To all Timothy Dalton fans (and especially, the TD Fishers).

INDEX

INDEX	7
INTRODUCTION	9
FILMS	11
TV SERIES	99
THEATRE	155
VOICE ACTING	231
BIBLIOGRAPHY	253
ABOUT THE AUTHOR	261

INTRODUCTION

Timothy Leonard Dalton-Legget was born in Colwyn Bay, North Wales, on March 21, 1946. He is the son of an advertising executive and the grandson of well-known music hall performers. When Dalton was about four years old, his family moved to Northern England. He decided to be an actor after attending his first play, an Old Vic production of *Macbeth*. He found the experience earth-shaking and at sixteen, while in school in Belper, he joined the school's drama group. After graduation, Dalton joined the local community theatre group, The Belper Players, and from there he joined the National Youth Theatre. 1964 was the year of his professional debut, a small role at the Queen's Theatre in *Coriolanus*. He spent two years studying acting at RADA, and he was given his first professional lead in the National Youth Theatre's production, *Little Malcolm and His Struggle Against the Eunuchs*. In 1967, just before graduating from RADA, he decided to hone his skills in the professional theatre and accepted a contract offer from the Birmingham Repertory Theatre with whom he appeared in a succession of classical plays. Dalton debuted on television also in 1967, in a series called *Sat'day While Sunday*, while still appearing in Birmingham. After finishing his first film, *The Lion in Winter*, in 1968, he went back to the Birmingham stage.

What follows is an accurate attempt to compile Dalton's entire career in cinema, television, stage and voice acting.

FILMS

THE LION IN WINTER	13
CROMWELL	16
THE VOYEUR	17
WUTHERING HEIGHTS	19
MARY, QUEEN OF SCOTS	24
PERMISSION TO KILL	26
SEXTETTE	27
EL HOMBRE QUE SUPO AMAR (THE MAN WHO KNEW LOVE)	30
AGATHA	32
THE FLAME IS LOVE [TV]	33
FLASH GORDON	34
CHANEL SOLITAIRE	38
THE MASTER OF BALLANTRAE [TV]	40
FLORENCE NIGHTINGALE [TV]	41
THE DOCTOR AND THE DEVILS	42
THE LIVING DAYLIGHTS	44
HAWKS	53
BRENDA STARR	57
LICENCE TO KILL	59
THE KING'S WHORE	67
THE ROCKETEER	70
LARK COMMERCIAL [TV]	74
NAKED IN NEW YORK	74
SALT WATER MOOSE [TV]	75
THE BEAUTICIAN AND THE BEAST	76

THE INFORMANT [TV]	79
MADE MEN [TV]	82
PASSION'S WAY [TV]	83
TIME SHARE [TV]	84
POSSESSED [TV]	86
AMERICAN OUTLAWS	88
LOONEY TUNES: BACK IN ACTION	90
HOT FUZZ	92
THE TOURIST	95

THE LION IN WINTER

1968

Avco Embassy Pictures Corp.

CAST

Peter O'Toole (King Henry II), Katharine Hepburn (Queen Eleanor), Anthony Hopkins (Richard), John Castle (Geoffrey), Nigel Terry (John), Timothy Dalton (King Philip II), Jane Merrow (Alais), Nigel Stock (Captain William Marshall), Kenneth Ives (Queen Eleanor's guard), O. Z. Whitehead (Hugh de Puiset)

CREDITS

Director: Anthony Harvey | Producers: Joseph E. Levine, Jane C. Nusbaum, Martin Poll | Writer: James Goldman | Based on the play *The Lion in Winter* by James Goldman | Cinematography: Douglas Slocombe | Edition: John Bloom | Art Direction: Peter Murton, Gilbert Margerie | Set Decoration: Peter James | Costume Design: Margaret Furse | Music: John Barry | *Running Time*: 134 min.

THE FILM

In 1183, King Henry II of England calls a Christmas Court at Chinon Castle. He assembles his estranged wife (Eleanor of Aquitaine, whom he has imprisoned for ten years) and their three surviving sons – the impetuous Richard, the scheming Geoffrey and the clumsy John – to decide which one would be the successor to the crown. Also, there are present Henry's mistress, Princess Alais, and her 18-year-old brother, Philip, the king of France.

DALTON:

"More realism could be aimed at in most historical films. In *Lion* the costumes had mud around the bottoms however rich or opulent they were. One could have gone further by having straw on the floors and grease in people's hair. I think audiences would really like to see how people actually lived in the past."

    PLAYS AND PLAYERS

"In my very first camera shot on my very first day of my very first film, I worked with her [Katharine Hepburn]. I was supposed to be introduced to her, and had one brief line acknowledging that introduction. When it came time for my close up shot, the director said there was no reason for her to stay. Someone else could read her lines off camera. But she not only insisted on staying, but also, to get the proper angle so I would be looking at her in a sitting position, she crawled on her hands and knees behind and under the camera and crouched down. Then I said my line. It was truly extraordinary. In all the films I've done since then, very few actors would have done that."

CELEBRITY

"He (Peter O'Toole) was fantastic, I owe him an enormous debt, simply because of my admiration and excitement in his work, but also because he looks after us, and when I say us it was my first movie it was Anthony Hopkins, Sir Anthony Hopkins, first movie and we were just kids you know, and he was an established star 'Lawrence of Arabia,' 'Becket' you know all these great, great, great movies, and he looked after us, he looked after us, like a dad, he made sure that we were good, he gave us all he had to give, whether he was on screen or off screen."

KLOS LA Radio interview

"The Director of the movie Tony Harvey had decided to have a rehearsal period which is not normal and we met at a theatre in London called the Haymarket Theatre for a read through of this very dense script. I mean a wonderful script written by James Goldman one of the last sort of talking movies in a way, I mean a real fabulously written script and I think I and Tony Hopkins was in it, Tony's first movie, my first movie an actor, John Castle, Nigel Terry, Jane Merrow were the main people in it, and it was all our first movies, apart from Hepburn and O'Toole and I think in those days we were sort of a little overcome by this notion that you really took your text, you thought about it, you tried to allow it to seep and work its way inside your personality, you were very tentative and you mumbled a little bit, you kind of searched for your character the sense what it was you were doing through the rehearsal process. I am sure we were influenced by, you know, probably nonsense we were hearing about method acting, and Marlon Brando, and all sorts of things [laughs] so we came to this read through on the stage of the Haymarket and there was Katharine Hepburn 'Good Morning' and there was Peter 'Good Morning how are you, good to see you' and we sat down fully prepared all of us, you know boys to kind of, you know, mumble and be very professional, and all that. Well, Peter O'Toole started reading as though he has been blasted by a rocket into the room he came out exploding with passion and vigour and style and anger and panache and Katharine Hepburn burst after him and we were amazed it was the scariest thing I think we were seeing better then performance on our first read through, we kind of shrivelled, we didn't know it, we couldn't read it, we couldn't match it. Every one of us came back the next day knowing every word of the entire script totally prepared to give as good as we got."

Savannah Acting Class

[Was that overwhelming at the time? Daunting?]

"Oh, no, I was far too young and naive and stupid. I thought it was the way films were... great to be part of it. I knew that I might fail but I thought, 'I'm just going to get in there and do my best.' Katherine Hepburn was fantastic. I never forget my first day's work on the movie. I was about 19 or 20 years old and very nervous. My first scene was facing her and Peter O'Toole and all their family...being introduced and they worked all day photographing them. And I was hoping they'd get to me and they didn't. At the end of the day they said, 'Okay, we'll do Tim tomorrow. We'll turn the cameras around. Katherine, you have the day off.' She only had one line to me. You know, that lady said, 'But I talk to Tim in the scene. I am coming in tomorrow morning.' And she came in, sixty-one years old. A great star. There was no room for her to sit. She had to squeeze her way through the lighting stands and she got herself to just to be there for me, and she said something like, 'Hi, I'm Eleanor. If things had worked out differently, I might have been your mother.' That was the only line she had. It was not only professional, it was a woman who cared about a young, scared kid doing his first movie."

Regis and Kathie Lee Interview [TV]

REVIEWS

"The acting – Anthony Hopkins, as a queer, manly Richard the Lionhearted; Nigel Terry, as a caricatured, spastic adolescent Prince John; John Castle, as an almost too attractive, scheming Prince Geoffrey; and Timothy Dalton, as a sensitive, regal, embittered Philip of France – is joyful and solid."

Renata Adler, THE NEW YORK TIMES, 31 October 1968

"I'm not convinced it's the best picture of the year, but I think Peter O'Toole's performance is of Oscar quality, and Anthony Hopkins and Timothy Dalton deserve nominations for their supporting roles as Richard and Philip."

Roger Ebert, CHICAGO SUN-TIMES, 4 November 1968

"He [Peter O'Toole] is superb. And so are others in the company – Anthony Hopkins as Richard, John Castle as Geoffrey, Nigel Terry as John, Jane Merrow as the mistress who is not as simple as she seems, Timothy Dalton as the French king who is not quite the 'boy' Henry chooses to think him."

Judit Crist, NEW YORK MAGAZINE, 4 November 1968

"Superb acting by Katharine Hepburn and Peter O'Toole, and good individual studies by John Castle, Anthony Hopkins and Nigel Terry as the sons, and by

Timothy Dalton as the king of France."

    Michael Beale, EVENING CHRONICLE, 21 March 1969

"Princess Alais and her brother, Young King Philip of France (a telling performance by Timothy Dalton)."

    THE AUSTRALIAN WOMEN'S WEEKLY, 20 August 1969

CROMWELL

1970

Columbia Pictures

CAST

Richard Harris (Oliver Cromwell), Alec Guinness (King Charles I), Robert Morley (Earl of Manchester), Dorothy Tutin (Queen Henrietta Maria), Frank Finlay (John Carter), Timothy Dalton (Prince Rupert of the Rhine), Patrick Wymark (the Earl of Strafford), Patrick Magee (Hugh Peters), Nigel Stock (Sir Edward Hyde), Charles Gray (the Earl of Essex), Michael Jayston (Henry Ireton), Douglas Wilmer (Sir Thomas Fairfax), Geoffrey Keen (John Pym), Anthony May (Richard Cromwell), Stratford Johns (President Bradshaw), Ian McCulloch (John Hampden), Patrick O'Connell (John Lilburne), Anna Cropper (Ruth Carter), Jack Gwillim (General Byron), Stacy Dorning (Mary Cromwell)

CREDITS

Director: Ken Hughes | Producer: Irving Allen | Writer: Ken Hughes | Cinematography: Geoffrey Unsworth | Editing: Bill Lenny | Art Direction: John Stoll, Herbert Westbrook | Set Decoration: Arthur Taksen | Costume Design: Vittorio Nino Novarese | Music: Frank Cordell | *Running Time*: 139 min.

THE FILM

In 1640, Oliver Cromwell, a Puritan member of England's Parliament, is disturbed by the growing injustices of King Charles. Encouraged by the strong influence of his Catholic queen and the loyal Earl of Strafford, Charles demands the Parliament to finance a war on Scotland; when Parliament refuses it, Charles sends the troops to regain control, and Cromwell accuse him of treason. A civil war is born between the forces of Parliament and the king's troops.

DALTON:

"At a preview I'm told several film producers went around saying: 'Who's the new chap playing Prince Rupert?' Me! It would have been *more* gratifying if they'd connected me with the name that got a lot of praise in *The Lion in Winter*."

　　　　WOMAN

REVIEWS

"People like Dorothy Tutin, Robert Morley (in for the few laughs in the film), Nigel Stock, Charles Gray, Timothy Dalton and Michael Jayston are among those who circle the stars strongly."

　　　Dick Richards, DAILY MIRROR, 16 July 1970

"No-one else gets much chances to establish a character but there are brief, effective appearances by Robert Morley as the Earl of Manchester, Dorothy Tutin as Queen Henrietta Maria and Timothy Dalton as a suitably dashing Prince Rupert."

　　　Michael Billington, THE BIRMINGHAM POST, 18 July 1970

"Nigel Stock contributes another notable character study as the righteous Edward Hyde and Timothy Dalton, surely one of Britain's most compelling young actors, gives a splendid arrogance to the foppish Prince Rupert of the Rhine."

　　　Peter McGarry, COVENTRY EVENING TELEGRAPH, 8 February 1971

THE VOYEUR

1970

Produzione Intercontinentale Cinematografica

CAST

Marcello Mastroianni (Sandro), Virna Lisi (Claude), Timothy Dalton (Mark)

CREDITS

Director: Franco Indovina | Producers: Franco Indovina, Adriano Magistretti, Danilo Marciani | Writers: Tonino Guerra, Franco Indovina | Cinematography: Arturo Zavattini | Editing: Roberto Perpignani | Costume Design: Adriana

Berselli | Music: Ennio Morricone | *Running Time*: 105 mins.

THE FILM

[aka *GIOCHI PARTICOLARI*] Forty-year-old Sandro is married to Claude, and they live in an isolated country house. Sandro has one strange obsession – he is a self-confessed voyeur. He films his wife in all phases of life on his handheld camcorder. But everything changes when Mark, a young student, enters in their life and Sandro conceives a plan.

DALTON:

"It's about people-watching, or looking at other people, striving to find a reality, a truth."

    SEVENTEEN

"The Italians want to get their soul on film, which I think is the height of pompousness."

    NEW YORK POST SATURDAY

"An Italian film which I don't speak about."

    PLAYS AND PLAYERS

REVIEWS

"Sandro's desperation, in conclusion, is not the desperation of the voyeur or the husband but the desperation of the artist who is not able to establish fertile links with the right matter. (...) Timothy Dalton is not very convincing as the hippy."

    Alberto Moravia, L'ESPRESSO, 6 December 1970

"Sharp parable about alienation."

    Umberto Cantoni, LA REPUBBLICA, 4 May 2014

"Film with an existential and introspective perspective, where an Antonioni's figure can be recognised."

    Eleonora Sforzi, gothicnetwork.org, 18 June 2015

WUTHERING HEIGHTS

1970

AIP

CAST

Anna Calder-Marshall (Catherine), Timothy Dalton (Heathcliff), Harry Andrews (Mr. Earnshaw), Pamela Brown (Mrs. Linton), Judy Cornwell (Nelly Dean), James Cossins (Mr. Linton), Rosalie Crutchley (Mrs. Earnshaw), Hilary Dwyer (Isabella Linton), Julian Glover (Hindley Earnshaw), Hugh Griffith (Dr. Kenneth), Morag Hood (Frances Earnshaw), Ian Ogilvy (Edgar Linton), Peter Sallis (Mr. Shielders)

CREDITS

Director: Robert Fuest | Producers: Samuel Z. Arkoff, James H. Nicholson | Writer: Patrick Tilley | Based on the book *Wuthering Heights* by Emily Brontë | Cinematography: John Coquillon | Editing: Ann Chegwidden | Music: Michel Legrand | *Running Time*: 104 mins.

THE FILM

Mr Earnshaw, a Yorkshire farmer, returns one day from a trip to the city with a ragged boy called Heathcliff. Earnshaw's son, Hindley, dislikes the child, but Heathcliff becomes companion and soulmate to Hindley's sister, Catherine. After her parents die, Cathy and Heathcliff grow up wild and free on the Moors, and despite the continued hostility between Hindley and Heathcliff, they're happy – until Cathy meets Edgar Linton, a very wealthy neighbour.

DALTON:

"That is why it [Heathcliff's character] interested me. Because it was difficult to do, it was worth doing. I will use myself more if I choose the difficult part. If I do the easy, it will be a waste of my time here."

THE DAY

"Emily Bronte's imagery is so superb, so moving, so grand. She wrote such a gigantic, powerful novel. Some people think it all beautiful and romantic, but her characters are the product of a strange, disturbed mind. It's a deeply disturbing book, black and sadistic, and at the same time such an incredible story of a great love. What those people go through - oh, it's extraordinary! The old film with Laurence Olivier and Merle Oberon was like a drawing-room romance, nice and polite, nothing to do with the actual story. I think Heathcliff is something inhuman, something other than reality. On a superficial level one knows what Heathcliff looks like, how he changes, but that's not enough. One has to explore and understand him and share his emotions and feelings. He's so cruel and hard, yet he has this overriding love for Cathy. You can't play a role like that intellectually. It's not a thing one understands or can really put into words. It's a happening inside of one's body. You read the book, you read the script and they entwine themselves together inside of you. I am constantly grasping, groping, emotionally searching for little bits and pieces of character. All the elements are there, but as an actor, I don't really know what's going to happen, which creates a great sense of excitement."

SEVENTEEN

"Why does everyone want to compare us? Sure, Sir Laurence played Heathcliff and now I'm playing him, but the characters are really completely different people. His Heathcliff was a romantic; mine was a bit of a moody bastard. I hope mine will be more in keeping with Emily Bronte's book, although Sir Laurence's was right at the time and in the mood of the film as it was made for audiences of the 1930s. But they are still two different roles, even if they have the same name. It's pointless comparing the two Heathcliffs. As far as I'm concerned, I can only do my best. I can't work looking over my shoulder. I just hope I do well, and that young people will then know me as the actor who made Heathcliff a character with whom they could identify."

American International Pictures Press Information

"Being out here on the moors is a whole physical experience. You can't tell what it's actually like until you get here. It makes you realise just how hardy the people that Emily Brontë wrote about must have been. We've filmed under weather conditions that were absolutely ghastly, yet whenever it rained, and we all got soaked through, everyone laughed. That's the sort of extraordinary effect the place has on you. The physical presence of the Brontë country strikes you with tremendous force. And the weather is quite unbelievable. It changes about every ten minutes. On any one day you can almost guarantee you'll get the complete four seasons! (…) Heathcliff, as portrayed by Sir Laurence was totally romantic. Now I'm playing him as a rebellious, brooding character. There's really no resemblance between the two. His performance suited the mood of the 1930s. It was right for what audiences wanted at that time. I am hoping that my Heathcliff will be more in keeping with the character as he is described in Emily Bronte's book. She called him 'a man's shape dominated by demon life'. And that's how I'm aiming to play him on the screen. They are two totally different roles, even if they have the same name. (…) With Heathcliff, it's slightly different. Emily

Bronte did all the hard work, and I'm simply re-creating what she fashioned. *My* hard work in this film is in reading and re-reading her great novel every evening to make sure I *do* get what was written into the character. Let's remember that we have a great debt to Emily Bronte for writing these wonderful characters for us play-actors to perform. It takes a great deal of courage to make a challenging classic like *Wuthering Heights*, and I am grateful to American International for giving me chance to be part of the challenge."

ABC FILM REVIEW

"The power, the magnitude, the immense proportion is so evocative. How people can fail to be disturbed by it, I can't understand. Someone else might read it, dream about him [Heathcliff], or want to paint him. I wanted to play him."

NEW YORK POST SATURDAY

"We tried very hard to do… to bring to the screen what she had written so our focus was on those pages of Emily Bronte, so really I mean she gives the interpretation and it is our job to try and bring it to life… I think we fell somewhat short because of how modern film commercial necessities, because at the time 'Love Story' broke and we cut out so much of what we had done which was hard and tough, and *lovingly* difficult. I mean it is a very tough seemingly hard painful book. I mean that love story I mean that hating each other an awful lot of the time as well as being passionately, madly in love with each other and… I think a lot of the perhaps more difficult stuff was taken out because… commercial films at that time would be rather romantic in the idealistic sense, but it was a wonderful film to do. (…) At the time I mean one worked very hard and I was very thrilled doing it and… I think captured certainly a lot of the qualities she was writing about. I think one of the most interesting things that took people by surprise was… the fact that we were rather young because if you have seen the Olivier, Merle Oberon I mean, you know, they were mature people… And of course when you read the book Catherine dies at the age of 19, the story is a story of teenagers, not a story of… healthy adult mature people, so that I think surprised people, but I think what we did we got a lot of what Emily Bronte was after."

JCET's Celebrity Spotlight

"In one sense *Wuthering Heights* was put down by the critics quite justifiably. But I'd like to get the record straight on two points. Firstly, Anna Calder-Marshall and I were damned for playing Catharine and Heathcliff as too young. But Catharine died at the age of nineteen in the novel. The first part of the book covers them as teenagers. It's in the second part, after her death, that Heathcliff grows into this towering, awful man. We based the relationship on a physical toughness which is there in the language and landscape of the book. It's a savage, analytical book. Now just at this time the film *Love Story* came out. The producers decided that this is where the money was - and they cut 30 minutes, key scenes of the film. All the 'nicer' scenes were left in. We filmed an ending of total despair – Heathcliff collapsing on the moors haunted by Catherine's ghost. Three months later the producers went off and filmed two extras running down a hill hand in hand as ghosts living happily after. But those producers could never understand that the greatest romance is the *hardest* romance – the one that goes through the trails and the bad times, and ends up as some kind of torture. That's what the great poets have always talked about."

    PLAYS AND PLAYERS

REVIEWS

"The Heathcliff of this version is portrayed by Timothy Dalton, an in his twenties Welsh actor whose striking face greatly helped him to project the passionate animality and sensitive humanity Emily Bronte wanted Cathy's lover to evince alternately. (...) He seems to have intelligence and acting ability as well as a memorable face. As I watched him work in this film I became convinced he was capable of more than the director was allowing him to attempt."

    Gloria Ives, FILMS IN REVIEW, February 1971

"Timothy Dalton and Anna Calder-Marshall play the star-crossed lovers in degrees of effectiveness that depend largely on camera angles. Dalton, under certain conditions, bears a remarkable resemblance to the young Laurence Olivier for whom the Wyler version was a triumph."

    Vincent Canby, THE NEW YORK TIMES, 19 February 1971

"Timothy Dalton plays Heathcliff, and one suspects that he was picked because of a resemblance to Laurence Olivier who played the part in the 1939 screen version. The resemblance is purely physical. Looking dour and menacing is not enough."

    Tony Mastroianni, CLEVELAND PRESS, 11 March 1971

"Timothy Dalton in the Heathcliff part captures the stallion-like side of the character, but other aspects often escape him."

    Arthur Thirkell, DAILY MIRROR, 10 June 1971

"Timothy Dalton is a fine-looking Heathcliff, satanic and broody, if stronger in silence than in speech."

David Robinson, FINANCIAL TIMES, 11 June 1971

"Timothy Dalton does actually work quite well as Heathcliff, aided no doubt by an appearance and some mannerisms very reminiscent of Olivier in the role. But the important big-star magnetism just does not yet come across; he remains a small figure in a big screen."

John Russell Taylor, THE TIMES, 11 June 1971

"Timothy Dalton may not be a deeply subtle actor but he looks very like one's idea of Heathcliff — dark, slant-eyed and dangerous — while Anna Calder-Marshall, though inexperienced, does well with Cathy's wild, unhappy frustration."

Winefride Wilson, THE TABLET, 12 June 1971

"Anna Calder-Marshall and Timothy Dalton, while certainly the right age, just haven't got the dramatic equipment to convince us that their affair wouldn't be more appropriate to the King's Road. (...) Mr Dalton, although modest enough to pay an almost extravagant of homage to Lord Larry, seems little more than petulant and narcissistic."

George Melly, THE OBSERVER, 13 June 1971

"Anna Calder-Marshall, as Catherine, does the best she can, but is given no time to develop the role, so that, as the script rushes her on from outcry to outcry, she can't help sounding like a homely, southern-counties girl out of her depth in a welter of emotionalism. For the same reasons Timothy Dalton's Heathcliff, sullen, wild, moody and the rest of it, appears faintly absurd much of the time."

Christopher Hudson, THE SPECTATOR, 18 June 1971

"Timothy Dalton, heavy-browed, broods and glowers like a threat of thunder that produces a squeak, doing nothing for Heathcliff except make him a frustrated teenager."

Michael Billington, THE BIRMINGHAM POST, 26 June 191

"Heathcliff and Catherine are played by Timothy Dalton and Anna Calder-Marshall very much in the modern mode. His dark-eyed looks and fiery temperament strike me as more the angry young man than the strange and haunted Heathcliff, though at times he certainly resembles the young Olivier in the earlier film. (...) Both performances have their own measure of strength and depth, however, and both are governed to a large extent by Patrick Tilley's screenplay."

Peter McGarry, COVENTRY EVENING TELEGRAPH, 28 June 1971

"Timothy Dalton (last seen as the young King of France in *The Lion in Winter*) makes a fine Heathcliff, brooding, powerful, malign yet vulnerable, and succeeds in living up to the memory of Laurence Olivier in the earlier film."

Anne Thoms, THE PRESS AND JOURNAL, 30 June 1971

"Timothy Dalton is also a technically capable actor, with a dark gipsy brooding look that is appropriate for Heathcliff. But his sullen, almost sulking portrayal is often that of a hurt boy rather than a man seething with resentment and a frustrated passion, a powder keg ready to explode."

VARIETY, 1971

MARY, QUEEN OF SCOTS

1971

Universal Pictures Ltd.

CAST

Vanessa Redgrave (Mary, Queen of Scots), Glenda Jackson (Queen Elizabeth), Patrick McGoohan (James Stuart), Timothy Dalton (Henry, Lord Darnley), Nigel Davenport (Lord Bothwell), Trevor Howard (William Cecil), Daniel Massey (Robert Dudley), Ian Holm (David Riccio), Andrew Keir

(Ruthven), Tom Fleming (Father Ballard), Katherine Kath (Catherine de Medici), Beth Harris (Mary Seton), Frances White (Mary Fleming), Bruce Purchase (Morton), Brian Coburn (Huntly), Vernon Dobtcheff (Duc de Guise), Raf de la Torre (Cardinal De Guise), Richard Warner (Walsingham), Maria Aitken (Lady Bothwell), Jeremy Bulloch (Andrew), Robert James (John Knox), Richard Denning (Francis, King of France)

CREDITS

Director: Charles Jarrott | Producer: Hal B. Wallis | Writer: John Hale | Cinematography: Christopher Challis | Editing: Richard Marden | Art Direction: Terence Marsh, Robert Cartwright | Set Decoration: Peter Howitt | Costume Design: Margaret Furse | Music: John Barry | *Running Time*: 128 mins.

THE FILM

Mary Stuart, who was named Queen of Scotland when she was only six days old, is the last Roman Catholic ruler of Scotland. Her cousin Elizabeth Tudor, the English Queen and her arch adversary, plots against her because she fears Mary could encourage the Catholic English population against her. Meanwhile, Mary's exiled cabinet of Lords also hatches its plan to dethrone her.

DALTON:

"When I think a part is like myself I've got nothing to hold on to. (...) Even Darnley in *Mary Queen of Scots* – I could go back and discover things about. I enjoy those parts most – like putting on the blond wig and all that crap."

PLAYS AND PLAYERS

REVIEWS

"With fine actors involved along the way, Trevor Howard's on hand as William Cecil, Daniel Massey as Elizabeth's Dudley, Timothy Dalton – and very good he is – as Mary's deservedly ill-fated Darnley."

Judit Crist, NEW YORK MAGAZINE, 14 February 1972

"Particularly good is Timothy Dalton as the weak-willed, pox-ridden Lord Darnley. Not a sympathetic character, but Dalton makes him flesh and blood in a film notable deficient in both."

Arthur Thirkell, DAILY MIRROR, 28 March 1972

"The most successful performance, to my mind, is Nigel Davenport's rough, masculine Bothwell, though Timothy Dalton is surprisingly good as Darnley."

Maryvonne Butcher, THE TABLET, 8 April 1972

"The only character who really comes to life, however, is Timothy Dalton's weak and vicious Lord Darnley."

Malcolm Grey, EVENING CHRONICLE, 14 April 1972

"And poor Timothy Dalton, usually so good, slinks around those gloomy castle corners like a first-year student in Vincent Pricery."

Peter McGarry, COVENTRY EVENING TELEGRAPH, 6 June 1972

"Timothy Dalton as Darnley brings out the twisted soul of the man. Now, Darnley was just about the most repulsive character in the whole affair. Of this, Dalton leaves you in no doubt. His performance is more filled with understanding than any other in the film."

Dougal Macdonald, THE CANBERRA TIMES, 18 July 1972

"Timothy Dalton impresses as the wilful and spiteful Darnley."

EVENING CHRONICLE, 2 November 1972

PERMISSION TO KILL

1975

Avco Embassy Pictures

CAST

Dirk Bogarde (Curtis), Ava Gardner (Katina Petersen), Bekim Fehmiu (Diakim), Timothy Dalton (Charles Lord), Nicole Calfan (Melissa Lascade), Frederic Forrest (Scott E. Allison), Klaus Wildbolz (Muller), Anthony Dutton (Jennings), Peggy Sinclair (Lily), Dennis Blanch (Brewer), John Levene (Adams), Alf Joint (MacNeil), Vladimir Popovic (Kosta), Ratislav Plamenac (Pavlos), Oliver Schott (François Diderot), Erna Riedl-Tichy (Mme Diderot)

CREDITS

Director: Cyril Frankel | Producer: Paul Mills | Executive Producers: Robert Jungbluth | Heinz Lazek | Writer: Robin Estridge | Based on the book *W.I.L. One to Curtis* by Philip Loraine | Photography: Freddie Young | Art Direction: Elliot Scott | Theo Harisch | Herwig Libowitzky | Film Editing: Ernest Walter |

Set Decoration: Walter Knaus | Costume Design: Franka | Music: Richard Rodney Bennett | *Running Time*: 93 mins.

THE FILM

(aka *THE EXECUTIONER*) Agent Alan Curtis of the Western Intelligence Liaison blackmails five people to help him stop revolutionary exile Alexandre Diakim to return to his home country. They are a French-Algerian assassin; a former follower of Diakim, now a journalist; an eight-year-old French boy; a British foreign officer, whose homosexual affairs threaten his career; and Diakim's former lover, an American expatriate living in Milan. Curtis gathers them in Gmunden (Austria) where Diakim plots his homecoming.

DALTON:

"I might have an early script with *The Executioner* on it, but it was *Permission To Kill* when I made it… with Ava Gardner! A magnificent woman. (…) So many of the people I've worked with have been fabulous people, as well as wonderful actors and actresses, and Ava Gardner was magnificent. What a woman. [*Takes a deep breath, then exhales*.] Gosh. I mean, there's nothing much more I can tell you about her than that. She was just… oh, you know, she was just big and warm and wonderful and… *fun*. She was simply magnificent."

   A.V. Club

REVIEWS

"As things stand, one is glad at least of the occasionally pleasing scenic view of Gmunden in Upper Austria, and a welcome infusion of lightness here and there by nimble-tongued Timothy Dalton, doing minor wonders with corny lines as a British Foreign Office under-secretary who happens to be a homosexual but refuses to be dumped between the stools of *Angst* and campery."

  Gordon Gow, FILMS AND FILMING, January 1976

SEXTETTE

1978

Crown International Pictures

CAST

Mae West (Marlo Manners), Timothy Dalton (Sir Michael Barrington), Ringo Starr, (Laslo Karolny), George Hamilton (Vance), Tony Curtis (Alexei Karansky), Alice Cooper (Waiter), Dom DeLuise (Dan Turner), Keith Allison (Waiter), Rona Barrett (Rona Barrett), Van McCoy (Delegate), Keith Moon (Dress designer), Regis Philbin (himself), Walter Pidgeon (The Chairman), George Raft (himself), Gil Stratton (himself), Harry Weiss (The Don)

CREDITS

Director: Ken Hughes | Producer: Daniel Briggs, Robert Sullivan | Associate producer: Harry Weiss | Executive producer: Warner G. Toub | Writer: Herbert Baker | Photography: James Crabe | Art Direction: James F. Claytor | Film Editing: Argyle Nelson | Set Decoration: Reg Allen, Bob Chitwood, Paul Cunningham, Norman Tuers | Costume Design: Thad Prescott, Edith Head | Music: Artie Butler | *Running Time*: 91 mins.

THE FILM

Marlo Manners is enjoying her honeymoon with Sir Michael Barrington, husband number 6. An international conference is also taking place in the same hotel, and the Russian delegate (one of Marlo's former husbands) is threatening to frustrate the negotiations unless he can have one more date with his ex. Also, Marlo's manager is desperately trying (and failing) to destroy a tape where she has recorded all the details of her affairs and scandals.

DALTON:

"The film was made as some sort of tribute to Mae, with all the old lines. But it went beyond that. It was a bizarre, extraordinary, mad film, with Mae as a sort of centrepiece. If you took it seriously you'd think it was grotesque. I mean here's this very old woman supposedly with six men all in love with her!"

    PHOTOPLAY

"Ken Hughes, for whom I'd made *Cromwell*, took me out to California for the Mae West *Sextette*, which was really bizarre; every night after shooting we'd go out to eat and she would read poems she'd written about New York before World War One. She didn't admit to ninety-one so everyone had to pretend she was eighty-seven, and the producers just thought she might be good for a last buck, but in fact she was this highly intelligent lady who'd been working on her own image since 1900 when, on Broadway, she'd seen an old hooker with a sailor on each arm standing in that arms-akimbo posture which then became her trademark."

THE TIMES

"We had a great time on that film. Tony Curtis, George Hamilton, Dom De Luise, Ringo Starr, we all approached it as a funny, send-up tribute to her. But I suppose a lot of people who might have seen it, could think it's rather grotesque. An old lady in her eighties, attempting to be a twenty-five-year-old beauty queen with seven husbands! You have to approach it with the premise that here's a grand old lady with a history to have fun with. A lot of people – perhaps rightly, I don't know – took it the other way."

FILMS ILLUSTRATED

"That's what a call a silly role. But to be honest, I admired her nerve, and enjoyed working with her [MW] – I was even interviewed by Rona Barrett in the picture! It was a real stretch for me, and, frankly, after making love to a woman in her mid-80's, I knew I could handle any assignment!"

PREVUE

"She claimed to be 84 but some old-timers said she was 90. It was amazing to be working at her old studio, Paramount, and see her come to life every day as she did the thing she loved."

ASSOCIATED PRESS

"She [Mae West] was, she was quite extraordinary she was very witty, very funny... we didn't have much of a script to go on so a lot of it was being made up as we went along, it was full of bizarre, bizarre people I mean the cast list was hundreds of very famous people including George Raft came and did a couple of lines and there were pop stars like Ringo Starr and Alice Cooper. It was just a very strange odd experience, but she was smashing, she was sadly I mean very old and... you know, no one can defeat age, but she was charming and fun and... she was doing the best she could do. It's an odd film, isn't it? [laughs]"

JCET's Celebrity Spotlight

REVIEWS

"The remainder of the cast – Tony Curtis as a Soviet delegate to the peace conference, Timothy Dalton as West's new husband, Ringo Starr and George Hamilton as former husbands, among others – hardly enhance their reputations."

VARIETY, 1978

"In addition to Mr Dalton, *Sextette* features a number of other people who, in happier circumstances, are decent actors."

Vincent Canby, THE NEW YORK TIMES, 8 June 1979

"Dalton tries his best, but the script keeps him busy with a pointless 'is he or is he not gay' angle that's as old as dinosaur dung."

Bill Gibron, dvdtalk.com, 7 November 2000

EL HOMBRE QUE SUPO AMAR (THE MAN WHO KNEW LOVE)

1978

General Film Corporation, S.A.

CAST

Timothy Dalton (Juan de Dios), Antonio Ferrandis (Dr Cabrales), Jonathan Burn (Antón Martín), José María Prada (Great Inquisitor), Queta Claver (Inés), Antonio Iranzo, José Vivó (Luis Gómez), Fernando Hilbeck (Yusuf), Marc Gimpera, Pilar Bardem (wench), Antonio Casas (Commissioner), Alberto Mendoza (Juan de Ávila), Ángela Molina (Jazmín), Victoria Abril (Amelia), Isabel Mestres (Elvira), Félix Dafauce (Bishop García), Luis Ciges (exorcist), Paco Valladares (Juan's voice)

CREDITS

Director: Miguel Picazo | Producer: Eduardo Bussalleu, Jose María Carcasona | Writer: Santiago Moncada | Based on the book *Una aventura iluminada* by José Cruset | Cinematography: Manuel Rojas | Editing: Pablo G. Del Amo | Art Department: Julián Arribas, Juan de la Flor | Art Direction: Eduardo Torre de la Fuente | Music: Antonio Pérez Olea | *Running Time*: 141 mins.

THE FILM

In 1539, in Granada (Spain), a Portuguese librarian named Juan Ciudad is taken for a fool when he tries to denounce the acts of injustice around him. When he gets released from the horrifying asylum, he decides to dedicate his life to take care of the poorest people.

DALTON:

"I'm not Catholic, but Jesus wasn't it either. Not being a believer won't diminish my acting."

BLANCO Y NEGRO

"Actually, I don't play a saint. Juan Ciudad was made saint later on. I play the character in his time, when he was living, like a splendid fighter inside the XVI century society that he was even quite apart from the Church."

IDEAL

"Picazo is a man of talent. Working next to him was a fantastic experience. Because, at that moment, I realised Spain was starting to live a new era. It allowed me to meet very important actors. Besides, I was impressed by the power of the Spanish cultural and artistic world, unknown to me."

LA VANGUARDIA

REVIEWS

"Good performances from Timothy Dalton, Antonio Ferrandis, Jonathan Burn, José María Prada, Alberto de Mendoza, Ángela Molina, Queta Claver, Antonio Casas and Antonio Iranzo, some of many actors that participate in the film."

Vicente Quiroga, ODIEL, 12 October 1976 *

"In this impressive fresco from the XVI century, Picazo has moved the actors accurately; Timothy Dalton is good at playing the passionate Juan de Dios."

A.Colón, ABC, 27 February 1977 *

"The film has an excellent actor, Timothy Dalton, who develops the leading role with expressivity, firmness and, at the same time, with all the sweetness that the part demands."

Ángeles Masó, LA VANGUARDIA, 2 April 1977 *

"Among the cast, it needs to be highlighted Timothy Dalton's great creation, Ángela Molina's good work and a brief but accurate performance by the late José María Prada."

Hermes, ABC, 24 August 1978

"And, in a terrible cast that values most the quantity than the quality, only Timothy Dalton – from time to time – can be saved."

Fernando Trueba, EL PAÍS, 1 September 1978

"A remarkable film, wisely directed, and with a very inspired group of actors."

A.F., REVISTA CINEMATOGRÁFICA ESPAÑOLA, September 1978

*Despite some previews, the film wasn't officially released in Spain until 1978.

AGATHA

1979

Warner Bross., Inc

CAST

Vanessa Redgrave (Agatha Christie), Dustin Hoffman (Wally Stanton), Timothy Dalton (Col. Archibald Christie), Helen Morse (Evelyn Crawley), Celia Gregory (Nancy Neele), Paul Brooke (John Foster), Carolyn Pickles (Charlotte Fisher), Timothy West (Kenward), Tony Britton (William Collins), Alan Badel (Lord Brackenbury), Robert Longden (Pettelson), Donald Nithsdale (Uncle Jones), Yvonne Gilan (Mrs. Braithwaite), Sandra Voe (Therapist), Barry Hart (Supt. MacDonald), David Hargreaves (Sgt. Jarvis), Tim Seely (Capt. Rankin), Jill Summers (Nancy's Aunt), Chris Fairbank (Luland), Liz Smith (Flora), Peter Arne (Hotel Manager)

CREDITS

Director: Michael Apted | Producers: Jarvis Astaire, Gavrik Losey, David Puttnam | Writers: Kathleen Tynan, Arthur Hopcraft | Cinematography: Vittorio Storaro Editing: Jim Clark | Production Design: Shirley Russell | Art Direction: Simon Holland | Costume Design: Shirley Russell | Production | Music: Johnny Mandel | *Running Time*: 98 mins.

THE FILM

Crime writer Agatha Christie is in shock when her husband Archibald demands a divorce, and she promptly vanishes. She signs into a Harrogate hotel under the name of a relative of Archie's lover and, as the country gets full of rumours regarding her disappearance, she secretly plans dark revenge against him that can only be averted by Wally Stanton, an ambitious American journalist who falls in love with her.

REVIEWS

"In a few short scenes of almost sadistic emotional violence, Timothy Dalton recreates the look and sound of the young, devastatingly attractive Laurence Olivier (in his darkly sever *Rebecca* period) – only this is an Olivier without the tenderness beneath the anger."

David Denby, NEW YORK MAGAZINE, 19 February 1979

"Ironically, arrogance is the quality Dalton uses against her [Agatha] and the one Hoffman uses to wind his way into her life and win her confidence."

Ed Blank, THE PITTSBURGH PRESS, 2 March 1979

"Dalton, as the erring husband, reflects not guilt but austere displeasure."

Little Elgin, THE CITIZEN (Ottawa), 6 March 1979

"Earlier in the day she [Agatha] learned that husband Archie (Timothy Dalton, looking remarkably like a young Laurence Olivier) had asked for a divorce."

Arthur Thirkell, DAILY MIRROR, 4 May 1979

"Timothy Dalton, as the philandering husband, gives the best performance, or at least the most entertaining."

John Hindle, THE AGE, 14 June 1979

"Costumes, locations and appropriate social niceties are all scrupulously observed and, thanks chiefly to Timothy Dalton's vignette of Christie and Helen Morse's of Agatha's friend, Evelyn, much is implied about the roles of the sexes in the first 'modern' decade."

Michael Rowberry, COVENTRY EVENING TELEGRAPH, 2 July 1979

THE FLAME IS LOVE [TV]

1979

NBC

CAST

Linda Purl (Emmaline Nevada 'Vada' Holtz), Shane Briant (Pierre), Timothy Dalton (Marquis de Guaita), Richard Johnson (narrator), Joan Greenwood (Duchess of Grantham), Paul Lavers (Duke of Grantham), Kathleen Barrington (Nancy Sparling), Helena Carroll (Charity), Godfrey Quigley (M. Worth), John Franklyn (Verlaine), Jim Fitzgerald (Toulouse-Lautrec), Maureen Toal (La Goulue), Alain Christie (Arthur Rimbaud), Meryl Gourley (Mrs. Holtz)

CREDITS

Director: Michael O'Herlihy | Producers: Ed Friendly, Michael O'Herlihy | Writer: Hindi Brooks | Based on the book *The Flame Is Love* by Barbara Cartland | Cinematography: John C. Flinn III | Editing: Paul LaMastra | Art director: Alan Pleass | Music: Morton Stevens | *Running Time*: 104 mins.

THE FILM

Vada is an innocent American heiress travelling with a chaperone that has to remain temporary in Paris. There, she decides to experience life in a way she never had before, and she meets two different men: a nobleman who hides a horrifying secret and a bohemian journalist.

REVIEWS

"The leads are nicely cast. Linda Purl as Vada, Shane Briant as Pierre and Timothy Dalton as the marquis are admirably attractive and straight-faced in their endeavors."

John J. O'Connor, THE NEW YORK TIMES, 15 October 1979

FLASH GORDON

1980

Universal Pictures

CAST

Sam J. Jones (Flash Gordon), Melody Anderson (Dale Arden), Max von Sydow (Emperor Ming the Merciless), Chaim Topol (Dr. Hans Zarkov), Ornella Muti (Princess Aura), Timothy Dalton (Prince Barin), Brian Blessed (Prince Vultan), Peter Wyngarde (General Klytus), Mariangela Melato (General Kala), Richard O'Brien (Fico), John Hallam (General Luro), John Morton (Airline pilot), Robbie Coltrane (Man at Airfield), William Hootkins (Munson), Leon Greene (Colonel of Battle Control Room), Tony Scannell (Ming's officer), Bogdan Kominowski (Lieutenant of Ming's Air Force), George Harris (Prince Thun), John Osborne (Arborian priest), Deep Roy (Fellini), Peter Duncan (Treeman), Bob Goody (Azurian Man), Philip Stone (Zogi the High Priest), Kenny Baker (Dwarf)

CREDITS

Director: Mike Hodges | Producers: Dino De Laurentiis, Bernard Williams | Writers: Lorenzo Semple, Jr., Michael Allin | Based on the comic strip *Flash*

Gordon by Alex Raymond | Photography: Gil Taylor | Art Direction: Danilo Donati | John Graysmark | Film Editing: Malcolm Cooke | Set Decoration: Danilo Donati, Ted Michell | Costume Design: Danilo Donati | Music: Queen | Orchestral score: Howard Blake | *Running Time*: 111 mins.

THE FILM

Flash Gordon, a famous football player, and Dale Arden, a travel agent, unwillingly fly with Dr Zarkov on his rocket ship to an unknown planet. Arriving on Mongo, Flash and his companions learn that this world is under the ruler-ship of the evil Emperor Ming the Merciless who is attacking Earth with natural disasters to destroy it. Realising that Earth and the human race is in mortal danger, Flash decides to unite the kingdoms of Mongo and combine the forces of rivals Prince Barin and Prince Vultan to defeat Ming and save Earth from annihilation.

DALTON:

"The costumes are knockout, too. I was lucky. I didn't have any plastic wings to flap around in. Nor lizard scales! I got the Robin Hood outfit! (...). Anyway, to describe the story is silly. It's comic cartoon time. In fact, when Dino de Laurentiis first offered it to me, I said, 'Dino, I can't say if I can do this or not – let me see a script'. He went over to the sideboard and got out all the Alex Raymond comic books. 'Look!' he said. 'Looka here. This – you! Fantastic.' And, of course, it *is* fantastic. Saturday morning picture stuff. And I grew up on those. So did Mike Hodges, the director. It's a wonderful thrill to be part of something that is so strong in your childhood consciousness. (...) Obviously, no one has any idea what kind of film Nic Roeg would have made of it, but Mike Hodges, more than anybody, is responsible for the humorous, funny, witty, marvellous film it is now. Nothing like *Star Wars* or any of those *Aliens*. It's not science-fiction, or any modern-day prediction of how space is going to be. I mean, it's rooted in the past, the '30s, '40s of Alex Raymond. No-one wears space helmets – they can go on space motorbikes and just have their hair blowing in the breeze. To make a film like this, a huge budget, with the shooting lasting so long, with such technical problems, is an enormous task anyway. A monstrous thing to try and make. Not only did Mike conquer that, but his wonderful sense of humour and sensitivity to the thing is, I'm sure, going to make it a popular success."

  Films Illustrated

"It's a flashy, dashing-about sort of movie, big feathers and long hair and swords."

  Seventeen

"I fought with a whip I think if I remember rightly. I had to learn how to do that, and we had that fight on the tilting disc. (...) There was one shot I didn't do... which was going over the edge, that had to be done about 60 feet up in the air and they tilted the disc and they asked me if I would roll down and fall off the edge and hang on to a... one of these spikes that were coming up through it and I said 'no I really don't think so, I don't want to try that, I am sure I can catch the spike but I don't know if I can hold my own weight', and they said 'of course you will give it a go' and I said 'no I think not' and they said 'Well there are boxes down below' you know this is 60 feet below I mean it is a long way so anyway I said no and a stuntman did it and he couldn't hold his own weight either and he was taken to hospital sadly but he was alright."

    JCET's Celebrity Spotlight

"It was one of my favourite films, too. It did wonderfully well around the world. It was the #2 film in Europe, but for some reason -possibly spaceships that were red and gold; it didn't seem to do too well in the States."

    Hollywood Online

"I enjoyed being a comic book character. Besides, salary does become a consideration at times."

    PREVUE

"He's not the stiff, hero cartoon caricature type of person, which I find very funny! [Laughs] Unless you're playing in a cartoon, human beings are complex."

    USA TODAY

"You know you're having fun, you know you're hoping to make people laugh and, you know, a lot of the time you're laughing yourself inside but you can't! You know, if you could do it in a nudged way, you know, tip the audience off, it doesn't work, you've just got to play it for what it is and hope that the sense of humour people watching it... (...) It [the movie] is so refreshing, so uplifting, so exhilarating!"

    Flash Gordon Q&A

"I think it's wonderful. Now it's huge. Everybody loves *Flash Gordon*. (...) I'm astonished by what a huge cult film it is. But I have to say that the Americans didn't get it at all at the time. It's taken maybe 30 or 40 years to realise it's a joke! I was astonished reading the horror with which the American press vilified the movie. 'How can they have a spaceship that looks like a '50s motorcar? I mean, spaceships don't look like that! And the Wingmen—or the

Birdmen or Eaglemen or *whatever* they are—you can tell that their wings are paper-mâché! This is an awful film!' And it wasn't just one, you know. It was a whole bunch of them who didn't realise that it was kind of a marvellously funny and imaginative way of depicting a cartoon that in itself is rather silly. 'Come on, Flash! We've got 10 minutes to save the universe!' [Laughs.] The dialogue is awful! (...) So the world laughed... but not a lot of American movie critics did! But I was Prince Barin, the sort of wooden... oh, I'm trying to think of a word. Pompous? Self-important? Arrogant? Narcissistic? [Laughs.] Really, it was a lovely role to play! (...) Ah, he [Brian Blessed] is great fun. And Max von Sydow, he's just sensational. And then you've got Topol and Ornella Muti and Mariangela Melato as well. I have to say, I'm beginning to hear myself keep repeating this phrase, but I loved being in that movie! (...) *Flash Gordon*, I just thought was a fabulous film, and as I say, I was disappointed, but now I laugh about the fact that it was, I think, the second highest-grossing film in the world that year... and it bombed in the United States!"

    A.V. Club

REVIEWS

"Timothy Dalton's dashing, enthusiastic Prince Barin of Arboria wears the green tunic of Robin Hood, and his woodland moon where his men are a companionable band, suggest Sherwood Forest. Arboria has a dark, macho rite, though. Prince Barin and Flash are pitted against each other in a fairy-tail form of Russian roulette. They take turns putting a hand into the crevices of a gnarled tree trunk, risking the fatal bite of the resident monster. This sequence, which evokes the illustrations in old book of children's stories, is much scarier than the futuristic torments. (...) When Princess Aura pledges her love to her handsome fiancé, Prince Barin he says, 'Lying bitch', admiringly, in tribute to her polymorphous perversity. No woman with such hot-tomato lip gloss could be faithful."

    THE NEW YORKER, 5 January 1981

"My objection is that a lot of skill is lavished on something pretty worthless and that the square, good-versus-evil contest of the original 30s strip is now treated as pure camp. Tongues are kept firmly in cheeks as, for instance, Timothy Dalton's Flynn-like Baron [sic] is chained to a wall and merrily quips to his captive companion, 'Tell me about this man Houdini.'"

    Michael Billington, ILLUSTRATED LONDON NEWS, 01 February 1981

CHANEL SOLITAIRE

1981

United Film Distribution

CAST

Marie-France Pisier (Coco Chanel), Timothy Dalton (Boy Capel), Rutger Hauer (Etienne de Balsan), Karen Black (Emilienne d'Alencon), Brigitte Fossey (Adrienne), Leila Frechet (young Coco Chanel)

CREDITS

Director: George Kaczender | Producers: Larry G. Spangler, Eric Rochat | Writer: Julian More | Based on the book *Chanel solitaire* by Claude Delay | Photography: Ricardo Aronovich | Art Direction: Jacques Saulnier | Film Editing: Georges Klotz | Set Decoration: Gerard Viard, Marc Frederix | Costume Design: Rosine Delamare | Music: Jean Musy | *Running Time*: 120 mins.

THE FILM

Biographical film about the French fashion designer Coco Channel, from her unfortunate youth to her success in the design world, focusing on her relationship with the wealthy textile heir Etienne de Balsan and her tempestuous love affair with his friend, the English polo player Boy Capel. Both men played an important role in setting her up as an independent businesswoman.

DALTON:

"It's fascinating to be in France, working with a Hungarian-Canadian director, other leading actors who are French, Dutch and American, an American producer and a French supporting cast. I feel there's good cause for real optimism about the film. And the food's very good!"

    FILMS ILLUSTRATED

"I've always liked the concept of multinational films, and when they sent me the script it was with an absolute promise to rewrite, which innocently I believed. Then I got into the studio in Paris and found they hadn't changed a word of it, and we started from there. After two weeks they did get around to sacking the writer but, as the crew were all either French or Hungarian-Canadian, they didn't know many other authors, so I was despatched to

London to find one while they all stood around the set waiting for the action. The only writer I really wanted said he was already having a nervous breakdown and didn't need *Chanel* as well, so in the meantime the lady playing Chanel and I sat up most of the night trying to get it right and then in came Julian More, who used to write the scenes ten minutes before we had to shoot them. "

THE TIMES

"[*About Marie-France Pisier*] Our approach to work was very different, but we were getting along well by the end of the film. She's got a great face. Absolutely stunning."

PHOTOPLAY

"Capel wrote this book about a federation of Europe, and sixty years later we get into the Common Market! And he did encourage Chanel to work which was unusual in those days. One didn't have a mistress that worked. It was a bad reflection on one's own social standing. He was even part of the Versailles Peace Treaty so he was obviously a man of substance. He was a man who was making his fortune rather than a man who was idly frittering it away in country houses with horses. Sure, he wanted to get on."

CINEMA

REVIEWS

"The script never gives gorgeous-looking Marie-France Pisier a chance to suggest what really made Coco Chanel tick, though Timothy Dalton conveys swarthy ruthlessness as the self-made millionaire Boy Capel."

Richard Barkley, EXPRESS ON SUNDAY, 14 October 1981

"More appealing and plausible are Timothy Dalton as Capel and Rutger Hauer as Etienne De Balsan, both of them doing highly successful matinee-idol turns. As Chanel's one true love and her debonair mentor, respectively, Mr Dalton and Mr Hauer help the movie work at least at the level of a schoolgirl romance. "

Janet Maslin, THE NEW YORK TIMES, 16 October 1981

"Hauer and Dalton are superb. Once best friends, they confront each other in rivalry over Coco. Hauer (the loser) breaks down and weeps, asking his friend to embrace him. It's a moving moment."

PEOPLE, 7 December 1981

THE MASTER OF BALLANTRAE [TV]

1984

CBS

CAST

Michael York (James Durie), Richard Thomas (Henry Durie), Timothy Dalton (Col. Francis Burke), Finola Hughes (Alison Graeme), John Gielgud (Lord Durrisdeer), Ian Richardson (Mr. MacKellar), Kim Hicks (Jessie Broun), Nickolas Grace (Dass), Brian Blessed (Captain Teach), Ed Bishop (Pinkerton), Nick Brimble (Chew), Brian Coburn, (John Mountain), Pavel Douglas (Bonnie Prince Charlie), Richard Driscoll (McGregor), Donald Eccles (John Paul), John Hallam (Captain Harris), Don Henderson (Hicks)

CREDITS

Director: Douglas Hickox | Producers: Hugh Benson, Patrick Dromgoole, Peter Graham Scott, Larry White | Writer: William Bast | Based on the book *The Master of Ballantrae* by Robert Louis Stevenson | Cinematography: Bob Edwards | Production Design: John Biggs | Editing: Geoff Shepherd | Art Direction: Derek Nice | Costume Design: Olga Lehmann | Music: Bruce Broughton | *Running Time*: 150 mins.

THE SERIES

In 1745, Bonnie Prince Charlie lands in Scotland breaking out the last Jacobite rebellion. James, the Master of Ballantrae, is a brave but foolish and hot-headed young man. He decides to join the uprising, against the advice of his father and younger brother. Eventually, the family agrees that one brother must join the Jacobites, but the other must remain loyal to the government so that, no matters who wins, the family's future will be safe.

DALTON:

"It was one of the few roles I've done where there was no romantic involvement. It was quite a relief! It was much closer, in fact, to the sort of character I would really like to be playing. I can remember as a kid going to the Saturday-morning flicks and seeing people on pirate ships and riding horses, and thinking, 'Gosh, wouldn't I love to do that!' And *The Master of Ballantrae* had it all. We went on real square-riggers in the English Channel, fighting sea battles, and we played Cowboys and Indians through the North American wilderness, which was actually filmed in the Wye Valley in South Wales. Great fun!"

WOMAN'S WEEKLY

REVIEWS

"When James first travels to America, he is accompanied by Col. Francis Burke, played by Timothy Dalton as the most winsome of rapscallions."

Janet Maslin, THE NEW YORK TIMES, 31 January 1984

FLORENCE NIGHTINGALE [TV]

1985

NBC

CAST

Jaclyn Smith (Florence Nightingale), Claire Bloom (Fanny Nightingale), Timothy Dalton (Richard Milnes), Timothy West (William Russell), Peter McEnery (Sidney Herbert), Stephan Chase (Dr Sutherland), Ann Thornton (Parthe Nightingale), Jeremy Brett (William Nightingale), Jeremy Child (Dr Hall), Brian Cox (Dr McGregor), Patrick Drury (Henry Nicholson), Lesley Dunlop (Joanne), Michael Elwyn (Dr Menzies), Julian Fellowes (Charles Bracebrige), Lorna Heilbron (Selina)

CREDITS

Director: Daryl Duke | Producers: Gerald W. Abrams, Ron Carr, Jennifer Faulstich, Anthony B. Richmond | Writers: Ivan Moffat, Rose Leiman Goldemberg | Cinematography: Jack Hildyard | Editing: Bill Lenny | Production Designer: Harry Pottle | Art Direction: Mark Nerini | Set Decoration: Terry Parr | Costume Design: Marit Allen | Music: Stanley Myers | *Running Time*: 140 mins.

THE FILM

Florence Nightingale is an aristocratic woman who defies Victorian society and starts to reform hospital sanitation. After rejecting a comfortable life, she volunteers to travel to Scutari to care for the wounded soldiers of the Crimean War. However, she will be scorned by her community, and she will face great opposition for her new way of thinking.

REVIEWS

"When Mr Milnes, played by the dashingly handsome Timothy Dalton, finally drops out of the marriage picture by announcing his engagement to another woman, he is quickly replaced by a Dr Sutherland."

    John J. O'Connor, THE NEW YORK TIMES, 7 April 1985

"Her [Jaclyn Smith] initial scene with Dalton (soon to debut as Bond that year; he's both feline and bored at the same time here) has some awkward exchanges."

    Paul Mavis, dvdtalk.com, 27 July 2009

THE DOCTOR AND THE DEVILS

1985

Twentieth Century-Fox Film Corp.

CAST

Timothy Dalton (Dr Thomas Rock), Jonathan Pryce (Robert Fallon), Twiggy (Jennie Bailey), Julian Sands (Dr Murray), Stephen Rea (Timothy Broom), Phyllis Logan (Elizabeth Rock), Lewis Fiander (Dr Thornton), Beryl Reid (Mrs. Flynn) T. P. McKenna (O'Connor), Patrick Stewart (Prof. Macklin), Siân Phillips (Annabella Rock), Philip Davis (Billy Bedlam), Philip Jackson (Andrew Merry-Lees), Danny Schiller (Praying Howard), Bruce Green (Mole), Toni Palmer (Rosie), David Bamber (Cronin), Nichola McAuliffe (Alice), Deidre Costello (Nelly), Terry Neason (Kate), Paul Curran (Tom the Porter)

CREDITS

Director: Freddie Francis | Producers: Jonathan Sanger, Mel Brooks | Writer: Ronald Harwood | Based on the script by Dylan Thomas | Cinematography: Gerry Turpin, Norman Warwick | Editing: Laurence Méry-Clark | Art Direction: Robert Laing, Brian Ackland-Snow | Set Decoration: Peter James | Costume Design: Imogen Richardson | Music: John Morris | *Running Time*: 93 mins.

THE FILM

Dr Thomas Rock is a respected 19th-century anatomist lecturing at a prominent medical school. He is genuinely passionate about improving medical knowledge, a pursuit for which he believes "the ends justify the means." Unfortunately, due to the laws of the time, very few cadavers are legally available to the medical profession, so the use of grave robbers is required to procure additional corpses.

DALTON:

"Dylan Thomas, he wrote as a film script it is... I think a marvellous piece of work; it would also make a wonderful play actually. (...) At that time no doctor could do an operation...because he did not know what was inside the human body, it was illegal to dissect human bodies... he went into a very very tricky ethical area, and that is really what the film is about. The real doctor was ruined, disgraced but ultimately cleared but for the fact that he was cleared, doesn't mean to say, no, he must have known, he must have known. (...) The film was about 3 minutes shorter than it should have been because there is a marvellous scene in Dylan Thomas which was shot where the doctor comes face to face with the consequences of his actions and his own responsibility and I mean recognises, there is a scene where he has lost everything."

> JCET's Celebrity Spotlight

"I once went into an operating theatre together with the surgeon and once, into pathology department for an autopsy, that was just research for a film."

> Flicks And The City

REVIEWS

"As guardian of the film's moral issues, Mr Dalton - who assisted with an autopsy to help prepare himself for his role - is provided with soliloquies that, for the most part, match the language of Dylan Thomas's screenplay."

> Fabienne Marsh, THE NEW YORK TIMES, 14 August 1985

"All of the performances are good and, in the case of Mr Dalton, Mr Pryce, Mr Rea and Twiggy, they're also funny without condescending to the material."

> Vincent Canby, THE NEW YORK TIMES, 4 October 1985

"Timothy Dalton, who plays the mad doc, acts as though this were a role that the young Laurence Olivier overlooked. The difference is that Olivier would have played the part; Dalton merely poses for it."

> Ralph Novak, PEOPLE, 28 October 1985

"Dr Rock (Timothy Dalton) comes across as a constipated prig."

> Roger Ebert, CHICAGO SUN-TIMES, 11 November 1985

"Timothy Dalton with a decent role for once."

> NEWCASTLE EVENING CHRONICLE, 29 May 1986

"It is like a Hammer horror film perfunctorily warmed up and unredeemed by try-hard performances from Dalton, Jonathan Pryce and Twiggy."

Nigel Andrews, FINANCIAL TIMES, 30 June 1986

THE LIVING DAYLIGHTS

1987

United International Pictures & MGM/UA Communications Company

CAST

Timothy Dalton (James Bond), Maryam d'Abo (Kara Milovy), Jeroen Krabbé (General Georgi Koskov), Andreas Wisniewski (Necros), Art Malik (Kamran Shah), John Rhys-Davies (Gen. Leonid Pushkin), Joe Don Baker (Brad Whitaker), Thomas Wheatley (Saunders), Desmond Llewelyn (Q), Robert Brown (M), Geoffrey Keen (Minister of Defence), Walter Gotell (General Anatol Gogol), Caroline Bliss (Miss Moneypenny), John Terry (Felix Leiter), Virginia Hey (Rubavitch)

CREDITS

Director: John Glen | Producers: Albert R. Broccoli, Michael G. Wilson | Writers: Michael G. Wilson, Richard Maibaum | Cinematography: Alec Mills | Editings: John Grover, Peter Davis | Production Design: Peter Lamont | Art Direction: Terry Ackland-Snow | Set Decoration: Michael Ford | Costume Design: Emma Porteous | Music: John Barry | *Running Time*: 130 mins.

THE FILM

James Bond helps Russian officer Georgi Koskov to make defection to the West, but after the MI6 hides him, Koskov is abducted. Bond jumps into action, following a trail that leads him to the beautiful cello player Kara in Bratislava. After crossing the Austrian border and losing a fellow agent, Bond and Kara travel to Tanger where they find out a complex weapons plot with global implications.

DALTON:

"I don't think this is paper thin at all. I think it's a wonderful action adventure story. And one must remember also that the British film industry is not what it used to be. People might try and con you that it's in fine fettle, but it's not. And Mr Broccoli, for 25 years, has produced a British product, with British crew, British directors, and a major leading part for a British actor. And the longevity of this film series is a testament to how good and how exciting and how interested an audience is in watching them. And I don't think any actor should dismiss such an opportunity lightly. I mean it's a great thrill to be doing such a popular and an exciting film, which I embrace with joy and enthusiasm. (...) I think the essential quality of James Bond is that he's a man who lives on the edge, you never know, when at any moment he might be killed, therefore I think some of the qualities we associate with Bond, the qualities we've seen in this series of movies, the qualities that Ian Fleming wrote so well about, reflect that sense of danger in his own life."

Vienna Press Conference [THE MAKING OF *TLD*]

"I wanted to capture that occasional sense of vulnerability, and I wanted to capture the spirit of Ian Fleming."

Inside The Living Daylights

"The only way I can work as an actor is to find out what the man is I've got to play. In this instance, it's right there in the Ian Fleming books. (...) I cut most of those flippant lines. They had to go. There's still good humour in the movie, but it's not humour in the flip sense – it comes from the situation and from the believability of it. I think what we did was right, but there are still some terrific one-liners, aren't there? Some big laughs. (...) I had never done anything like a Bond movie before. It was the first modern contemporary action role I had ever done. There is also the challenge of pulling off a major international picture, one of the few that offers a leading part to a British actor. (...) I hope the audiences get a cracking good piece of entertainment from *The Living Daylights*. It's a movie that I feel is more believable, more watchable, more interesting, and much more realistic."

STARLOG

"I'm trying to bring something new to the role, so that neither the audience nor can I get bored; I'm attempting to inject something different - an expression, some humour, and interesting nuance - into every take, into every scene. Perhaps the 007 image will get a tad more intellectual. Who knows? They may tag me the 'thinking man's James Bond.'"

PREVUE

"Bond is rather humourless and deadly serious about his work, at least in the books. I definitely wanted to recapture the essence and flavour of the books, and play it less flippantly. After all, Bond's essential quality is that he's a man who lives on the edge. He could get killed at any moment, and that stress and danger factor is reflected in the way he lives, chain-smoking, drinking, fast cars and fast women. (...) He's someone I can relate to. After all, he's essentially, an old-fashioned hero, and I think that's his great appeal, to both men and women. He's steadfast, loyal, tenacious, and in the great tradition of British romantic heroes that probably started with Sir Galahad and The Knights of the Round Table, and who were epitomised by the Spitfire pilots in The Battle of Britain. (...) He's a ladies' man, but he's also a very male member of the species. He's the ultimate romantic, for Christ's sake, always out there rescuing the damsel in distress, usually at great personal risk. Let's face it; I'm sure an awful lot of feminists who accuse him of being macho and chauvinistic wouldn't half appreciate being saved from death from him. (...) He uses his brains and ingenuity as much as his fists. And Bond would never, ever spend hours in some gym pumping iron - Christ, Stallone will probably kill me for saying all this! No, you're far more likely to find him in a casino with a beautiful girl on his arm or at his club with a stiff Scotch in his hand; none of this carrot juice and celibacy nonsense. "

PLAYGIRL

"I think the Bond films did perhaps overexploit some of the very qualities that made them successful. But I'm delighted to see that we've brought back certain things that are redolent of Bond and Bond movies - the Aston-Martin car is back, and though we have far fewer gimmicks and tricks, we have some wonderfully inventive and ingenious ideas. (...) It's incorrect to think of Bond as a chauvinist. He often puts his life in more danger by helping the woman. He's the ultimate romantic, for Christ's sake, always out there rescuing the damsel in distress - and usually at great personal risk. He could often make his escape swifter if he didn't do the gentlemanly thing and wait for or protect the safety of his female accomplice. However, if the lady is a villain and gets in his way, she will be treated exactly the same manner as Bond treats a male villain. If, at the end of the adventure, Bond and the leading lady tumble into bed, it's because the lady wants to, as well as Bond. Both are falling in love, or should I say in lust."

NEW WOMAN

"My approach can't be 'How am I going to play it?' but 'What did Fleming write about? What made these stories work?' (...) When there's danger he's frightened. Every time you pick up Fleming, he's talking about the stomach getting wrenched knotted with anxiety. There are pills being taken. A glass of booze, just to get him through a moment. You can't identify with someone who doesn't feel relief or fear. (...) He's [Bond] like a knight. Not shining, but tarnished. (...) Bond was never flash or ostentatious. In fact, he really wore a uniform, a dark suit, navy blue. He was very navy blue. He wasn't a wealthy man. He used his money to buy the best that he needed, but then he kept it. For example, his suitcase. At one time it was a very good suitcase. But he's had it for ten years."

Rolling Stone

"First and foremost, I wanted to make him human. He's not a Superman; you can't identify with a Superman. You can always identify with the James Bond of the books, he's very much a man, and a tarnished man really, he's not perfect. I wanted to give him variety. I wanted to capture that occasional sense of vulnerability, and the sense that you could be allowed inside him, but there was something that was in there that you wanted to perceive, that that kind of man must have, and I wanted to capture the spirit of Ian Fleming."

Official UIP, Publicity Interview Transcript

"I felt it would be wrong to pluck the character out of thin air, or to base him on any of my predecessors' interpretations. Instead, I went to the man who created him, and I was astonished. I'd read a couple of the books years ago, and I thought I'd find them trivial now, but I thoroughly enjoyed every one. It's not just that they've a terrific sense of adventure and you get very involved. On those pages I discovered a Bond I'd never seen on the screen, a quite extraordinary man, a man I really wanted to play, a man of contradictions and opposites. He can be ruthless and determined, yet we're constantly shown what a serious, intelligent, thinking, feeling human being he is. He's a man of principle too, almost an idealist, but one who sees that he's living in a world without principle, in which ideals are cheaply bought and sold. He's a man who wants human contact; the need for love seems to overflow from him. Yet he can't afford emotional involvement; he can't fall in love or marry or have children, because that would prevent him functioning in a world where the possibility of his death is ever-present. Above all, I realised that he hates to kill. He recalls that when he was young, he thought it was all in the cause of righteousness, but now he perceives his assassinations as dirty murders. He kills himself by killing someone who's himself on the other side. Yet he carries on, always regretting it, always trying to shut it out of his mind. Altogether, it seemed to me that Bond was a complex man, with many more facets than I'd realised. Not a shining knight, but someone deeply unhappy with his job, suffering from confusion, ennui, moral revulsion and what Fleming calls accidie. (...) And of course, he's fun; he has a lust for life. He gambles, he drinks, he drives fast cars, he has casual sex or at least falls in love for a rather limited time. But that's because he lives on the edge of life and wants to live it to the full while he's still got it. To me, that's perfectly human."

The New York Times

"The James Bond character, of necessity, is involved in a lot of action. This movie is an adventure thriller, with a sense of humour, and if that is part of my role, then I should at least attempt as much of it as I can. In this James Bond film, it's especially important that the audience identify with this new man playing an established character. And the more they perceive Bond to be me, the more they will get caught up in the excitement. The action is necessary to the role, so I do as much as I can. (...) The differences between James Bond and myself are extreme. It's strange, because, as an actor, I must look for common identities in order to express Bond through me - but it isn't easy. Obviously, I don't know what it's like to be a secret agent, and I'm certainly not licensed to kill. And I don't know if I would *want* to be licensed to kill. Well, you never know, do you? There are odd times when it *has* flashed across my mind."

> TLD: THE OFFICIAL POSTER MAGAZINE

"The Bond movies are fantasies but I think in order to enjoy the fantasy you've got to hold into the reality and I was very, very influenced as a young kid by the movies of Sean Connery, *Dr No, From Russia with Love*, and *Goldfinger* and so I wanted to bring, at least be able to contribute a sense of reality, a sense of involvement, a sense of excitement, hopefully some danger and possibly some risk".

> James Bond – A BAFTA Tribute

REVIEWS

"Timothy Dalton looks more likely to last. He is handsome, square-jawed, dashing, suitable English, and technically a better actor than his predecessors. Some of the comedy, though, has gone with the change of star. (...) Dalton, though, has the classlessness of the classical actor. (...) While Connery was ironic and throwaway, and Moore flip and insolent, Dalton gives the impression of taking the secret agent's responsibilities seriously: he spends a lot of his time being intense and shifting his dark eyes suspiciously from side to side."

> David Robinson, THE TIMES, 30 June 1987

"Still, there's a new 007 to talk about and he's Timothy Dalton. And the formula has changed a bit, both to accommodate him and to take suitable cognisance of the post-permissive society. Dalton hasn't the natural authority of Connery nor the facile charm of Moore, but George Lazenby he is not. He is, in fact, four-square on the Balham Line – decent, daring, not above unorthodoxy but unlikely to ask Q for a fool-proof condom for the Aids era. The caveat is that a good actor has to have lines, and Richard Maibaum and

Michael G. Wilson let him invent the character again only in the barest outline. It's an able first go in the circumstances, though perhaps it could do with a bit more humour."

> Derek Malcolm, THE GUARDIAN, 2 July 1987

"Dalton here, though on trial, looks the part. His face has the handsome, chiselled wryness of Connery, with a cheek ready to dimple at the drop of an epigram. The voice is a soft but virile burr. And he wears the black tie and DJ without looking, as George Lazenby die, like a plumber surprised by tickets to a May Ball."

> Nigel Andrews, FINANCIAL TIMES, 3 July 1987

"When we eventually get a good look at him [TD] he appears lithe enough to do his own stuntwork, and is indeed a darkly handsome public-school type, with straight-hair and square-jaw, much like the Bond on the covers of the 1950s Pan paperbacks. He's a graver figure than Connery, Lazenby or Moore, and the screenwriters have given him a few funny lines, which also constitutes a return to Fleming. There are no Donald McGill *double entendres* and few of those callous wisecracks over the corpses of his victims. The humour is in Dalton's attractive personality, the wit in the extravagant action. (...) They [villains] are working heavies like Timothy Dalton's intense, dedicated secret agent."

> Philip French, THE OBSERVER, 5 July 1987

"Timothy Dalton makes a solemn Bond after Roger Moore, but the exotic location, action & stunts are as spectacular as ever in John Glen's film."

> ILLUSTRATED LONDON NEWS, 25 July 1987

"Dalton, with his lean and hungry look, is much nearer the Fifties character of Ian Fleming's books while being in a film that is very much for the Eighties. (...) Dalton has restored a vital element to 007 – the very best of British, the amateur gentleman who is better than any professional. He is kinder, more human, charming and low-profile. For me he is Bond, James Bond."

> Victoria Mather, DAILY TELEGRAPH, 1987

"He [Dalton] is a strong actor, he holds the screen well, he's good in the serious scenes, but he never quite seems to understand that it's all a joke. (...) Dalton is rugged, dark and saturnine, and speaks with a cool authority. We can halfway believe him in some of his scenes. And that's a problem, because the scenes are intended to be preposterous."

> Roger Ebert, CHICAGO SUN-TIMES, 31 July 1987

"Mr Dalton, the latest successor to the role of James Bond, is well equipped for his new responsibilities. He has enough presence, the right debonair looks and the kind of energy that the Bond series has lately been lacking. If he radiates more thoughtfulness than the role requires, maybe that's just gravy. (...) Mr Dalton, who trained at the Royal Academy of Dramatic Arts and has had a lot of experience playing Shakespeare, has a more sombre, reflective acting style than the ones Bond fans have grown used to; he's less ironic than Sean Connery, less insistently suave than Roger Moore. Instead, Mr Dalton has his own brand of charm. His Bond is world-wearier than others, but perhaps also more inclined to take the long view (as well he might, after all these years). In any case, he has enthusiasm, good looks and novelty on his side."

    Janet Maslin, THE NEW YORK TIMES, 31 July 1987

"Dalton, no waffler, develops the best Bond ever. He's as classy as the trademark tuxedo, as sleek as the Aston-Martin. Like Bond's notorious martini, women who encounter his carved-granite good looks are shaken, not stirred. Dalton does not play a pompous, mean-spirited Bond like Sean Connery or a prissy, sissy Bond like Roger Moore. Both were as aggressively heterosexual as pubescent Playboy subscribers. Calling on a background that includes everything from the Joan Collins' pot boiling mini-series *Sins* to a stint with the Royal Shakespeareans, Dalton creates a dashing and endearing secret agent. And unlike the creaky Connery and the mushy Moore in their later years, he looks fit for derring-do. He fleshes out the caricature that had evolved over the past 25 years. For inspiration, Dalton went back to the original 007 created by writer Ian Fleming, a character who endures, like such British perennials as Sherlock Holmes, for his audacity, élan and idiosyncrasies."

    Rita Kempley, WASHINGTON POST, 31 July 1987

"Dalton, with his athletic sort of Brit-yuppie work ethic and romantic streak, comes out all right. He's spindly but energetic and enthusiastic. The eyes are scintillating, green and squinty. The accent's as refined as Moore's, but free of aloofness. He doesn't have the hairy-chested exuberance of Connery, but there's a warmth trying to get out. (Are we talking about an actor or a racehorse?)."

    Desson Howe, WASHINGTON POST, 31 July 1987

"Hail, the new James Bond! Timothy Dalton is the classiest heir to the mantle of England's sexy secret agent since Sean Connery really said never again. He's serious... instinctive and appealingly heroic. (...) Smart enough not to copy the originator and also to eschew the hamminess of Moore that sent 007 into a weird orbit, Dalton makes the part his own. If anything, he underplays, but is never overshadowed by gadgets, gorgeous women or awesome stunt work. "

Candice Russell, THE SUN SENTINEL, 31 July 1987

"Indeed, the most impressive factor in the film, the one on which its success depends more than the story, is on Timothy Dalton, who is so damn good as James Bond, you feel like asking where he's been hiding since Connery left. Although he's so far only done this one, I feel safe to proclaim Dalton the best of the four, and one that Ian Fleming would have approved of... All in all, *The Living Daylights* has paved the way for a further twenty-five years of good James Bond films, and that is largely due to Timothy Dalton, who deserves as much as credit as possible. (...) Dalton puts back into Bond that unpredictability and ruthlessness that Roger Moore and, to an extent, Sean Connery lacked. "

Gary Russell, STARBURST, August 1987

"A very handsome actor, Dalton looks a little like the young Olivier, and he has fine voice. But there's a spark missing. Dalton has played classical roles in the theater; he's a serious man, and he seems to be trying to play Bond thoughtfully, which is almost a certain mistake. (...) So it seems odd that Dalton as Bond is so straight and businesslike, and at times almost angry, as if he didn't quite approve of the frivolousness of the material. He grows impatient, irritable, but he can't do anything with his mood. After all, what thoughts *could* Bond have except disgust? But disgust would be a betrayal, of himself and of us. For a quarter century, Bond has flourished as the only happy Englishman in the movies. We don't want to know what's 'inside' him. Bond is rakish or he's nothing."

David Denby, NEW YORK MAGAZINE, 10 August 1987

"In Timothy Dalton's interpretation of 007 in *The Living Daylights*, one finds some of the lethal charm of Sean Connery, along with a touch of crabby Harrison Ford. This Bond is as fast on his feet as with his wits; an ironic scowl creases his face; he's battle ready yet war-weary. And in the age of AIDS, even Bond must bend to serial monogamy; this time, for reasons of plot and propriety, he's a one-gal guy. Dalton performed a lot of his own stunts, and he looks great in a tuxedo – especially the one with the Velcro lapels that folds over to give him the guise of a priest-assassin."

Richard Corliss, TIME, 10 August 1987

"Timothy Dalton is a huge improvement on Roger Moore; for one thing, he's the right age for an active secret agent who spends considerable time dangling from a flying transport plane. But more than that he has the cool, coiled élan that Connery used to such advantage. Like the original Bond, Dalton jaunts through the action with an air of imperturbable calm, with only an occasional raised eyebrow or droll remark to indicate his intellectual engagement in the action."

      Henry Sheehan, THE CHICAGO READER, 13 August 1987

"The actor looks appropriately debonair in the role, and he 'commits' more to the character. Except for an occasional flash of his Cheshire cat's smile, Dalton gives us a more serious, edgy and far less facetious Bond."

      Robert Dimatteo, NEA, 14 August 1987

"In *The Living Daylights*, Dalton gives us a Bond who is less world-weary than Roger Moore and more realistic about life than the daring Sean Connery. He takes risks out of necessity, not just for fun."

      Linda Deutsch, THE ASSOCIATED PRESS, 23 August 1987

"Timothy Dalton, the fourth Bond, registers beautifully on all key counts of charm, machismo, sensitivity and technique. In *The Living Daylights* he's abetted by material that's a healthy cut above the series norm of super-hero fantasy. (...) Belatedly, the Bond characterization has achieved appealing maturity."

      VARIETY, 1987

"After an absence of nearly twenty years the real James Bond has returned to the screen in the guise of Timothy Dalton. All credit must go to Dalton for keeping his portrayal of Bond as close to Ian Fleming's original conception as possible. (...) I believe Timothy Dalton is the most human and emotional James Bond yet. (...) Both Dalton and the creative talent behind the camera have given the Bond series a much-needed shot in the arm."

      Kevin Harper, 007, March 1988

HAWKS

1988

J. Arthur Rank Film Distributors

CAST

Timothy Dalton (Bancroft), Anthony Edwards (Deckermensky), Janet McTeer (Hazel), Camille Coduri (Maureen), Jill Bennett (Vivian Bancroft), Robert Lang (Walter Bancroft), Pat Starr (Millie Deckermensky), Bruce Boa (Byron Deckermensky), Sheila Hancock (Regina), Geoffrey Palmer (SAAB Salesman), Caroline Langrishe (Carol), Benjamin Whitrow (Mr. Granger), Robyn Moore (Second Bridesmaid), Connie Booth (Nurse Jarvis), Julie T. Wallace (Ward Sister)

CREDITS

Director: Robert Ellis Miller | Producers: Richard Becker, Keith Cavele, Morrie Eisenman, Steve Lanning | Writers: Roy Clarke, Barry Gibb, David English | Cinematography: Douglas Milsome | Editing: Malcolm Cooke | Production Design: Peter Cooke, Peter Howitt | Costume Design: Catherine Cook | Music: Barry Gibb, John Cameron | *Running Time*: 110 mins.

THE FILM

Two terminally ill patients in a London hospital – a British solicitor and an American football player – with no friends or family near, form an uneasy alliance and plot an escape to Amsterdam's biggest brothel for one last wild time. On their trip, they will meet two English girls and their adventure will be very different from what they expected.

DALTON:

"It's probably the most enjoyable experience I've had making a film. *Hawks* is about two men who are facing a premature death, since they have cancer—and that puts life into focus. It's provocative, a serious comedy, a black comedy. It deals with ordinary people who are going slightly crazy because of the situation they're in—it's somewhat life-affirming, challenging, aggressive. And it says: Fight for your life; don't give in!"

> STARLOG

"He [Anthony's character] is a really good, nice, straight, honest character, and goes through a process that is very common. He gets very, very indulgent and very, very depressed. Very depressed. And my character, you know, uses all the means at his disposal to kind of spark and prod and poke and provoke. And he does the same for me at a later date, you know? I mean, we start to learn to need each other. (...) I think this [work] has got something more important to say. I mean, it is dealing with a much more important subject than a lot of others, certainly. I mean, you know, you've got to treat life with some humour, haven't you? I mean, you know, that's a good attitude to take - pugnacious, tough, have a laugh, be good-humoured, resourceful, and resilient."

> The Making of *Hawks*

"*Hawks* deals with the subject of extraordinary relevance: Why does it take a crisis to make you realise how bloody precious life is? Unfortunately, it's about cancer, which is a not a word the film business thinks of as being particularly commercial."

> LIFESTYLES

"*Hawks* is a story about two young cancer victims who decide to… well, they're young, foolish, they're full of braggadocio and balls, and they're gonna die, and they just do what they wanna do. Rather than lie about and die in hospital and do chemotherapy or whatever, they decide to just get out and do a little bit of living. The studio changed it around a bit, unfortunately, but it was a sad, tragic comedy, and at the time I was overwhelmed with letters by cancer victims and the husbands, wives, and children of cancer victims who were just saying, 'Thank you so much'."

A.V. Club

"He's a man faced with a huge problem and he faces it with great pugnacity, verve and humour. *Hawks* is really more about life than death. The lives of Bancroft and Decker have been brought into very sharp focus through their illness. The film is about the course of action that they take and how they deal with it. It's a film of resilience and courage, good humour and toughness. It's a terrific story, a worthwhile story."

Film Review

"Roy Clarke's *Hawks* is one of the best scripts I've seen, which makes it much easier for me to use myself as the vehicle to convey the part and identify with it. It invigorates your thinking. If we do this film well, it will be a complex, richly textured piece of work. It's a story so international in its theme, it should touch everybody: there's prognacity, learning, wisdom, dependence, independence, need...all about life in the little time they've got, and it's all enchanted by Barry Gibb's haunting score."

Hello!

"For some dumb reason, the Americans have decided to cut out the parents from the movie, and that I think is important because it gives the two guys their world of loneliness. I'm very proud of it – it's a wonderful film. (...) You're talking about two guys who have cancer. It's not actually about death; it's in fact about life, how precious life is and how it should be seized and grasped and how. Why do we always take tomorrow for granted? Why does it always take a crisis like a war or some doctor telling you have a dicky heart or a cancer to make us value what it is we've got. The premise of that, of course, is death, so I'm sure people think it's not particularly a commercial subject, although it's relevant to every single human being on the face of this earth! We all know people, who have been affected by cancer, and we all have a life to live and we all waste a lot of it."

007

"There's been some resistance to it from the distributors because its basic premise is that two men are looking at a foreshortened life because of cancer. And cancer effects just about everyone on the globe. We all know someone who's got it, had it, died of it. But a lot of people don't seem to think that one should mention the word. It's a good film, very provocative. It's about how life is thrown very sharply into focus and how two guys try to get on with it and learn a lot about life and life's values. The situation they're in is very poignant, because when you discover good, and you know you're losing it... Some people think that one should not use comedy to examine anything that's serious, and of course, no one is poking fun at cancer. Comedy is used as an expression of courage, and as an expression of vigour, determination to live. It's a good film; I like it very much and was extremely happy making it. It should be coming out. It was shown recently at the Toronto Film Festival and did *extraordinarily* well."

BONDAGE

REVIEWS

"Dalton, whose superglued jaw-muscles suit James Bondery better than jollity, does wonders in inviting sympathy for a character I would have no hesitation in asking to have removed from my terminal ward."

Nigel Andrews, FINANCIAL TIMES, 5 August 1988

"Dalton goes a bit overboard as Bancroft, occasionally stretching believability."

VARIETY, 1988

"Timothy Dalton plays the afflicted solicitor, Bancroft, turned maudlin philosopher and sarcastic critic of the cards that life has dealt him. Followers of Dalton's recent performances might only associate him with the suave, sophisticated new, new, new James Bond. But I remember his dark, brooding, mysterious good looks as Heathcliff in *Wuthering Heights*, an image which more suits his pale, hollow-cheeked appearance here."

Cass Hampton, THE CANBERRA TIMES, 7 August 1989

"Mr Dalton is asked to spout an incessant stream of cloying chatter, but he does this with grace and good humor."

Janet Maslin, THE NEW YORK TIMES, 10 November 1989

"Dalton manages to rouse himself out of the stupor that undermines his performances in the James Bond films. But though this means that he's more animated and hits his consonants with a little more verve, it doesn't mean that he's any more expressive. Edwards, on the other hand, is too lightweight for his assignment – in every sense of the word. The notion that he is a football player is ludicrous, but he doesn't have the emotional weight either. Dalton, at least, has some stature."

Hal Hinson, THE WASHINGTON POST, 10 November 1989

"As Bancroft, Dalton thumbs his nose at the ogre of typecasting and takes an axe to his image of suave romantic. As an eloquent, high-spirited victim of bone cancer, complete with thinning scalp, the star devours the screen with hungry gulps of over-acting. He is immensely watchable, but his is a stage performance."

James Cameron Wilson, FILM REVIEW, 1989

BRENDA STARR

1989

Triumph Releasing

CAST

Brooke Shields (Brenda Starr), Tony Peck (Mike Randall), Timothy Dalton (Basil St. John), Diana Scarwid (Libby "Lips" Lipscomb), Jeffrey Tambor (Vladimir), Nestor Serrano (Jose), June Gable (Luba), Charles Durning (Editing Francis I. Livright), Kathleen Wilhoite (Reporter Hank O'Hare), John Short (Cub Reporter Pesky Miller), Eddie Albert (Police Chief Maloney)

CREDITS

Director: Robert Ellis Miller | Producer: Myron A. Hyman | Writer: Noreen Stone, James David Buchanan, Jenny Wolkind | Based on the characters of

Brenda Starr by Dale Messik | Cinematography: Freddie Francis, Peter Stein | Editing: Mark Melnick | Production Design: John J. Lloyd | Art Direction: Tim Boxell, Michael Brunsfeld, William Groshelle, Steven Schwartz | Set Decoration: William Anderson, Craig K. Brown, Michael E. Campbell, Norman C. Dulaney, Audie Gibson, Christy Richards, Ana Berta Vazquez, Richard A. Villalobos | Costume Design: Peggy Farrell | Music: Johnny Mandel | *Running Time*: 94 mins.

THE FILM

Mike is the author of the *Brenda Starr* comic strip for a newspaper. Suddenly Brenda comes to life and leaves the comic strip. To keep his job, Mike draws himself into the strip and pursues Brenda who is heading to the Amazon jungle, to find a scientist with a secret formula which will create cheap and powerful fuel from ordinary water. There, she must steal the formula from her competition and foreign spies.

DALTON:

"[I play] a man who has one eye and lives in the depths of the Amazon jungle, where he drinks the juice of black orchids to avoid going insane. I mean, certainly, there's a curiosity to that."

>STARLOG

"Brooke is a beauty who hasn't yet had a role worthy of her. I doubt *Brenda Starr* is that role, but the picture should put her back on the cinematic map – and may also do me some good, too."

>PREVUE

"It's funny, charming, light. The problem – I have to be careful what I say – is a contractual and legal problem between the investors and producers."

>THE MILWAUKEE JOURNAL

REVIEWS

"Timothy Dalton is apt casting as dashing Basil St. John, the mystery man with the signature black orchids who beguiles Starr."

>Kevin Thomas, LOS ANGELES TIMES, 15 April 1992

"The plot's unfortunate resemblance to Disney's vastly superior *Rocketeer** is further underscored by the presence of Timothy Dalton, whose wickedly funny turn as the Nazi villain in that film only makes his walk-through as Brenda's twitty, eye-patch-wearing love foil, Basil St. John, seems twice as leaden."

Peter Travers, ROLLING STONE, 15 April 1992

"Also on hand, though not able to rise above the film's dull and scenery-logged adventure plot, are Timothy Dalton as the terminally dashing Basil St. John and Diana Scarwid as Libby Lips, Brenda's archrival in the reporting game."

Janet Maslin, THE NEW YORK TIMES, 19 April 1992

"Dalton, who trots out the rascal persona he used in *The Rocketeer**, is a free-lance-hero type who becomes Shields' Lois Lane. Like the film's writers, though, he seems to take the plot way too seriously."

Ralph Novak, PEOPLE, 11 May 1992

*In the USA, *Brenda Starr* was not released until 1992.

LICENCE TO KILL

1989

United International Pictures & MGM/UA Communications Company

CAST

Timothy Dalton (James Bond), Carey Lowell (Pam Bouvier), Robert Davi (Franz Sanchez), Talisa Soto (Lupe Lamora), Anthony Zerbe (Milton Krest), Frank McRae (Sharkey), David Hedison (Felix Leiter), Wayne Newton (Professor Joe Butcher), Benicio Del Toro (Dario), Anthony Starke (Truman-Lodge), Everett McGill (Ed Killifer), Desmond Llewelyn (Q), Pedro Armendáriz Jr. (President Hector Lopez),Robert Brown (M), Priscilla Barnes (Della Churchill Leiter), Don Stroud (Heller), Caroline Bliss (Miss Moneypenny), Cary-Hiroyuki Tagawa (Kwang)

CREDITS

Director: John Glen | Producers: Albert R. Broccoli, Michael G. Wilson | Writers: Michael G. Wilson, Richard Maibaum | Cinematography: Alec Mills | Editings: John Grover, Peter Davis | Production Design: Peter Lamont | Art Direction: Dennis Bosher, Michael Lamont | Set Decoration: Michael Ford | Costume Design: Jodie Tillen | Music: Michael Kamen | *Running Time*: 133 mins.

THE FILM

James Bond is suspended from MI6 when he doesn't want to give his pursuit of drugs lord Franz Sanchez who has ordered an attack against his CIA friend Felix Leiter and rape and murder on Felix's wife during their honeymoon. Working on his own, Bond travels from Key West to the Republic of Isthmus where he will receive the help of ex-CIA agent Pam Bouvier and an unexpected Q.

DALTON:

"You can't relate to a superhero, to a superman, but you can identify with a real man who in times of crisis draws forth some extraordinary quality from within himself and triumphs but only after a struggle. Real courage is knowing what faces you and knowing how to face it."

    THE MAKING OF LICENCE TO KILL

"There won't be much hardware in this one at all. As the title would imply he's lost his licence so he hasn't got that much access to it. But it's still full of action, and it's a good story. These are escapist fantasies and my belief has always been that you will only enjoy a fantasy if you can be made to be involved, and identify with the people in it. You have to *believe* them."

    FILM MONTHLY

"He's not behaving as a professional. Normally in any other story and in any other future story, one would presume that Bond would behave as a professional, detached, objective, skilled agent, but this time he's personally involved. He becomes consumed by this mission, backed by fury because nobody is going to do anything about it. A good man's been viciously maimed and his wife's been murdered. Don't forget, Bond's been married and his wife was murdered, too, and because of the corruption, the drug money and the influence of that corruption, no one's going to do anything. So he becomes very, very involved, and he f**** up. It's a destructive course of action. It's very understandable; in a pragmatic sense commendable. Maybe not from an idealist viewpoint, where you're supposed to arrest people and let justice take its course. In this case he kills them, but then he changes his tact because he's gone down that course almost to the point of self-destruction. But he realizes it, and then he broadens out the view of what he's after, and he behaves much more objectively, because he realizes that he just doesn't have to go against the man, he's got to go against what the man stands for and what the man is, and his empire as well. Bond is very clever, preying on the man's weakness which the man thinks as being his strength, and planting that paranoia, allowing the man to destroy himself. "

    EMPIRE (1)

"Bond movies at their inception, whilst having a sense of fantasy, were definitively exciting adventure thrillers that grown-up audiences loved. We have made a step away from the comedic type of Bond which Roger Moore did very well. (...) He [Bond] goes around looking like a bad guy, but is fact a good guy. He is not the perfect white shining knight, Bond is far more genuine. The great thing about any hero is what he has to face to overcome the great odds in his path. (...) We were just determined to make a real James Bond movie for grown-ups, but I have not spoken to a single person who thought the certification [15] was correct. There is nothing in the film I wouldn't take my own son to see and there is nothing you haven't seen before in a Bond movie. People are always being eaten by sharks and burned alive. (...) I put as much into Bond as anything. I would be letting myself down if I didn't."

  EVENING CHRONICLE

"In essence, every Bond film is new. But it's like playing Hamlet. Everybody's watched 'Hamlet' - but they want to see what someone new does with it."

  LIFESTYLES

"I tried to bring some dimension to James Bond, to make him a human being. He is determined, often very ruthless, by no means a white knight. If you're going to deal with villains, you have to be villainous to beat them. I take my cue from the novels and the very early Bond movies. "

  THE NEW YORK TIMES

"The film is a different kind of film – more straightforward in its motive. (...) *Licence to Kill* is about vengeance, retribution and setting a wrong – a personal grievance – right, but it broadens, expands and takes on a larger perspective. Ultimately, as in all good Bond films, good does triumph over evil on a better basis than just one of personal revenge. I mean, one's own scope, one's own awareness of how he's behaving is enlarged and is brought back to something that is much more calculating and striving for a good end. (...) The movies themselves had the evolution. (...) In *Licence to Kill*, too, I hope you see a different Bond."

  Official UIP, Publicity Interview Transcript

"If my contribution was anything, it did sort of move towards a change of focus and change of direction and gave it a new lease of life. We put in place the blocks that allowed the series to grow. That I'm happy for".

  THE JAMES BOND CAR COLLECTION

"She [costume designer] wanted to put me in pastels. Can you imagine? I thought, 'No, we can't have that.' The clothes say so much about Bond. He's got a naval background, so he needs a strong, simple colour like dark blue."

TODAY

"If you're going for something current, you have to go with what is perceived as a universal threat – and the drug mobs certainly are. We hope that the story will be more interesting than the locations – and that's not always been true. It's still an escapist fantasy movie, of course. (...) That [Fleming's] Bond is capable of behaving in an objective way, as a professional, but he can respond with revulsion to the terrible things that happen. (...) Man should be able to identify with his heroes. A hero has to be the same as you, but capable of being able to pull something special out when he needs to. (...) I went into this with my eyes wide open, having turned it down twice before. And actually, I'm very happy with the side effects."

KNT News Service

"If you're going to do a James Bond film, he exists in a world of danger and violence. That should be given. It's just for the past 10 years, the films have been more light-hearted and comedic – to fit Roger's style. But if you go back to Ian Fleming's novels and the early films, people were always being eaten by sharks, shot, set on fire, tortured or killed in horrendous ways. (...) Bond is generally monogamous. There have been occasions when he has been to bed with another woman, it's true, but generally, he has his leading lady and that's his relationship."

NEA

"It's still the same man, only here he's driven less objectively and professionally than he might be if he was working on a mission or a job. It comes from a personal source, but of course he's still Bond. (...) I would like to mention that this movie will be a harder, grittier, darker, and perhaps more realistic film than we've seen before. Alec Mills, who's lighting it, and the very texture of the story, both guarantee that. (...) I was gratified that so many people *did* enjoy *The Living Daylights*, but the responsive has *not* been 100 per cent, because everybody has their preconceptions of how James Bond should be. But overall, there has been an overwhelming sense of pleasure at the direction the last movie took and how it was received but the audience. But it doesn't have five one greater ease at all!"

STARLOG

"What one must face today is that we've got something new, something different... This is a new style of Bond. It isn't a light-hearted, comic, spoofing Bond. It's not a technological extravaganza. I think it's back down to its origins, its basics, trying to capture the spirit of Ian Fleming, and of the early movies. (...) *Licence to Kill* started to do extremely well in Europe. If it does well here, I'm sure there will be another one. But for how long I'll continue, I don't know."

ASSOCIATED PRESS

"Bond exists in a violent world and had to use violence against violence. However light-hearted and funny the middle section of movies were [played by Roger Moore], they lost what was essential to anyone who knows what Bond films and books were all about. (...) All I want is for them [the writers] to write a bloody good Bond history and I'll come and act it. Once you start writing for someone, then you miss the unpredictability and lose a certain edge."

DAILY EXPRESS (1)

"This [15 certificate] has never happened before to a Bond film. When you consider what children can watch on television these days, there is nothing in this movie which could cause problems. We have standards on Bond films, and this does not breach them – even if it is more realistic than previous pictures."

DAILY EXPRESS (2)

"A lot of people have said *Licence to Kill* was forerunner of Bond today [*2012*] and in a sense that is what Cubby and I were trying to do. The Bond movies were becoming pastiches of themselves but they were still successful and people were not ready to embrace a new formula. There was a lot of innate resistance to change."

EXPRESS ON SUNDAY

"Benicio Del Toro cut off my finger! It wasn't really his fault, but we were doing the scene in Licence to Kill where I'm hanging over a meat-grinder and he's cutting away at the wires holding me, and something went wrong. Come to think of it, we probably shouldn't have had a sharp knife! (...) For the finale, I had to jump from one moving tanker to another. I leap across, climb this ladder while all these bullet hits are going off – BAM! BAM! BAM! BAM! BAM! – and the klaxon that means 'cut' goes off. I'm thrilled. I know I've done a good job. But when I look around, everyone's pissing themselves. I look down and I'm in my underpants. My trousers are hanging down off my ankles. My very beautiful suit – made of strong serge, as Fleming specifies in the books - was in shreds! (...) One critic complained that it was no longer a film six-year-olds could go to. Well, Bond movies, when they opened in the '60s, were not for six-year-olds. They were grown-up adventures. (...) I'm very lucky – I've had a good life and a good career. And Bond has brought me a lot of joy."

Empire (2)

REVIEWS

"Here, as played by Timothy Dalton, he goes about his business with a grim determination that is out of key with the plot, which is absurd but fundamentally dull."

Ian Christie, Daily Express, 14 June 1989

"Tim Dalton's 007 has, in Biblical parlance, developed into a hairy rather than a smooth man, apt to be sparing with the quips, earnest with the women and positively angry with the villainous perfidy of his opponents. He is not so much the latterday Errol Flynn of MI5 but a tepider version of Humprey Bogart, prepared to tell the British Secret Service to bugger off when it's not prepared to do the decent thing."

Derek Malcolm, The Guardian, 15 June 1989

"Dalton brings to the role a clenched, scarce-smiling intensity."

Nigel Andrews, Financial Times, 15 June 1989

"The previous James Bonds were obvious *parvenus* and social frauds; Timothy Dalton has more class; you can believe he went to a good school, even if a provincial accent creeps in now and then. He is a warmer personality, too; and perhaps in consequence the script makes him markedly less callous in his killings and in his one-line comments on sudden death."

David Robinson, The Times, 15 June 1989

"Despite the playful sparkle in his eyes, Timothy Dalton's Bond is even more serious here than in *The Living Daylights*. He beds only two women, unseen and without accompanying fireworks or crashing waves, both nobly in the interests of the plot. When Sanchez refers to 007's 'big cojones' it is a tribute to his courage rather than his manifest virility, and the old *doubles entendres* have been dropped."

Philip French, The Observer, 18 June 1989

"Dalton gives the character greater depth than before: he bleeds, both externally and internally, and has moments of introspection worthy of his Hamlet-like black shirt."

Iain Johnstone, Sunday Times, 18 June 1989

"Mr Dalton glowering presence adds a darker tone. (…) Mr Dalton is perfectly at home as an angry Bond and as a romantic lead and as an action hero, but he never seems to blend any two of those qualities at once. He does not seem at ease with all of Bond's lines and to the actor's immense credit he seems least comfortable when M meets him at Hemingway's house, a Key West tourist attraction and tells him to turn over his gun 'I guess it's a farewell to arms' says Mr. Dalton not quite cringing. They have to stop writing lines like that for the Dalton Bond or he'll really be full of angst. Meanwhile he is beginning to hold his own with the shadows of his former self..."

Caryn James, THE NEW YORK TIMES,12 July 1989

"On the basis of this second performance as Bond, Dalton can have the role as long as he enjoys it. He makes an effective Bond - lacking Sean Connery's grace and humor, and Roger Moore's suave self-mockery, but with a lean tension and a toughness that is possibly more contemporary. The major difference between Dalton and the earlier Bonds is that he seems to prefer action to sex. But then so do movie audiences, these days. *Licence to Kill* is one of the best of the recent Bonds."

Roger Ebert, CHICAGO SUN-TIMES, 14 July 1989

"For *Licence to Kill*, the 16th installment in the Cubby Broccoli-produced series, the filmmakers and their star, Timothy Dalton, have entered into a sort of grim collusion, building the film to the actor's stern specifications. As a result, Dalton plays a straight-faced, humorless, no-nonsense Bond – all guns and no play – and it makes for a very dull time. The blame falls as much to the creators' conception of their hero as to the actor playing him. It's not that Dalton, who's making his second appearance in the role, isn't actor enough for the job. It's that Bond himself now seems prosaic, earthbound, in serious need of a superhero transfusion. (...) Also, although there's grace and agility in Dalton's physical work, in repose he nearly ceases to exist. That Dalton hasn't emerged as a Bond to be reckoned with, a star to juice the character's EKG back onto the scale, is a shocking disappointment. With his deep-clefted, cruelly handsome features, Dalton held out the promise of a return to Connery form, to a time in Bond's movie life when both danger and wit were part of his secret agent accessory kit. But playing Bond doesn't seem to spark anything special in Dalton. Even though this is only his second shot at the role, there's nothing new to discover in him. Dalton plays the part as if it were an unpleasant chore – he doesn't seem to be having any fun – and there's an air of condescension in his performance, as if somehow his classical training made the character beneath him. He acts as if he's slumming. Dalton actually gets the dangerous part, it's the essential wit that's missing. (...) Dalton turns Agent 007 into a brooding blue-collar grunt. (...) Dalton doesn't seem to find any greater thrill in these erotic encounters than he does in Bond's other chores. It's all heavy lifting to him. Not all the film's problems can be blamed on Dalton; his presence merely brings them into focus."

    Hal Hinson, THE WASHINGTON POST, 14 July 1989

"But director Glen has also taken advantage of Bond's new interpreter, Timothy Dalton, to introduce a fresh emotional angle. (...) Dalton revives the cool, ironic detachment of the Connery years, but he also allows a touch of obsession to show through Bond's surface aplomb. Though he's hardly the raving neurotic of Keaton's *Batman*, this Bond does have a loose screw or two, and the deepening of the character adds immeasurably to impact of the action scenes, as superbly filmed as they are."

    Dave Kehr, CHICAGO TRIBUNE, 14 July 1989

"To diehards who didn't want Moore to succeed Connery and didn't want anyone to succeed Moore, Dalton will never be right, but he is a first-rate actor, is physically convincing and should seem more like the 'authentic' movie Bond the longer he stays in the role."

    Ralph Novak, PEOPLE, 17 July 1989

"Timothy Dalton treads uneasily in the footsteps of Sean Connery and Roger Moore. His Bond has an unfamiliar brooding quality, the suave assurance that characterised his predecessors displaced by a degree of vulnerability that makes him a little more human. Of course, the new Bond does all the old things, but when he does them, there's more than a suggestion that he's not quite sure he has them under control. (...) Dalton is all dark hair and eyebrows with a perpetually worried look. There's no way he could be as crisp and untroubled as Connery or as foppish and frothy as Moore."

    Tom Ryan, THE AGE, 3 September 1989

"Timothy Dalton frankly does not fulfil the promise he showed the first time he played Bond. The only thing in his favour is that he is a better actor than Roger Moore (but still less definitively Bond than Sean Connery). Which is not saying all that much."

    Dougal Macdonald, THE CANBERRA TIMES, 9 September 1989

"Dalton plays 007 with a vigor and physicality that harks back to the earliest Bond pics, letting full-bloodied actions speak louder than words."

    VARIETY, 1989

THE KING'S WHORE

1990

Miramax Films

CAST

Timothy Dalton (Vittorio Amadeo), Valeria Golino (Jeanne de Luynes), Stéphane Freiss (Count of Verua), Robin Renucci (Charles de Luynes), Margaret Tyzack (Dowager Countess), Eleanor David (Queen), Paul Crauchet (Duke Luynes), Amy Werba (Heloïse), Franco Valobra (Duke of Aoste), Francesca Reggiani (Marie Christine), Leonardo Ruta (Prince Vittorio), Luigi Bonos (2nd Priest), Elisabeth Kaza (Countess Trevie), Lea Padovani (Countess Cumiana), Anna Bonaiuto (Countess Longhi)

CREDITS

Director: Axel Corti | Producers: Maurice Bernart, Wieland Schulz-Keil, Paolo Zaccaria | Writers: Axel Corti, Frederic Raphael, Daniel Vigne | Based in the book *Jeanne de Luynes* by Jacques Tournier | Cinematography: Gernot Roll | Editings: Bryan Oates, Joële Van Effenterre| Production Design: Michèle Abbé-Vannier, Francesco Frigeri | Art Direction: Pierfranco Luscrì, Atos Mastrogirolamo | Set Decoration: Lorenzo D'Ambrosio, Jacques Leguillon |

Costume Design: Carlo Diappi | Music: Gabriel Yared | *Running Time*: 138 mins.

THE FILM

Jeanne is an impoverished countess who marries an Italian nobleman at the end of the 17th century. Very soon the King of Piedmont is attracted to her and tries to get rid of her husband. Jeanne faces the pressure from the entire court to succumb to his wishes as the King, obsessed with Jeanne, ignores the threats of war against his kingdom.

DALTON:

"I've come to like the title. I wasn't sure about it at all in the first place. It may have to be changed in America. There has been some talk that his word 'whore' is not suitable for cinema marquees. I mean, only in America, for some bizarre reason. (...) He [the King] is in love. People do crazy things when they're in love. (...) I think the theme of love and what you do when you're in love and how you react to each other is universal and across all time. This may be set in period, but the story is quite contemporary. We are talking about passion, obsession, jealously, love, revenge, abuse of power, a relationship that doesn't work for all the wrong reasons."

> THE MILWAUKEE JOURNAL

"I did this because I thought it was a great love story – the best I've ever come across. (...) Ultimately, it's a tragedy because they are actually right for each other and the love each other. He wants her; he needs her. He falls in love with her later but he can't help that. What he does is to abuse every power he's got and he corrupts and destroys her. You have to recognise he cannot help himself. The very thing you want, you sometimes destroy. That is life – that is everyone's life. In the film, the King is a victim as much as the perpetrator of it. He can't help wanting love."

> DAILY EXPRESS

"One of my recent favourites is a movie called *The King's Whore,* a very disturbing story about love and obsession."

> HOLLYWOOD ONLINE

"I made a movie once called *The King's Whore* with an Austrian Director who I thought, he is dead now sadly, who I thought was who had the most profound insight into, I mean far greater than mine, which is why I respected and admired him so much into how human beings are, how they work, what the layers of relationship between people are and the intelligence to know how to try to develop those, you know in a communicative story. And he also, he was working again with a wonderful Director of Photography, one of the great European Directors of Photography, so it is beautifully shot, and it is also, you know, given our own limitations and there are weakness's in the movie, and failures in the movie, but, you know, the work was about really, with real insight, I mean, as I say, far more profound then I could have brought to it, you know, insight into the personal nature of it."

Savannah Acting Class

REVIEWS

"In this last part, Timothy Dalton, having brought in Frederic Raphael and Derek Marlowe as additional writers, tries to avoid the inherent pitfalls of a Euro-pic (it's a Franco-Italian-British production) but only with difficulty. He lets the dialogue fall from his lips with the clipped economy of an early Olivier but communicates the uneasy feeling that he wishes he were somewhere else sipping a dry martini, perhaps."

Iain Johnstone, SUNDAY TIMES, 20 May 1990

"To reproach Axel Corti, as some people have done, for having hired Timothy 'James Bond' Dalton is absurd, as the actor, who has played Hamlet and Heathcliff and has a Shakespearean training, is remarkable in his role of the master attached to his prey."

M.C., POSITIF, July 1990

"The talent of the actors saves the film. Even though the (rare) mass of extras is not enough, Timothy Dalton, who 'unluckily' has been James Bond twice, has performed Shakespeare during ten years, and he composes with conviction this absolutist monarch, object of a duplicated devotion due to the insignificance of his kingdom and the bigotry. And he remains, as he says himself, a peasant, prey of a fixed desire, only 'moderated' by lucidity."

G.L., POSITIF, January 1991

"The acting, besides Timothy Dalton who shows an unexpected disposition, is as dull as the film."

H.P., FICHES DU CINEMA (TOUS LES FILMS 1990), 1991

"I think about it [Goytisolo's novel *El rey mendigo*] when I see that Vittorio Amadeo that so intensively creates Timothy Dalton."

Jordi Batlle Caminal, FOTOGRAMAS, October 1992

"The film tells the tempestuous relationships between King Vittorio Amadeo of Piemonte (an extraordinary Timothy Dalton) and a French courtier woman, Jeanne de Luynes (an exciting Valeria Golino)."

Ruiz de Villalobos, Imágenes de Actualidad, October 1992

THE ROCKETEER

1991

Buena Vista Pictures

CAST

Bill Campbell (Cliff), Jennifer Connelly (Jenny), Alan Arkin (Peevy), Timothy Dalton (Neville Sinclair), Paul Sorvino (Eddie Valentine), Terry O'Quinn (Howard Hughes), Ed Lauter (Fitch), James Handy (Wooly), Robert Miranda (Spanish Johnny), John Lavachielli (Rusty), Jon Polito (Bigelow), Eddie Jones (Malcolm), William Sanderson (Skeets), Don Pugsley (Goose), Nada Despotovich (Irma)

CREDITS

Director: Joe Johnston | Producers: Lawrence Gordon, Charles Gordon, Lloyd Levin | Writers: Danny Bilson, Paul De Meo, Danny Bilson, Paul De Meo, William Dear | Cinematography: Hiro Narita | Editing: Arthur Schmidt | Production Design: James D. Bissell | Art Direction: Christopher Burian-Mohr | Set Decoration: Linda DeScenna | Costume Design: Marilyn Vance | Music: James Horner| *Running Time*: 104 mins.

THE FILM

Cliff Secord is a 1930's LA young pilot who stumbles on a top secret rocket-pack. With the help of his mechanic and mentor, Peevy, he learns how to use the rocket-pack and becomes a famous hero after saving a pilot. However, he will also have to rescue his girl from a Hollywood star's clutches and to stop, as The Rocketeer, the Mafia, and the Nazis, who also want the rocket-pack.

DALTON:

"You've got to enjoy a villain, I think. I mean, in a certain kind of movie, a bad guy can be just a really hateful sort of guy, but in this kind of movie, you know – it's entertainment, it's a wonderful sort of show...you've got to like the villain. The difficult thing for me was how to create a situation where you don't like him too much...You essentially should love the performance and not the guy, not the man. Because, after all, he is a Nazi. You shouldn't miss him when he goes; you should miss the performance. (...) You've got this wonderful thing of an actor who pretends for a living, and, of course, a spy or an agent pretends for a living, so you mix the two together and you get a wonderful world of illusion and reality, truth and lies, acting and real life. And that, for me, was what I thought should be the foundation of the way I played the part. (...) That [the nightclub scene] was filmed on the back lot at Warner Bros., and it was kind of like being in an old theater, an old stage theater, when you suddenly get all these kinds of echoes and reverberations of history, of the past, of the great actors that have been there."

  LOS ANGELES DAILY NEWS

"*That* was a comedy, or at least it was the way I played it! [Laughs.] I enjoyed it hugely, and I loved working with Joe [Johnston]. It's not every day that you get to do a big Hollywood studio movie. I mean, most movies are made out of Hollywood, away somewhere. And that was made in Hollywood. It was a great experience to do that and be part of it, and I thought it was a terrific film. But the one odd experience—I was having as much fun as I could squeeze out of this Errol Flynn-type character and hoping to make audiences smile and, at best, make them laugh from time to time. The problem is, it turns out your man is a Nazi at the end! You know, we don't want to make the idea of Nazis in any way appealing or in any way fun. I was kind at a bit of a loss as to what to do. I was like, 'How am I going to reconcile this?' If you're going to play a bad guy in this kind of movie, you've got to make your audience enjoy him, which I think I did, but how to finally put a nail in the coffin? And I just thought, out of interest, I'd go and find out what people thought about Nazis. So every time I was in the street or in a bar or restaurant, I'd lean over and say to somebody, 'What do you know about the Nazis? I'm just conducting my own informal poll.' [Laughs.] I tried to do it with relatively young people—people up to, say, 30 years old or whatever—and it was really disappointing that the most common answer I got was, 'Weren't they the bad guys in movies?' (...) So anyway, I thought I'd try to make him go a little bit mad at the end, make it seem he'd gone crazy—because that is a craziness, and not an appealing craziness—and then, of course, he gets his comeuppance by blowing the end of the 'Hollywoodland' sign off and crashes! [Laughs.] But, no, that was a lovely experience. I think Joe was a terrific director, and I liked him very much."

  A.V. Club

REVIEWS

"Dalton plays the Errol Flynn-ian Sinclair with twinkling malice and oozing schmooze. He should seriously consider dumping James Bond and playing bad guys from now on."

    Joe Brown, THE WASHINGTON POST, 21 June 1991

"Timothy Dalton, playing an Errol Flynn-like movie star who is actually a Nazi spy, shows far more looseness as a decadent villain than he's ever had as James Bond. His performance comes to life when he slips into a German accent (though this makes absolutely no sense – was he planted in America by proto-Nazis 30 years before?)."

    Owen Gleiberman, ENTERTAINMENT WEEKLY, 21 June 1991

"Arkin has some fun as the eccentric codger, and Dalton makes a sly villain."

    Roger Ebert, CHICAGO SUN-TIMES, 21 June 1991

"The acting is uniformly good, but part of the credit belongs to casting director Nancy Foy, who picked precisely the right types of people to play Secord, Peevy, Secord's girlfriend Jenny Blake (Jennifer Connelly), Valentine, Sinclair (Dalton, the new James Bond, makes a deliciously oily villain) and Howard Hughes (O'Quinn's a generally good lookalike)."

    Lloyd Paseman, THE REGISTER-GUARD, 28 June 1991

"Dalton, in a role that could have been modeled on rumors of Errol Flynn's Nazi sympathies, brings out the delectable qualities of evil."

    Ralph Novak, PEOPLE, 1 July 1991

"But *The Rocketeer*'s champagne lynchpin is Dalton's hissably slimy secret agent masquerading as the devil-may-care, Errol Flynn inspired matinée idol – a neat bending of the real controversy over Flynn's political leanings. Whether sword fighting his way through of Flynn's *The Adventures of Robin Hood* (titled 'The Laughing Bandit' here) spitting out evil German orders to zeppelin henchmen, or flouncing around his luxury mansion trying to seduce Connelly with old movie lines, Dalton reigns supreme in a terrific Summer treat that will leave you gasping and then begging for more."

    Alan Jones, STARBURST, August 1991

"All the same, Bill Campbell's Rocketeer and Jennifer Connelly's Jenny make a pretty anodyne romantic pairing, and it is left to Timothy Dalton's Errol Flynn-type film star and Paul Sorvino's cigar-toting crook to inject some colour into proceedings which look good but feel samey."

    Derek Malcolm, THE GUARDIAN, 1 August 1991

"The trouble is, the missing machinery is also being hunted down by the FBI, the mob, and a Hollywood superstar (played in dashing form a la Errol Flynn by Timothy Dalton)."

NEWCASTLE EVENING CHRONICLE, 1 August 1991

"A secret Nazi screen superstar played with consummate overdone charm by Timothy Dalton."

Harriet Waugh, THE SPECTATOR, 2 August 1991

"The film postulates that, back in the 1930s, such technical know-how would have the strategic significance of an Iraqi supergun, so the Feds and the Nazis close in on its accidental possessor, Bill Campbell, who just wants to use it to snatch his best girl, Jennifer Connelly, out of the clutches of the evil English swashbuckler, Timothy Dalton. All understandable enough, except that if I had been Jenny, I think I would rather have stuck with Tim."

Iain Johnstone, SUNDAY TIMES, 4 August 1991

"The best thing about *The Rocketeer* is Timothy Dalton enjoying himself as a Thirties Hollywood film star who is really a Nazi spy."

Yves Baigneres, THE TABLET, 10 August 1991

"Those around him [Bill Campbell] come off to better advantage, notably Dalton as the deliciously smooth, insidious Sinclair."

VARIETY, 1991

LARK COMMERCIAL [TV]

1992

Japanese TV and cinemas

CAST

Timothy Dalton

CREDITS

Director: Russell Mulcahy | Kim Colefax | *Running Time*: 30 secs.

THE COMMERCIAL

An action scene, James Bond style, is set on the roofs of a city at night. Dalton is pursued by a baddie, who gets caught in the neon lights. "Need a light?" and then "Speak Lark" are his lines when he defeats him.

NAKED IN NEW YORK

1993

Fine Line Features

CAST

Eric Stoltz (Jake Briggs), Mary-Louise Parker (Joanne White), Ralph Macchio (Chris), Jill Clayburgh (Shirley), Tony Curtis (Carl Fisher), Timothy Dalton (Elliot Price), Lynne Thigpen (Helen), Kathleen Turner (Dana Coles), Roscoe Lee Browne (Mr. Ried), Whoopi Goldberg (Tragedy Mask), Paul Guilfoyle (Roman), Calista Flockhart (Acting Student), Arabella Field (Tammy Taylor), LisaGay Hamilton (Marty), David Johansen (Orangutang)

CREDITS

Director: Daniel Algrant | Producers: Carol Cuddy, Martin Scorsese, Frederick Zollo | Writers: Daniel Algrant, John Warren | Cinematography: Joey Forsyte | Editing: Bill Pankow | Production Design: Kalina Ivanov | Costume Design: Julie Weiss | Music: Angelo Badalamenti | *Running Time*: 91 mins.

THE FILM

Jake is a young playwright who wants to succeed on Broadway. Meanwhile, his girlfriend Joanne starts a career as an Art Gallery worker at home, in Massachusetts. In New York, Jake will have to deal with producers, divas and his childhood friend who wants to be the star of his play.

REVIEWS

"Joanne is a photographer, who catches the eye of a lecherous gallery owner (Timothy Dalton) at about the time Jake leaves for New York with his best play under his arm."

> Roger Ebert, CHICAGO SUN-TIMES, 29 April 1994

"The cast makes the movie interesting in a party-trick way–hey, isn't that Timothy Dalton? But I don't think this cavalcade of talent serves the young filmmaker well."

> Lise Schwarzbaum, ENTERTAINMENT WEEKLY, 29 April 1994

"Curtis, Turner, Clayburgh, Thigpen, and Dalton all shine, and Macchio does a sensitive turn as Jake's steadfast actor pal."

> Robert Faires, THE AUSTIN CHRONICLE, 10 June 1994

"On the screen, Parker can project a seductive enthusiasm for life. She gets so involved, you can't help wanting to join her. Timothy Dalton is the one who does, however."

> Chuck Graham, TUCSON CITIZEN, 29 July 1994

SALT WATER MOOSE [TV]

1996

Hallmark Home Entertainment

CAST

Johnny Morina (Bobby Scofield), Katharine Isabelle ('Jo' Parnell), Timothy Dalton (Lester Parnell), Lolita Davidovich (Eva Scofield), Corinne Conley (Grandma), Maurice Godin (Richard), David Roemmele (Luke), Dan Warry-Smith (Slug), Michael Colton (D.J. Barnes), Quinn Simpson (Zoe), Ashley Brown (Ormond), Dennis O'Connor (Norbert), Zeus (Beatrice the Moose)

CREDITS

Director: Stuart Margolin | Producers: Steve Beeks, Bruce McKenna, Ray Sager, Peter R. Simpson | Writer: Bruce McKenna | Cinematography: Vic Sarin | Editing: Nick Rotundo | Production Design: Jasna Stefanovic | Art Direction: Ingrid Jurek | Set Decoration: Jim Lambie | Costume Design: Joyce Schure | Music: Paul Zaza | *Running Time*: 93 mins.

THE FILM

Bobby and his mother travel from Toronto to a small town in Nova Scotia to spend the summer with his grandmother. There, despite missing his baseball team, Bobby befriends with Jo, a very imaginative girl, and her father, Lester. Jo has spotted a solitary male moose on a small island nearby, and she intends to find a female moose for him.

REVIEWS

"Sentimental family caper, with Timothy Dalton and Lolita Davidovich."

>THE TIMES, 27 December 1999

"Harmless family adventure with Timothy Dalton."

>THE GUARDIAN, 18 August 2003

THE BEAUTICIAN AND THE BEAST

Paramount Pictures

1997

CAST

Fran Drescher (Joy Miller), Timothy Dalton (Boris Pochenko), Ian McNeice (Grushinksky), Patrick Malahide (Kleist), Lisa Jakub (Katrina), Michael Lerner (Jerry Miller), Phyllis Newman (Judy Miller), Heather DeLoach (Masha Pochenko), Adam LaVorgna (Karl Pochenko), Kyle Wilkerson (Yuri Pochenko), Tyler Wilkerson (Yuri Pochenko), Timothy Dowling (Alek)

CREDITS

Director: Ken Kwapis | Producer: Howard W. Koch, Jr., Todd Graff | Writer: Todd Graff | Cinematography: Peter Lyons Collister | Editing: Jon Poll | Production Design: Rusty Smith | Art Direction: Steve Cooper | Set Decoration: Sara Andrews | Costume Design: Barbara Tfank | Music: Cliff Eidelman | *Running Time*: 105 mins.

THE FILM

A resolute beautician from Brooklyn, after a heroic action, is mistakenly thought to be an academic teacher by a representative of an Eastern European dictator. She is invited to their country and asked to be the tutor of the dictator's children. While there, she will befriend the children, and she will soften the dictator. In short, she will try to Westernise the whole country.

DALTON:

"One of the reasons I took the role is because I'm rarely offered comedy. I really do want to do more. (...) The great thing about playing 'the beast' is that you have to spend a lot of time finding out what's nice and good in him. (...) All of them [kids] were wonderful. They each brought their own unique quality to the movie, and if they hadn't been likeable, there would have been no reason for Fran's story and mine to work".

    Hollywood Online

"I've done a lot of comedy. I just haven't done it in movies because I never get asked. Let me tell you, if I could be Leslie Nielsen and doing all those things, I'd be thrilled. (...) It's a wonderful role. It's the kind of role you can have a lot of fun with. He starts out as the archetypal, chauvinist dictator. Then this extraordinary bizarre woman from a completely different culture, who he can't stand, gets under his skin and liberates him and turns him into, I hope, quite a nice guy. It's not your normal kind of comedy. It's got something much more intelligent to say, even in this comedic, satiric sense, about men and women: don't fall in love with the superficial, fall in love with what's real. They get together hating each other, but there's a respect – which is much more mature and interesting."

    TV WEEK

"We're essentially doing a non-musical version of *The King and I* with Fran playing the teacher and me as the barbarian whose heart and country she softens. (...) You know from the moment you meet Fran that this is no little wallflower. She's a diva in the best sense of the word. She knows what she wants and is determined to get it. She's an incredible comedienne and she gives a great massage."

    CALGARY SUN

"That was fun. That was really nice. Yes. I liked that. (...) [Fran Drescher] is a wonderful comedian. She's really got a superb sense of timing. It's the old clichéd joke, isn't it? The secret of comedy: timing. But she's fabulous. Rock solid and always funny."

A.V. Club

REVIEWS

"As the old-fashioned, autocratic 'monster-leader,' former James Bond Timothy Dalton begins broadly and deliberately as a buffoon in order to make his transformation into a kinder and gentler ruler, and a dashing ladies' man, more credible."

Emanuel Levy, VARIETY, 3 February 1997

"Dalton, who was the grimmest of movie James Bonds, strikes a nice comic stance, too, awkward yet not buffoonish as Pochenko's tender tendencies emerge."

Bob Strauss, DAILY NEWS (LA), 7 February 1997

"As this fearsome frog metamorphoses into a prince who increasingly fits Joy's demanding specifications for a mate (...), Mr Dalton physically reverts from a Leonid Brezhnev caricature into a resemblance of one of his earlier roles, James Bond."

Stephen Holden, THE NEW YORK TIMES, 7 February 1997

"Dalton plays the role as if he had somehow found himself the villain in a James Bond film instead of the hero."

Roger Ebert, CHICAGO SUN-TIMES, 7 February 1997

"Dalton has plenty of charm and warmth; he's scarcely more severe than Robby Benson's growler in Disney's *Beauty and the Beast*. Dalton seems to think this movie benefits from first-rate, deeply felt acting, and he supplies some."

Lawrence Toppman, KNIGHT-RIDDER, 7 February 1997

"Think of Dalton as Drescher's Desi Arnaz, a hotheaded macho guy who is as crazy about his cohort as he is irritated by her. Dalton, who has unfortunately not done nearly enough comedy in his movie career (he was a great, funny villain in *The Rocketeer*), gets to show off his fine comic timing here. With a porcupine hairdo, black mustache, crockery blue eyes and a devilishly cleft chin, he looks like a cross between John Travolta and Joseph Stalin. It doesn't hurt that he is disturbingly handsome."

Barbara Shulgasser, SF EXAMINER, 7 February 1997

"Dalton, the grimmest of the cinematic 007s, succeeds with a campy approach to his role of a dour, Cold War relic, but then he goes all dewey and Bambi-eyed when he realizes he's in love with Joy. Talk about gagging on your Goobers."

    Rita Kempley, THE WASHINGTON POST, 7 February 1997

"Say what you will about Timothy Dalton as James Bond, the guy does a great job here as the country's bearish dictator. In fact, he almost steals the show out from under Drescher. Dalton does a fine job of being both fearsome and likeable in a role that could have been a general stereotype."

    Patrick Naugle, dvdverdict.com, 1997

THE INFORMANT [TV]

1997

Showtime Networks

CAST

Anthony Brophy (Gingy McAnally), Cary Elwes (Lt. David Ferris), Timothy Dalton (DCI Rennie), Maria Lennon (Roisin McAnally), John Kavanagh (IRA Chief), Sean McGinley (Frankie Conroy), Frankie McCafferty (Dalton), Stuart Graham (Det. Astley), Gary Lydon (Det. McDonough), Sean Kearns (Det. Prentice), B.J. Hogg (Constable Goss), Ciarán Fitzgerald (Gerard McAnally), Virginia Cole (Roisin's Ma), Gary Lammin (Cpl. Jones), James Gaddas

(British I.O.)

CREDITS

Director: Jim McBride | Producers: Leon Falk, Steven-Charles Jaffe, Paul Lowin, Nicholas Meyer | Writer: Nicholas Meyer | Based on the book *Field of Blood* by Gerald Seymour | Cinematography: Affonso Beato | Editing: Éva Gárdos | Production Design: Mark Geraghty | Art Direction: Conor Devlin | Costume Design: Joan Bergin | Music: Shane MacGowan | *Running Time*: 149 mins.

THE FILM

Gingy McAnally, an ex-IRA assassin, is caught by the Ulster police so to avoid long imprisonment he gives the name of his bosses. He and his family are then considered traitors to the Irish cause, despite Gingy's wife regrets, who was against the betrayal from the start. A British lieutenant will support and sympathise with the McAnally family.

DALTON:

"It is a disturbing film, and I think a very brave film. It's close to my heart. The world lives with that [Irish] situation. But if you spend time in the U.K., it's on your doorstep, and you can't escape it. I mean, how many people have been killed since Christmas? What I like about our film, for a start, it doesn't take sides. That's not because it is an easy, safe, political option. It's certainly not neutral about both sides. While it damns both sides, I think it deals with the complete abdication of morality. When two sides want to win a conflict, morality goes out the window. (...) [The actor chose to play the interrogator unshaven] because one doesn't want `handsome.' Handsome would deflect. You want a look that is jaded, probably worn, a man who drinks too much, smokes too much, has gone to seed. (...) People look at *The Informant* through the window of their own political prejudice. Everyone wants to take a side. But taking sides hasn't worked for the past 30 years of this present round of conflict, or the last 800 years of overall history. If you take a side and you can't win, let's stop taking sides. Let's try to understand the nature of the problem and try to solve it without being prejudiced. Otherwise, the bloodshed just continues."

ASSOCIATED PRESS

"I'm happy to have the opportunity [to do the film] because *The Informant* is a complex and gritty look at the violence in Northern Ireland, a subject that I have been intimately involved in for thirty years. (...). Cable networks have the courage to take on projects that the major studios would not have touched. Films such as *The Informant* are 'interesting and risky'. Hollywood has made movies about Ireland only when the coast looks clear. (...) *The Informant* wisely refuses to take sides. It's very easy and it's very expected that people will take one side or another. Taking sides is, I think, immature and irresponsible. People have been taking sides for thirty years. Taking sides has prolonged the conflict."

TORONTO STAR

"This is a great part for me. This is real. Everything in this movie is true... It's a very rare thing to be in a movie that's actually got something to say about something that's happening today. (...) I don't agree [*Seymour's book, McBride said, had a more pro-British position*] There you are. That's the kind of reaction this film gets whenever you show it. People look at it through the window of their own political prejudice. You can argue about it all day long. (...) This movie certainly exposes that neither side is good. And taking sides hasn't worked for centuries. But they are talking and most people want peace. We must hope there will be some resolution in the near future."

HOUSTON CHRONICLE

"I'm the security guy in charge of this case who is a profound and, probably bigoted, loyalist protestant."

Regis and Kathie Lee Interview [TV]

"One of the great things about some of the cable networks, particularly Showtime, is that they are making a lot of movies the studios wouldn't make. They're making controversial movies, they're making movies about current political topics, politically sensitive issues, which I think is a great thing. This movie, *The Informant*, is a Northern Irish movie, set in Belfast, about how the security forces and the IRA manipulate a terrorist that has been caught and his family - wife and child - children. (...) About my hero... Well, you know, it lays like real life. You know, if you're a bigot, if you support one point of view, I guess he's a good guy. If you're kinda reasonable, like most the rest of us are, you'd have to say he's kinda bent. And if you're on the other side, he's a real bad guy, deserves to be killed."

KSD Radio interview

REVIEWS

"Gingy is quickly arrested and grilled by the formidable Chief Inspector Rennie (Dalton), a brutal officer with an understandable hatred of IRA assassins. (...) Brophy is extremely good as the tormented tout. Dalton is eminently hissable and seems to relish his role as the tough cop, while Lennon, in a relatively small part, sharply evokes the anguish felt by the wife of a traitor."

David Stratton, VARIETY, 28 September 1997

"The detective is manipulative, violent and sneaky. He is played by an unshaven Dalton with a lot of pleasure and with so greasiness and obscenity that every scene in which he appears belongs to him."

Christian Heller, critic.de, 15 March 2007

MADE MEN [TV]

1999

HBO

CAST

James Belushi (Bill Manucci), Michael Beach (Miles), Timothy Dalton (Sheriff Dex Drier), Steve Railsback (Kyle), Carlton Wilborn (Felix), Vanessa Angel (Debra), Jamie Harris (Royce), David O'Donnell (Nick), Tim Kelleher (Deputy Conley), Skip Carlson (Bobby), Susan Isaacs (Darla), Oscar Rowland (Old Timer), Chad Lillywhite (Nathan), Cissy Wellman (Frances), Don Shanks (Caleb)

CREDITS

Director: Louis Morneau | Producers: Dan Cracchiolo, Richard Donner, Steve Richards, Joel Silver | Writers: Robert Franke, Alfred Gough, Miles Millar | Cinematography: George Mooradian | Editing: Glenn Garland | Production Design: Philip Duffin | Art Direction: Kelly Potter | Set Decoration: Warren Sewell | Costume Design: Susan L. Bertram | Music: Stewart Copeland | *Running Time*: 91 mins.

THE FILM

Bill Mannuci stole 12 million dollars from the mob and turned over information to the FBI about the boss, the mysterious Skipper. Now four of Skipper's men have tracked down Bill to his new home in a small country town. Bill has been warned of this and sends his wife Debra away. Captured by Skipper's men, Bill is forced to take them to the money.

DALTON:

"It is an American modern gangster movie, which is loyalist and subversive and anarchic; very funny, and I played an Oklahoma sheriff."

    Conan O'Brien TV interview

REVIEWS

"Jim Belushi is strong; Michael Beach, Steve Railsback, and Timothy Dalton add interesting performances to a fun yet intense screenplay, backed by two of the biggest producers of action movies today. (...) For spice, let's see, my second favorite James Bond Timothy Dalton as a corrupt southern sheriff."

    Norman Short, dvdverdict.com, December 1999

PASSION'S WAY [TV]

1999

CBS

CAST

Timothy Dalton (Charles Darrow), Sela Ward (Anna Leath), Alicia Witt (Sophy Viner), Jamie Glover (Owen Leath), Cynthia Harris (Adelaide), Leslie Caron (Regine De Chantelle), Hannah Taylor Gordon (Effie Leath), Rupert Frazer (Mr. Farlow), Jane Bertish (Mrs. Farlow), Robert Russell (Messenger), Lori Wyant (Embassy Secretary), Marcos Márquez (Hotel Concierge).

CREDITS

Director: Robert Allan Ackerman | Producer: Gideon Amir, Freyda Rothstein | Writer: William Hanley | Based on the book *The Reef* by Edith Wharton | Cinematography: Sandi Sissel | Editing: Susan B. Browdy | Production Design: Barbara Dunphy | Art Direction: Jindrich Kocí | Costume Design: Barbara Lane | Music: Patrick Williams | *Running Time*: 120 mins.

THE FILM

(aka *THE REEF*) In early 1900's, Anna, an American widow living in France, renews her former romantic interest with Charles, the American ambassador in London, until she discovers that he has had a recent fling with one of her new employees, a nanny. The two women have several well-mannered accusations and conversations, while Charles can only wait for Anna's decision.

REVIEWS

"*Passion's Way* is an earnest but turgid adaptation of Edith Wharton's 1912 novel *The Reef*. (...) Though the drama has wisdom to offer concerning the power of love and the futility of seeking perfect relationships, all the hand-wringing may give you a craven impulse to change channels."

    Erik Meers, PEOPLE, 26 July 1999

TIME SHARE [TV]

2000

B & H Entertainment / Constantin Film

CAST

Nastassja Kinski (Dr. Julia Weiland), Timothy Dalton (Matt Farragher), Kevin Zegers (Thomas Weiland), Cameron Finley (Max Weiland), Billy Kay (Lewis Farragher), Natalie Marston (Daphne Farragher), Kelli Garner (Kelly), Geoffrey Lower (Russell), Randolph Mantooth (Ken Crandall), George Murdock (Cedric Templeton), Richard Tanner (Smythe), Manny Fernandez (Ferry Worker), Frank Cavestani (Store Owner), Larry Robbins (Judge), Chez Starbuck (Tan Jock)

CREDITS

Director: Sharon von Wietersheim | Producers: Jeanette Buerling-Milio, Joseph P. Genier, Alexandra Hoesdorff, Martin Moszkowicz, Lance H. Robbins | Writer: Eric Tuchman | Cinematography: Christian Sebaldt | Editing: John Gilbert | Production Design: Clare Brown, Ernestine Hipper | Costume Design: Tanja Weck | Music: Larry Seymour | *Running Time*: 87 mins.

THE FILM

(aka *BITTER SUITE*) Two very different families have to share a house for their summer holidays involuntarily. Matt and his kids are spontaneous and impulsive, but Julia and her kids are organised and follow the rules. The initial quarrels between the two families get transformed into the friendship of the kids and the attraction of the parents, even though Julia's fiancée, and co-worker, is about to arrive.

DALTON:

"The story, I hope, it's going to be entertaining and amusing and, in a sense you'll look at how the mother of one family is good for the boys of the other... and the father of the second family is good for the kids of the other. Anybody needs a mum and a dad. (...) She is very... she is a logician, she is a scientist, somebody, I guess, who tries to understand and control the world through order. He is exactly the opposite, rather loose; someone who doesn't go by any rules. (...) Basically, it's about two adults needing each other and about kids actually needing a mother and a father, or a mother and a father figures, people who will take those positions. (...) I know lots of people like Matt and, you know, you can have a great time with them, I know friends like Matt, but they're unreliable."

    Interviews [DVD]

REVIEWS

"His [Timothy Dalton's] agitation and seduction as casual chef Matt are as credible as an elephant on a tightrope."

    Oliver Hüttmann, cinema.de, 2000

"War and romance ensue after sparks fly between the children – and the parents."

    THE FREE LANCE-STAR, 3 August 2002

POSSESSED [TV]

2000

Showtime

CAST

Timothy Dalton (Fr. William Bowdern), Henry Czerny (Fr. Raymond McBride), Jonathan Malen (Robbie Mannheim), Michael Rhoades (Karl Mannheim), Shannon Lawson (Phyllis Mannheim), Christopher Plummer (Archbishop Hume), Michael McLachlan (Halloran), Richard Waugh (Reverend Eckhardt), Deborah Drakeford (Mrs. Eckhardt), Piper Laurie (Aunt Hanna)

CREDITS

Director: Steven E. de Souza | Producer: Jane Bartelme, Barbara Title | Writer: Michael Lazarou, Steven E. de Souza | Based on the book *Possessed: The True Story of an Exorcism* by Thomas B. Allen | Cinematography: Edward J. Pei | Editing: Anthony Redman | Production Design: John Dondertman | Art Direction: James Oswald | Set Decoration: Rosalie Board | Costume Design: Michael Harris | Music: John Frizzell | *Running Time*: 107 mins.

THE FILM

In St. Louis, 1949, little Robbie Mannheim exhibits signs of demonic possession. When psychologists fail to find an answer for Robbie's unexplainable behaviour, such as moving objects with preternatural force, his parents turn to the Catholic church. The person in charge of the exorcism will be Father William Bowdern, a troubled priest wrestling with his demons.

DALTON:

"I don't know if the boy was possessed or not. He certainly was suffering, whether it was possession or some mental illness. The people back then believed he was [possessed]. (...) I get the sense that these men [Jesuits] were pragmatic and real, honest and good. Strong and tough. You may disagree with them on the nature of God, but their souls were in the right place. (...) This kind of film is hard to make. To keep an audience involved in the story of a possession, you want them to have some level of belief in what's going on. There are no heads spinning around or lots of other special effects. You [the viewer] wonder, 'Is my belief misleading me? (...) We didn't want to be scarier than *The Exorcist* because that was a horror movie dealing with the subject of an exorcism. We're actually taking this real exorcism and trying to give it to you with all its complexity, hoping to provoke you into wondering what it was really all about."

> RedZone

"If people are fascinated with *The Exorcist*, then they've got to be fascinated by the real story. We didn't want to be scarier than *The Exorcist* because that was a horror movie dealing with the subject of an exorcism. We're actually taking this real exorcism and trying to give it to you with all its complexity, hoping to provoke you into wondering what it was really all about."

> TV GUIDE

"When you mention things like the devil, possession, books flying across the room and windows bursting, it's hard to talk seriously about them, but the thing is true. Nothing is in this movie that hasn't been witnessed but at least three people. All those crazy things actually happened. At least, people would swear they witnessed it happen. I became very clear it's not a remake of The Exorcist at all. It is a true dramatization of real events. We had access to historical details banned by the church. (...) The endurance and physical stamina and the unbelievable mental strength they [the priests] must have had, knowing they weren't winning. They faith was in question. They, as instruments of God, aren't beating the devil."

> TV DATA FEATURES SYNDICATE

"We should also mention that Steven E. de Souza who, who I think it's his first, it's his Directing debut, has done a fabulous job in condensing all these strange, strange events into a very gripping and suspenseful, true, story."

> KLOS LA Radio interview

"The most important thing for me in *Possessed* was to understand why a man becomes a priest. Then one has to explore and understand the conflict between faith and doubt and then guilt."

> Showtime Chat

REVIEWS

"Jonathan Malen, who plays Robbie, the 11-year-old boy possessed by a demon, looks more like an impish cherub than the devil incarnate while Timothy Dalton, as tormented priest Father Bowdern, vacillates between haunted and haughty all the while employing a wildly erratic accent."

> Laura Fries, VARIETY, 18 October 2000

"It has a good storyline, an intelligent subtext about a Catholic church battling communists and superstition, and a performance from Timothy Dalton full of attack and charisma."

Steve Grant, SUNDAY TIMES, 8 July 2001

AMERICAN OUTLAWS

2001

Warner Bros. Pictures

CAST

Colin Farrell (Jesse James), Scott Caan (Cole Younger), Ali Larter (Zee Mimms), Gabriel Macht (Frank James), Gregory Smith (Jim Younger), Harris Yulin (Thaddeus Rains), Kathy Bates (Ma James), Timothy Dalton (Allan Pinkerton), Will McCormack (Bob Younger), Ronny Cox (Doc Mimms), Terry O'Quinn (Rollin H. Parker), Nathaniel Arcand (Comanche Tom), Ty O'Neal (Clell Miller), Joe Stevens (Loni Packwood), Barry Tubb (Captain Malcolm)

CREDITS

Director: Les Mayfield | Producers: Bill Gerber, James G. Robinson, Jonathan A. Zimbert | Writer: Roderick Taylor, John Rogers | Cinematography: Russell Boyd | Editing: Michael Tronick | Production Design: John Frick, Cary White | Set Decoration: Barbara Haberecht | Costume Design: Luke Reichle | Music: Trevor Rabin | *Running Time*: 94 mins.

THE FILM

After returning from the civil war, a group of young Midwest farmers join forces to rebel against a corrupt railroad tycoon who intends to force them to sell him their land. The young and charismatic Jesse James leads the gang of the renegade farmers, and their main goals are the banks with the railroad money. Very soon they become famous and the targets of the biggest manhunt in the history of the Old West.

DALTON:

"It's a stylized script. We're not really talking God's honest truth. We are talking sort of romanticised adventure, which makes it exciting and allows you to go places. We're certainly not limited by the 'truth.' This is the Robin Hood Jesse James."

    HOUSTON CHRONICLE

"The railroad is moving west across the country, taking their land, so the railroad is the bad guy. (...) I play Allan Pinkerton who was a Scot who emigrated into the United States of America when he was about twenty-three years older and ultimately he formed the famous Pinkerton Detective Agency; and he's the man employed to hunt down Jesse James. (...) A real sense of glamourised adventure and fun with a satisfying end. // Les Mayfield; he and Jim Robinson have assembled a team that seems to be bringing a great sense of historical texture to the piece. I mean, look around, this town looks great; the costumes look great... it brings back my childhood, going to see all the western movies that were so popular when I was a kid. This makes me wonder just what these people's lives were like who, you know, forged the creation of the West of America. I guess they were though lives, hard lives, but it took courage to pioneer."

The Making of *American Outlaws* // Creating the Old West [DVD]

"I'm playing a guy you might have heard of; I am sure you've heard of called Allan Pinkerton who started the Pinkerton Detective Agency. He was a Scot who moved to Chicago and was hired by the railroads to chase down and capture Jesse James, which in history he never did, he never did. Our movie is the great; it's the romantic adventure, it's Jesse James as the hero you know? It's a great story. It is not the gritty realistic you know; cold bloodied outlaw story at all, and I play Pinkerton."

KLOS LA Radio interview

REVIEWS

"The only wrinkle in the extremely straightforward storytelling is allowing Pinkerton to feel some measure of admiration for his elusive adversaries, in the manner of gentlemen-warriors past, or at least of Tommy Lee Jones in *The Fugitive*. Dalton doesn't make this single kernel of dramatic possibility very interesting, however, even when he finally confronts the captured Jesse in a high-security prison, but it's worthy of Bret Harte compared to the limp conflicts between Jesse and Cole, which inspire nothing in Farrell and Caan but long, empty stares."

Robert Koehler, VARIETY, 16 August 2001

"As Pinkerton, Mr Dalton doesn't have nearly as much to work with, but he does well with what he is given. Pinkerton has a flinty charm, and Mr Dalton is smart enough to wait out a pause, dropping a line to best effect. He seems squandered as a supporting player, trotting out a Sean Connery impression to remind us that he, too, played James Bond."

Elvis Mitchell, THE NEW YORK TIMES, 17 August 2001

"The hired goons are led by Allan Pinkerton (Timothy Dalton), who spends most of the movie looking as if he knows a great deal more than he is saying, some of it about Jesse James, the rest about this screenplay."

Roger Ebert, CHICAGO SUN-TIMES, 17 August 2001

"Yulin and Dalton, the old pros in the cast, are saddled with limp dialogue and pat scenes. Dalton gets a few good moments bantering with Jesse, with whom he secretly sympathizes."

Louis B. Parks, HOUSTON CHRONICLE, 17 August 2001

"They are pursued by Timothy Dalton as a meticulously sour detective with an accent that slides alarmingly from Belfast to Dundee."

James Christopher, THE TIMES, 13 December 2001

"True, Timothy Dalton sports a beard as detective Allan Pinkerton, who doggedly hunts Jesse and his gang. But he stays on his horse and it's his daft Scottish accent that unintentionally provides most of the laughs."

Alan Frank, DAILY STAR, 14 December 2001

"In leaden pursuit of the gang is professional detective Pinkerton, played by Timothy Dalton in a Scots accent so broad you'd swear it was his Sean Connery Christmas party piece."

Anthony Quinn, THE INDEPENDENT, 14 December 2001

"It seems a bizarre choice for Timothy Dalton, who pops up as the notorious Allan Pinkerton in what, as far as I am aware, is his first film role in years."

Henry Fitzherbert, EXPRESS ON SUNDAY, 16 December 2001

LOONEY TUNES: BACK IN ACTION

2003

Warner Bros. Pictures

CAST

Brendan Fraser (DJ Drake/Himself/Tasmanian Devil/Tasmanian She-Devil), Jenna Elfman (Kate), Timothy Dalton (Damien Drake), Steve Martin (Mr.

Chairman), Joan Cusack (Mother), Bill Goldberg (Mr. Smith), Heather Locklear (Dusty Tails), Don Stanton (Mr. Warner / Mr. Warner's Brother), Dick Miller (Security Guard), Roger Corman (Hollywood Director), Kevin McCarthy (Dr. Bennell), Jeff Gordon (himself), Matthew Lillard (himself), Mary Woronov (Acme VP, Bad Ideas)

CREDITS

Director: Joe Dante | Producers: Christopher DeFaria, Larry Doyle, Joel Simon, Paula Weinstein, Bernie Goldmann | Writer: Larry Doyle | Cinematography: Dean Cundey | Editings: Rick Finney, Marshall Harvey | Production Design: Bill Brzeski | Art Direction: Paul Sonski, Stella Vaccaro | Set Decoration: Lisa K. Sessions | Costume Design: Mary E. Vogt | Music: Jerry Goldsmith | *Running Time*: 91 mins.

THE FILM

Daffy Duck, tired of Bugs Bunny's prominence, decides to leave the Warner Bros. Studio for good and the WB security guard/aspiring stuntman DJ Drake is ordered to "escort" him off the studio lot. While DJ is still with Daffy, he discovers that his famous movie star father Damian Drake, known for playing suave international spies onscreen, is actually a spy in real life and has been kidnapped by the nefarious Acme Corporation.

REVIEWS

"When that process goes spectacularly wrong, she [Kate] fires DJ, who ends up with Daffy on the road to Vegas, trying to rescue his dad (a self-spoofing Timothy Dalton) — another Warner Bros. star who, in fact, is a secret agent."

Brian Lowry, VARIETY, 9 November 2003

"Duck and wannabe stuntman end up as buddies on a mission to rescue D.J.'s father, Warner's super-spy actor Damien Drake (appropriately played by former James Bond Timothy Dalton), from the clutches of the evil Acme Co. boss (Steve Martin)."

David Germain, ASSOCIATED PRESS, 14 November 2003

"(...) heading to Vegas to rescue Drake's dad (a self-spoofing Timothy Dalton) who, it transpires, is not only the studio's biggest star with his suave spy movies but a real-life secret agent as well."

Mike Davies, THE BIRMINGHAM POST, 13 February 2004

"Martin turns away like a cross between Les Dawson and Dr Evil. By comparison, Timothy Dalton, who plays the hero's dad, is a barrel of laughs and this is the man who nearly killed off James Bond because he couldn't deliver a quip."

Henry Fitzherbert, EXPRESS ON SUNDAY, 15 February 2004

HOT FUZZ

2007

Universal Pictures / Rogue Pictures

CAST

Simon Pegg (Nicholas Angel), Nick Frost (PC Danny Butterman), Jim Broadbent (Insp. Frank Butterman), Paddy Considine (DS Andy Wainwright), Timothy Dalton (Simon Skinner), Rafe Spall (Andy Cartwright), Kevin Eldon (Tony Fisher), Olivia Colman (PC Doris Thatcher), Karl Johnson (PC Bob Walker), Bill Bailey (Desk Sgt Turner), Edward Woodward (Prof. Tom Weaver), Billie Whitelaw (Joyce Cooper), Eric Mason (Bernard Cooper), Stuart Wilson (Dr. Robin Hatcher), Paul Freeman (Rev. Philip Shooter), Rory McCann (Michael "Lurch" Armstrong), Kenneth Cranham (James Reaper), Maria Charles (Mrs. Reaper), Peter Wight (Roy Porter), Julia Deakin (Mary Porter), Ben McKay (Peter Cocker), Adam Buxton (Tim Messenger), David Threlfall (Martin Blower), Lucy Punch (Eve Draper), David Bradley (Arthur Webley), Martin Freeman (Met Sergeant), Bill Nighy (Met Chief Inspector)

CREDITS

Director: Edgar Wright | Producer: Nira Park, Tim Bevan, Eric Fellner | Writer: Edgar Wright, Simon Pegg | Cinematography: Jess Hall | Production Design: Marcus Rowland | Editing: Chris Dickens | Art Direction: Dick Lunn | Set Decoration: Liz Griffiths | Costume Design: Annie Hardinge | Music: David Arnold | *Running Time*: 121 mins.

THE FILM

PC Nicholas Angel bosses reassign him to the quiet town of Sandford for being a "too good" cop. He is paired with Danny Butterman, who endlessly questions him about the action-lifestyle in London. Everything seems quiet and idyllic in Sandford until some strange deaths start to take place in the town. Angel and Danny will have to fight with everyone to try to discover the truth behind the mystery of those apparent "accidents."

DALTON:

"Comedies don't come along every day and this is completely off the wall."

    THE TELEGRAPH

"He [Simon Pegg] ran very fast. I wish he'd slowed down a little. We had to time that scene from the moment I joined him. He had to train hard for the role; he's the hotshot super cop. He has to do all the physical stuff. I, on the other hand, only had to scamper down the road with him, so I was lucky."

    BBC

"I loved making the film. There were some fantastic people involved. I play a worthy, upright pillar of the community; at least that's what he thinks. He believes he's perfectly respectable - he runs the supermarket but he's not all that he seems. It was very good fun."

    METRO

"When I read it [the script] I realised I had read not anything like this ever before. It's really original, I mean, it's *really* original. And when you see something like that, and you know that the people who wrote it are going to be making it, are talented, as they obviously are, as we know, is something you jump at."

    Hot Fuzz [US DVD]

"Wonderful! Loved working with Edgar Wright, and Simon Pegg and Nick Frost. And I discovered that I was working with a whole crowd of actors that I'd known as some point in my history. Generally speaking, you never work with anybody you know. But I was working with people I'd known from the ages of 20, 21, and 22. And it was one of the most happy, joyous experiences I've had in movies, first of all because it's a comedy, and it's funny, which made it great to do. I love comedy, and I love working with people who are funny. But it was also the actors themselves. We all loved each other, in a way. We all had history together. So it was great. As well as, I think, being a terrific film."

    A.V. Club

REVIEWS

"Playing the town's senior citizenry is an A list of older British actors, including Jim Broadbent, as the head of the local constabulary, Billie Whitelaw, Edward Woodward, Paul Freeman and a marvellously evil Timothy Dalton."

    Patricia Nicol, SUNDAY TIMES, 4 February 2007

"Co-writers Simon Pegg and Edgar Wright have been allowed to make *Hot*

Fuzz on their terms with a roster of fine British actors, headed by Jim Broadbent, Billie Whitelaw, Edward Woodward and Timothy Dalton, in splendidly played supporting roles."

 Ethan Carter, MORNING STAR, 7 February 2007

"The supporting cast are all wonderful too (they include Martin Freeman, Steve Coogan, Billie Whitelaw and Edward Woodward), though special mention goes to the extremely game Timothy Dalton, playing the sly and dangerous boss of the local Somerfield supermarket with moustache-twirling glee."

 Mark Adams, SUNDAY MIRROR, 11 February 2007

"Timothy Dalton brings a lupine sneer to the role of a supermarket manager, keen fun-runner and all-around cad, Simon Skinner."

 Wendy Ide, THE TIMES, 15 February 2007

"And might the increasing number of gruesome 'accidents' have something to do with smarmy supermarket manager Skinner (Timothy Dalton in moustache twirling form) and his prescient puns about the deaths?"

 Mike Davis, THE BIRMINGHAM POST, 15 February 2007

"All of them, especially Dalton, are happy to poke fun at their previous screen incarnations without any trace of vanity."

 Andy Dougan, EVENING TIMES, 15 February 2007

"Former James Bond Timothy Dalton plays slippery supermarket boss Simon Skinner with immense relish."

 Allan Hunter, DAILY EXPRESS, 16 February 2007

"Timothy Dalton is superbly slimy as the local supermarket boss."

 David Edwards, DAILY MIRROR, 16 February 2007

"A crop of veteran Brit actors play the village elders: Billie Whitelaw, Paul Freeman, Edward Woodward, Anne Reid, and most notably Jim Broadbent as the police inspector and Timothy Dalton, splendid as a villainous supermarket manager who literally twirls his moustache."

 David Gritten, DAILY TELEGRAPH, 16 February 2007

"A spate of 'accidental' deaths suggests that not all may be as it seems in the village, but Angel's efforts are met with inertia by his colleagues and ridicule by the sinister supermarket tycoon Simon Skinner (a gleefully wicked Timothy Dalton)."

Henry Fitzherbert, EXPRESS ON SUNDAY, 18 February 2007

"The scope is larger, the gag rate faster, the casting more inspired (Timothy Dalton plays a dastardly supermarket manager/champion fun-runner)."

Catherine Shoard, SUNDAY TELEGRAPH, 18 February 2007

"Broadbent and Dalton are especially good as Angel's hail-fellow-well-met superior and oily No. 1 suspect."

Derek Elley, VARIETY, 20 February 2007

"The supporting cast is a Who's Who of UK comedy and drama: Bill Bailey, Steve Coogan, Stephen Merchant, Edward Woodward, Billie Whitelaw, Bill Nighy and Jim Broadbent all appear, and Timothy Dalton's turn as the sinister supermarket owner is an absolute riot."

Patrick Roberts, THE INDEPENDENT, 21 February 2007

"Timothy Dalton, in full 007 grandeur as a smarmy supermarket magnate."

Lisa Schwarzbaum, ENTERTAINMENT WEEKLY, 18 April 2007

"For the most part these are fine boys indeed, and in the wonderful, weird case of Timothy Dalton, an unctuous toff with a menacing twinkle in his eye, even better than that."

Manohla Dargis, THE NEW YORK TIMES, 20 April 2007

"The moment at which Dalton grabs hold of a redheaded boy and exclaims 'Stay back, or the ginger nut gets it!' is to my ears the noblest line reading since the demise of Sir John Gielgud."

Anthony Lane, THE NEW YORKER, 30 April 2007

"Ex-007 Timothy Dalton as a villain straight out of *Scooby-Doo*."

Chris Nashawaty, ENTERTAINMENT WEEKLY, 3 August 2007

THE TOURIST

2010

Columbia Pictures

CAST

Johnny Depp (Frank Tupelo), Angelina Jolie (Elise Clifton Ward), Paul Bettany (Inspector John Acheson), Timothy Dalton (Chief Inspector Jones), Steven Berkoff (Reginald Shaw), Rufus Sewell (The Englishman), Christian De Sica (Colonnello Lombardi), Alessio Boni (Sergente Cerato), Daniele Pecci (Tenente Narduzzi), Giovanni Guidelli (Tenente Tommassini), Raoul Bova (Conte Filippo Gaggia)

CREDITS

Director: Florian Henckel von Donnersmarck | Producers: Graham King, Tim Headington, Roger Birnbaum, Gary Barber, Jonathan Glickman | Writers: Florian Henckel von Donnersmarck, Christopher McQuarrie, Julian Fellowes | Cinematography: John Seale | Editing: Joe Hutshing, Patricia Rommel | Art Direction: Susanna Codognato, Marco Trentini | Set Decoration: Anna Pinnock | Costume Design: Colleen Atwood | Music: James Newton Howard | *Running Time*: 103 mins.

THE FILM

Frank is an American tourist who travels to Italy to try to recover from a breakup. In the train, he meets Elise, a stunning woman. With the unique setting of Venice as a backdrop, Frank is driven by the attraction of romance, but soon he and Elise will be involved in a storm of intrigue and danger as he is mistaken for an international thief and pursued by the police and gangsters.

DALTON:

"We got a criminal in the story, who's pull a big heist of a gangster, lots of money, millions, hundreds of millions. And my job is to get it. That's why the police is involved; we're trying to get it from this gangster, who is one of this wonderful... you know, the classic, fabulous, story tale, fantasy criminal, and I don't know how much I can't tell you about without spoiling it!"

    Critics Choice

"*The Tourist* for me was another example of wanting to work with people. It doesn't have to be a big part – I play a policeman in the film – but if someone like Donnersmarck asks you to come and it's with two actors that you've never met before but have always admired, Johnny Depp and Angelina Jolie, and it's being shot in Venice, you take it."

    ENTERTAINMENT WEEKLY

REVIEWS

"The supporting roles are filled by excellent actors, and it's a sign of the movie's haplessness that none of them makes a mark."

    Roger Ebert, CHICAGO SUN-TIMES, 8 December 2010

"She [Jolie] eludes Shaw while dodging assorted law enforcement agencies, including Scotland Yard, where Paul Bettany and Timothy Dalton curl stiff upper lips."

    Manohla Dargis, THE NEW YORK TIMES, 10 December 2010

"There's also the pleasure of an appearance by Timothy Dalton who plays an acerbic, not-to-be-messed-with Scotland Yard official, and Paul Bettany as his frustrated underling."

    Henry Fitzherbert, EXPRESS ON SUNDAY, 12 December 2010

"Timothy Dalton and Rufus Sewell are woefully underused."

    SUNDAY MERCURY, 12 December 2010

TV SERIES

SAT'DAY WHILE SUNDAY 101
JUDGE DEE 102
CENTENNIAL 103
CHARLIE'S ANGELS 105
JANE EYRE 106
MISTRAL'S DAUGHTER 109
HOOKED! INTERNATIONAL 111
SINS 111
TALES FROM THE CRYPT 112
FRAMED 113
IN THE WILD 116
LIE DOWN WITH LIONS 119
SCARLETT 120
CLEOPATRA 124
HERCULES 127
AGATHA CHRISTIE'S MARPLE 129
UNKNOWN SENDER 131
DOCTOR WHO 131
CHUCK 133
PENNY DREADFUL 136
DOOM PATROL 144

SAT'DAY WHILE SUNDAY

1967

ABC / ITV Anglia

CAST

Sarah-Jane Gwillim (Charlotte), Malcolm McDowell (Frankie), Timothy Dalton (Peter), Gordon Reid (Mike), Roger McGough (Narrator), John Wreford (Paddy) Sandra Bryant (Rita), George Betton (Frankie's Father)

CREDITS

Directors: Jim Goddard, Mike Vardy, Pamela Londsdale, Voytek | Writers: Roy Bottomley, Tom Brennand, Leslie Duxbury, John Finch, Roger McGough, Adele Rose | Series production: Reginald Collin | Series production design: Roger Burridge, Terry Gough, Malcolm Goulding, Neville Green, Mike Hall | Story Editing: John Kershaw | *Running Time*: 30 mins.

THE SERIES

A twice-weekly serial focused on first-year university students. Charlotte is a well-to-do student who has two boys in love with her: Frankie, the tough working-class son of a docker; and Peter, a mill owner's son.

Dalton participates in 10 out of the 14 episodes:

- Home Is Like No Place: Parts 1 & 2

- The Boss's Son: Parts 1 & 2

- Once a Year in the Season: Part 1

- I Love Me, Who Do You Love?: Parts 1 & 2

- Seminar on Communications: Part 2

- Two Smilin' Faces: Parts 1 & 2

DALTON:

"It was for British television, and it was my first TV. I don't remember the character being called Peter. I don't even remember who or what he was or what he did. But I remember being in it! And Malcolm McDowell was also in it, and it was his first television. And a lovely British poet called Roger McGough was in it. It was a strange sort of thing, one of those shows that try to break down conformity. You had poetry, you had a bit of music, you had this, that, and the other, but I can't really remember much about it. The only thing of note about it was that it was Malcolm McDowell's first TV as well as my own."

    A.V. Club

REVIEWS

"ABC's latest groovy weekending is a teenage-orientated semi-serial, *Sat'day While Sunday*, which is all about what provincial hippies do at the weekend. Despite their carefully varied backgrounds and attitudes, they're all terribly nice young things. The best thing to be said for it is that it appears to have replaced *Batman*. Let us hope that, despite its rather stilted production and dialogue, it continues to do so."

    Linda Dyson, BIRMINGHAM DAILY POST, 21 October 1967

JUDGE DEE

1969

Granada Television

CAST

Michael Goodliffe (Judge Dee), David Ashton (Kuan Lai), Penny Casdagli (Sun Dew), Timothy Dalton (?), Arne Gordon (Ma Joong), Alick Hayes (Monk), Richard Hurndall (Abbot), Susan Lefton (Innocence), Ralph Michael (Master Sun), John Moreno (Actor), Garfield Morgan (Tao Gan), Pamela Roland (Rose Tree), Alan Rowe (Prior), Norman Scace (Hoong)

CREDITS

Directors: Howard Baker, Richard Doubleday | Producer: Howard Baker | Writer: John Wiles | Based on the stories by Robert van Gulik | Production Design: Peter Phillips, Colin Rees | Music: Derek Hilton | *Running Time*: 60 mins.

THE SERIES

Black and white series of 6 episodes set in Tang Dynasty China that deals with various criminal cases solved by the upright Judge Dee, as judges in ancient China were investigating magistrates.

Dalton participates in the episode "A Place of Great Evil" (2): Dee discovers the awful secrets of the Monastery of the Morning Cloud.

REVIEWS

"I admire any TV attempt to get away from routine, but really this series looks as if it will just turn into an Oriental Western. If the Chinese, as alleged, invented the detective story, it doesn't seem to have moved on very much. (...). If you make up a lot of British actors to look like Chinese, they all look just as much alike as Chinese."

      James Thomas, DAILY EXPRESS, 9 April 1969

CENTENNIAL

1978

NBC

CAST

William Atherton (Jim Lloyd), Raymond Burr (Herman Bockweiss), Barbara Carrera (Clay Basket), Richard Chamberlain (Alexander McKeag), Robert Conrad (Pasquinel), Richard Crenna (Colonel Frank Skimmerhorn), Timothy Dalton (Oliver Seccombe), Lynn Redgrave (Charlotte Buckland), Cliff De Young (John Skimmerhorn), Chad Everett (Major Maxwell Mercy), Sharon Gless (Sidney Endermann), Andy Griffith (Professor Lewis Vernor), Gregory Harrison (Levi Zendt), David Janssen (Paul Garrett / Narrator), Alex Karras (Hans Brumbaugh), Brian Keith (Sheriff Axel Dumire), Stephanie Zimbalist (Elly Zahm), Dennis Weaver (R.J. Poteet), Donald Pleasence (Sam Purchas), Clint Ritchie (Messmore Garrett), Clive Revill (Finlay Perkin), Sandy McPeak (Soren Sorenson)

CREDITS

Directors: Virgil W. Vogel, Bernard McEveety, Harry Falk, Paul Krasny | Producers: Richard Caffey, George E. Crosby, John Wilder | Writers: Charles Larson, John Wilder | Based on the novel *Centennial* by James A. Michener | Cinematography: Duke Callaghan | Production Design: Jack Senter | Editing: Robert Watts | Art Direction: John W. Corso, Loyd S. Papez | Set Decoration: John M. Dwyer, Joseph J. Stone | Costume Design: Helen Colvig | Music: John Addison | *Running Time*: 120 mins.

THE SERIES

An epic miniseries of 12 episodes about the making of America that spans the decades from the late eighteenth century to the present (the 1970s).

Dalton is Oliver Seccombe, an English writer who establishes in Centennial, first, as an agent of several wealthy British investors, and later as a cattle rancher himself. He participates in the following episodes:

- The Wagon and the Elephant (3)
- The Massacre (5)
- The Longhorns (6)
- The Shepherds (7)
- The Storm (8)
- The Crime (9)

DALTON:

"I'd worked one time before in Los Angeles, but I had never been into America. I mean the real America, and on that series, we went to Colorado and Kentucky and down to Texas and we filmed a bit of it in Del Rio, right on the Rio Grande there as part of a cattle drive. (...) For the first time, in my life, I understood you know how Texans are always characterised as kind of talking slow and walking slow and choosing their words carefully. Well, you know, you just accept that you don't know why. When you are down there, and it is like 130 in the shade, and it is so hot the animals are falling over, and you can't move. I understood why you walk slowly and talk slowly, wear big hats and think about what you say."

INTERVIEW

"There was no money around on stage, so I had to rebuild a film career, and I discovered the wonderful world of international television mini-series, like *Centennial* and *Sins*, which pay enough to let you go back to the theatre whenever you like."

THE TIMES

REVIEWS

"A big piece of change also was spent on the big-name cast, including Conrad, Carrera, Richard Chamberlain, Andy Griffith, Raymond Burr, Donald Pleasence, William Atherton, Timothy Dalton, Mark Harmon, Dennis Weaver, Lynn Redgrave, Sharon Gless, Stephanie Zimbalist, Sally Kellerman, Richard Crenna, Cliff De Young, Merle Haggard, David Janssen, Alex Karras, Brian Keith, Lois Nettleton, Anthony Zerbe, Michael Ansara, Dana Elcar, Carl Franklin, Richard Jaeckel, Geoffrey Lewis, Doug McKeon, A Martinez, Pernell Roberts, Gale Sondergaard, Julie Sommars, Clint Walker, Alan Napier, Barry Cahill, Eric Server, James Best, Van Williams and an uncredited George Clooney. That is an amazing cast by any standard, but typical of what TV used to be capable of."

Nicholas Sheffo, fuelvuedrive-in.com, July 2008

CHARLIE'S ANGELS

1979

ABC

CAST

Jaclyn Smith (Kelly Garrett), Cheryl Ladd (Kris Munroe), Shelley Hack (Tiffany Welles), David Doyle (John Bosley), Farrah Fawcett (Jill Munroe), Timothy Dalton (Damien Roth), Marilù Tolo (Carla Leone), Michael DeLano (Michael Leone), Richard Roat (Mr. Nobbs), Jenny Neumann (Mrs. Nobbs), Sandra Caron (Costumer), Gregory Itzin (Waiter)

CREDITS

Director: Allen Baron | Producers: Leonard Goldberg, Robert Janes, Aaron Spelling | Writers: Ivan Goff, Ben Roberts, Katharyn Powers | Cinematography: Richard M. Rawlings Jr. | Editing: Stanley Frazen | Art Direction: Alfeo Bocchicchio, Paul Sylos | Set Decoration: Bonnie Dermer | Costume Design: Nolan Miller | Music: Jack Elliott, Allyn Ferguson | *Running Time*: 60 mins.

THE SERIES

Three beautiful women work in a private detective agency with a mysterious boss.

Dalton participates in the episode "Fallen Angel" (4x05): The Angels are hired to catch Damien 'Ice Cat' Roth, a millionaire playboy/jewel thief, who also happens to be the boyfriend of the former Angel Jill Munroe.

DALTON:

"It was a rather nice job in terms of the piece. I was a robber, the sort of debonair, sophisticated, charming thing at which David Niven or Cary Grant were so good. It was great fun to do, and I liked Farrah [Fawcett] very much. She was very fresh and didn't have any illusions about her fame: she knew that it was all due to Charlie's Angels, and she was very happy and grateful that was the case."

WOMAN'S WEEKLY

"He was sort of a cool European cat burglar, probably modelled after someone like Cary Grant, or the idea came from something like that. And she falls in love with him. Of course, she has to turn him in at the end. [Laughs.] And I thought, "Yes! Definitely! I'm on the next plane back out!" I thought, "I've got to do this! I've never done anything like this before!", I mean, the thought of doing an hour in seven days... You'd *rehearse* a scene for seven days in some movies, let alone actually shoot an hour in seven days!"

A.V. Club

REVIEWS

"*Fallen Angel* is a particular find, with not only a rare Season 4 cameo by Ms Fawcett-Majors as the titular character, but also Timothy Dalton foreshadowing his best-known role: nine years before *The Living Daylights*, Mr Dalton vexed the Angels as a jewel thief possessing 'James Bondian tastes, means, and charm.' The episode is watchable if only for a mesmerizing sequence of snake-fu on the part of Mr Dalton, and some suspiciously realistic bickering between Ms Fawcett-Majors and her former co-star, Jaclyn Smith, and replacement, Cheryl Ladd."

Emily Nussbaum, THE NEW YORK TIMES, 29 June 2003

"The mysteries are still flimsy, the dialogue stiff, but it's worth wading through to get to Fawcett's appearance as a lovesick accomplice to Timothy Dalton's jewel thief, just to see her face-off against the onetime 007 in a rooftop kung-fu fight."

Jennifer Armstrong, ENTERTAINMENT WEEKLY, 15 July 2009

JANE EYRE

1983

BBC

CAST

Zelah Clarke (Jane Eyre), Timothy Dalton (Edward Fairfax Rochester), Carol Gillies (Grace Poole), James Marcus (John), Jean Harvey (Mrs. Fairfax), Joolia Cappleman (Bertha), Eve Matheson (Leah), Damien Thomas (Richard Mason), Colin Jeavons (Briggs), Kate David (Bessie), Blance Youinou

(Adele), Elaine Donnelly (Diana Rivers), Morag Hood (Mary Rivers), Colette Barker (Helen Burns), Sian Pattenden (young Jane Eyre), Judy Cornwell (Mrs. Reed), Alan Cox (John Reed), Emma Jacobs (Eliza Reed), Gemma Walker (young Georgiana Reed), Katharine Irwin (young Eliza Reed), Robert James (Mr. Brocklehurst)

CREDITS

Director: Julian Amyes | Producer: Barry Letts | Writer: Alexander Baron | Based on the book *Jane Eyre* by Charlotte Brontë | Cinematography: David Doogood, John Kenway, Keith Salmon | Production Design: Michael Edwards | Editing: Ian Collins, Oliver White | Art Direction: David Ackrill | Costume Design: Gill Hardie | Music: Paul Reade | *Running Time*: 29 mins.

THE SERIES

TV series of 11 episodes.

Jane Eyre is a plain governess, with no immediate family and educated in a boarding school, who arrives at Thornfield Hall to tutor the young Adele. She finds herself intrigued by and attracted to Thornfield's owner, the dark and sardonic Mr Rochester. But a dread secret resides in Thornfield Hall.

DALTON:

"I am very proud of *Jane Eyre* because I think that was, well I think it is a bit arrogant to say so but it was, it was really good. I was very pleased once upon a time I was in America, and I discovered it was the New York Times 'Pick of the Week' on the Arts and Entertainment Channel."

>BBC's Newsroom

"I think why it worked so well was because, in truth, it's such a good part. What a blow to the image! Rochester is tough and hard, short-tempered and curt on the one hand, and concealing a soul that's been hurt and made sensitive. So you have a lot of the qualities that really appeal to women in Rochester, and I was simply lucky enough to be playing him."

>WOMAN'S WEEKLY

"That was a wonderful thing, and I'm quite gratified to see [people] even today voting it the best *Jane Eyre* ever. It was good, and one of the reasons was, obviously, it's got to be adapted from the novel to the screenplay, and any writer wants to impose their own mark on it. But it's very difficult to try and impose your mark on Chekhov or Tolstoy... or Charlotte Brontë! I mean, they kind of imposed their own mark already, and what people want to watch is that. So what we actually did was, we sat down with the novel and actually — is the word "extrapolated"? — her dialogue into our movie. So most of it —

a lot of it — is actually what she wrote, and it *is* five hours long, so you can actually get a good grasp on the story, which is very hard if you're just making a two-hour movie. But as ours was five, it was broken up into episodes. But, yes, I loved doing that, and I think we did very well."

A.V. Club

"*Jane Eyre* is a very special part of our English Literature... It's very good we talk about this novel now. I think it was of great importance not only in the literature but in the field of women' emancipation. What a wonder, this book was written still in 1847 and written by a woman. Jane Eyre was portrayed by wonderful actress Zelah Clarke... I think Zelah could show the real inner greatness and the delicacy of feeling and thought, reflecting the real character of her heroine. As to my hero... This is strange, unusual man, an awkward bedfellow, who was hardened in heart. But with any doubts he had the delicacy of his sense of right and wrong. I think, he doesn't esteem his own class. This is an amazing role for the actor, and I'm proud, I have done it."

TELEVISION AND RADIO

REVIEWS

"Timothy Dalton, always skilfully suggesting the woundedness behind his often wounding words, made a potently saturnine, Byronically erotic Rochester; it's impossible to imagine the role being played with more sensitive intensity."

Peter Kemp, THE TIMES LITERARY SUPPLEMENT

"The chemistry between these two players [Clarke and Dalton] worked wonderfully."

Judit Simons, DAILY EXPRESS, 17 December 1983

"Then there was Timothy Dalton in *Jane Eyre*, Tom Fleming as Lord Reith, Ben Kingsley as Edmund Kean and Nicol Williamson in *Macbeth*. All gave performances which help to prove that the small screen can stretch the finest actors."

James Murray, DAILY EXPRESS, 31 December 1983

"Speaking of things British, cable viewers can size up the brand-new James Bond, Timothy Dalton, if they come in on the superb mini-series re-run of *Jane Eyre*, with Zelah Clarke (a perfect Jane) and the magnetic Mr Dalton as Rochester."

Howard Thompson, THE NEW YORK TIMES, 6 September 1986

"Charlotte Brontë made it clear that her brooding, Byronic Mr Rochester in *Jane Eyre* wasn't 'handsome or heroic-looking,' but casting the smooth Dalton as the gothic brute in this 11-episode BBC miniseries still works. Intensely tormented, the future Bond storms around a set straight out of a high school production – often to the point of caricature – but his smoldering does manage to convey why his child's governess (a mousy yet limpid-eyed Clarke) loves him so."

Michelle Kung, ENTERTAINMENT WEEKLY, 18 April 2005

MISTRAL'S DAUGHTER

1984

CBS

CAST

Stefanie Powers (Maggy Lunel), Lee Remick (Kate Browning), Stacy Keach (Julien Mistral), Ian Richardson (Adrien Avigdor), Philippine Leroy-Beaulieu (Fauve), Robert Urich (Jason Darcy), Timothy Dalton (Perry Kilkullen), Stéphane Audran (Paula Deslandes), Stephanie Dunnam (Teddy Lunel), Cotter Smith (Frank), Pierre Malet (Eric Avigdor), Alexandra Stewart (Mary Jane Kilkullen), Joanna Lumley (Lally Longbridge), Caroline

Langrishe (Nadine), Jonathan Hyde (Philippe), Angela Thorne (Nanny Butterfield), Wolf Kahler (Major Schmidt), Michael Gough (Cardinal), Françoise Brion (Patricia Falkland), Shane Rimmer (Harry Klein), Victor Spinetti (Alberto Bianchi)

CREDITS

Director: Douglas Hickox | Producers: Herbert Hirschman, Steve Krantz, Suzanne Wiesenfeld | Writers: Terence Feely, Rosemary Anne Sisson | Based on the book *Mistral's Daughter* by Judith Krantz | Cinematography: Pierre Lhomme, Jean Tournier | Production Design: Alain Nègre | Editing: John Bloom, Barry Peters | Set Decoration: Jacques Bataille, Jacques Bourdin, Daniel Heitz | Costume Design: Michel Fresnay | Music: Vladimir Cosma | *Running Time*: 97 min.

THE SERIES

Dalton participates in episodes 1 and 2 of this four-episode miniseries.

Beautiful and naïve Maggy Lunel arrives in Paris completely broke. She becomes an artist's model attracting the attention of Picasso-like painter Julien Mistral, an arrogant and selfish man who places his work above everything. Their paths diverge as Mistral's art catches the eye of a rich American woman who becomes his patroness. Meanwhile, Maggy falls in love with an American banker.

DALTON:

"Stacy [Keach], as Mistral, represents that temperamental, artistic, dour, self-indulgent side of man that woman find attractive. I play the flip-side of the coin: a kind, gentle, sensitive man. Of course, that was quite a change for me, particularly after doing Rochester in *Jane Eyre*."

>WOMAN'S WEEKLY

REVIEWS

"When a heartbroken Maggy loses Mistral to the scheming Kate, she finds herself being wooed by the wealthy Perry Kilkullen (Timothy Dalton), a dashing Irish-American banker who wants to console her with "diamond bracelets up to your shoulders and chinchilla to the floor.'"

>John J. O'Connor, THE NEW YORK TIMES, 24 September 1984

HOOKED! INTERNATIONAL

1985

BBC

CAST

Derek Davis, Pete Thompson, Timothy Dalton

CREDITS

Director: Philip Franklin | Producers: Pebble Mill, Roy Ronnie | *Running Time*: 30 mins.

THE SERIES

Dalton participates in an episode of this fishing TV programme.

Away from the fishing competition between a team from Britain and Ireland and a team from Europe, actor Timothy Dalton takes time off – from filming in France with Joan Collins – to try his luck after the spring salmon in Beltra Lough, County Mayo.

SINS

1986

CBS

CAST

Joan Collins (Helene Junot), Timothy Dalton (Edmund Junot), Jean-Pierre Aumont (Count De Ville), Marisa Berenson (Luba Tcherina), Steven Berkoff (Karl Von Eiderfeld), Joseph Bologna (Steve Bryant), Élizabeth Bourgine (Jeanne), Judi Bowker (Natalie Junot), Capucine (Odile), Neil Dickson (Hubert De Ville), Arielle Dombasle (Jacqueline Gore), James Farentino (David Westfield), Paul Freeman (Mueller), Allen Garfield (Adam Gore), Giancarlo Giannini (Marcello D'itri), Lauren Hutton (ZZ Bryant), Gene Kelly (Eric Hovland)

CREDITS

Director: Douglas Hickox | Producers: Peter Holm, Joan Collins, Steve Krantz | Writer: Laurence Heath | Based on the book *Sins* by Judith Gould |

Cinematography: Jean Tournier | Production Design: François de Lamothe | Editing: Michael Brown | Art Direction: Jacques Brizzio | Set Decoration: Françoise Benoît-Fresco, André Labussière | Costume Design: Michel Fresnay | Music: Francis Lai | *Running Time*: 140 mins.

THE SERIES

A three-episode miniseries.

Young Helene Junot witnesses the death of her mother at the hands of Nazis. Separated from her brother, Edmund, by the war, Helene goes to work at the chateau of the Count De Ville. There she falls in love with his son, to the Count's objection. She leaves for Paris where she becomes a fashion model and moves up the ladder of success. As she builds a magazine empire, Helene looks for her lost brother and seeks justice for her family.

DALTON:

"I worked with Joan Collins and Giancarlo Giannini on that. If you've ever seen him in those Italian movies directed by Lina Wertmüller, he's fabulous."

  A.V. Club

REVIEWS

"Timothy Dalton is wonderful as Edmund, Ms Junot's long-lost brother. He is especially moving, and totally believable, as he agonisingly relives the horror of his Nazi captivity in an Emmy-caliber performance."

  Kay Masters, THE EVENING INDEPENDENT, 1 February 1986

"Timothy Dalton's character allowed him to try both his new Bondishness and old Shakespearian acting in a Poor-Tom-style breakdown."

  Andrew Hislop, THE TIMES, 8 September 1987

TALES FROM THE CRYPT

1992

HBO

CAST

Timothy Dalton (Lokai), Dennis Farina (Antoine), Walter Gotell (Mr. Hertz), Charles Fleischer (Carl Rechek), Reginald VelJohnson (Mercedes'

Husband), Lela Rochon (Mercedes), Beverly D'Angelo (Janice Baird), John Kassir (Crypt Keeper voice), Wolfgang Puck (himself), Jason Rainwater (Peiter), Marci Simon (Chamber Maid), Andre Bustanoby (Werewolf)

CREDITS

Director: Steve Perry | Producers: Gilbert Adler, Richard Donner, David Giler, Walter Hill, Joel Silver, Robert Zemeckis | Writer: Scott Nimerfro | Cinematography: Rick Bota | Production Design: Gregory Melton | Editing: Stanley Wohlberg | Art Direction: Phil Dagort | Set Decoration: Greg J. Grande | Costume Design: Warden Neil | Music: Rick Marotta | *Running Time*: 25 mins.

THE SERIES

Dalton participates in the episode "Werewolf Concerto" (4x13)

The clients of a remote hotel get terrorised by rumours of a werewolf around the area. Luckily, a self-appointed werewolf hunter is amongst them. But he might have a dark secret of his own.

DALTON:

"It was, I guess, an interesting experience. But not a very fulfilling one."

    A.V. Club

REVIEWS

"This one is another example of how good the series could be when the right people were put in the right roles with a good script. Dalton is great as Lokai while the rest of the cast, D'Angelo in particular, are a lot of fun while supporting him."

    Ian Jane, dvdtalk.com, 11 July 2006

"*Werewolf Concerto* features great performances by Timothy Dalton and the lovely Beverly D'Angelo."

    Chuck Aliaga, digitallyObsessed.com, 24 July 2016

FRAMED

1992

ITV

CAST

Timothy Dalton (Eddie Myers), David Morrissey (Sgt. Larry Jackson), Timothy West (DCI Jimmy McKinnes), Annabelle Apsion (Susan Jackson), Penélope Cruz (Lola Del Moreno), Trevor Cooper (DI Shrapnel), James Findleton (Tony Jackson), Barry Findleton (John Jackson), Rowena King (Charlotte Lampton), Glyn Grimstead (DI Jimmy Falcon), Wayne Foskett (DC Summers), Anthony Smee (Superintendent), Carol Holt (Nurse Jackie), Francis Johnson (DC Frisby), Angus Kennedy (Surveillance officer), Sheila White (Moyra Sheffield)

CREDITS

Director: Geoffrey Sax | Producers: Delia Fine, Brenda Reid, Guy Slater | Writer: Lynda La Plante | Cinematography: Barry McCann | Production Design: Kenneth Sharp | Editings: Jim Howe, Graham Walker | Art Direction: Steve Groves | Costume Design: Barbara Kidd | Music: Nicholas Bicat | *Running Time*: 60 mins.

THE SERIES

A four-episode miniseries.

While he is on holiday in Spain, DC Lawrence Jackson is alarmed when he believes he has spotted none other than Eddie Myers; a powerful man turned informant who was wanted for his involvement in a bank robbery some years ago. Although Myers was believed to be long since dead, after his wife identified a corpse found in Italy, DC Jackson captures the man.

DALTON:

"I was very impressed with her [La Plante] script. I read a lot of scripts. It's one of a handful that I loved the most. It's rare these days. What's distressing is the ones you do think are great, you don't get offered. The ones you do get offered are the ones that you don't want to do. So it's wonderful when something comes along you do want to do. (...) I'm sure most guys if you ask them if they would like to fantasise about pulling off the most wonderful robbery, they would all say yes. I don't know about the ladies. We think of how to rob Fort Knox or something and get away with it. Of course, we don't do it. So the criminal mentality is very fascinating."

    LOS ANGELES TIMES

"I'm intrigued by the idea of having enough money to change your life and start afresh. It takes a creative mind to pull off a top-quality scam. In a sense it is quite admirable, if you are prepared to put your life on the line and take risks."

DAILY EXPRESS

"I wanted to see where I could take the role. One of the things my character, Phillip Van Joel, is trying to do with this young policeman is find any way into him, just get inside the guy. It's actually, literally, a seduction, and a very dangerous one, because Van Joel knows if he doesn't succeed and has to go to jail, he'll be killed."

ARTS AND ENTERTAINMENT

"Often the villains are the most interesting parts to play, but if I'm offered anything challenging and new, I always consider it."

PLAYS AND PLAYERS

REVIEWS

"The crook is Timothy Dalton, darkly suave though given to devilish laughs, and the detective is David Morrissey, clean as a chisel or, indeed, whistle."

Nancy Banks-Smith, THE GUARDIAN, 28 November 1992

"So why did Det Sgt Larry Jackson get so excited in *Framed* when he spotted Spr Grs Eddie Myers having a good time off a Marbella beach? Was it because he couldn't believe, any more than me, that triple-tasty Timothy Dalton would accept a part that so far requires him to do little more than look pretty, snarl, laugh in a snarling sort of way, and try out several variations on a pretty criminal accent?"

Margaret Forwood, DAILY EXPRESS, 28 November 1992

"Lynda La Plante has created yet another meticulously constructed piece of drama and Anglia Films has assembled a matchingly professional cast of top actors to do her work proper justice."

Tony Barrow, THE STAGE, 3 December 1992

"You saw what Prime Suspect 2 would have been like without her [Helen Mirren], watching La Plante's *Framed* (ITV) – all sound and fury and Timothy Dalton fluttering his antelope eyelashes in a frenzy of male bonding."

Allison Pearson, THE INDEPENDENT ON SUNDAY, 20 December 1992

"Mr Dalton is riveting as the menacingly elegant and diabolical Eddie."

John J. O'Connor, THE NEW YORK TIMES, 17 September 1993

"Dalton's Eddie, commanding and sophisticated, is a rich study of an intricate personality dedicated to self-service."

Tony Scott, VARIETY, 17 September 1993

"Dalton is superb, a sacred monster of manipulation: James Bond and P. T. Barnum and Mephistopheles."

John Leonard, NEW YORK MAGAZINE, 20 September 1993

IN THE WILD

1993

PBS

CAST

Timothy Dalton, David Mech

CREDITS

Director: Jeremy Bradshow | Producers: Jeremy Bradshow, Karen Mellor | Writers: | Cinematography: | Production Design: | Editing: | Art Direction: | Set Decoration: | Costume Design: | Music: | *Running Time*: 54 mins.

THE SERIES

Dalton participates in the first episode of this TV-series documentary titled "In the Company of Wolves": Actor Timothy Dalton and wildlife expert David Mech travel from America's remote wolf habitats to Canada's barren Arctic wilderness in pursuit of a close encounter with wolves in the wild.

DALTON:

"I thought it would be interesting to show my reactions to what was happening, to let me become an active part of the journey, to filter the material through how I was feeling and what I was thinking. (...) Great God, what fortune. There I sat, freezing in that vast empty, desolate, savage landscape, surrounded by barren nothingness, and suddenly they appeared, come to check us out. They were very wary and very curious, and I'm sure they would have skedaddled had I moved or gotten off my snowmobile. I'm sure they were more scared of me than I of them. They marked their territory to let us know who was boss, and finally they moved away. It was one of the most memorable moments of my life. (...) The wolf is neither to be feared or hated. It's not dangerous, evil or malicious. It's simply the wolf, and that's a smart animal trying to make a living under tough conditions."

San Francisco Chronicle

"The wolf has a strange, almost mythic reputation. The first time in the Arctic, when the wolves came towards us, I couldn't escape a feeling of apprehension. It didn't matter what I'd been told - that they didn't associate the human shape with food - or what I felt or believed. I still felt nervous. (...) The wolves proved very elusive. We had to travel to places that were so remote to find them. When we went to one location, 600 miles from the North Pole, it took three days travelling from Montreal. It is very savage terrain and you know you have 1,0000 miles of travel ahead of you if you break a leg. But I learnt a lot. It was a terrific experience. (...) There was no big trailer and no central heating. And it's great to have the chance to make it up as you go along, rather than speaking words from a script. At night it was very strange, especially in the Arctic where it was permanently light. It made me feel very tired. I just crawled into my sleeping bag and went straight to sleep. It would be very difficult to stay alive without help."

Daily Mail

"I started out believing that the wolf was a dangerous animal, and found out that no human need to fear them, and we are not what they consider food. I grew quite fond of them. (...) I am selfish. I thought what a great chance it would be to be 600 miles from the North Pole in late winter and live with some Eskimos. It would be fascinating. I thought it would be a good idea to have someone there who could be an intermediary for the audience. (...) On the north slope of Alaska, where it is 40 below zero and the cold is almost visible in the air and the harshness of the territory is right in front of you, you feel very, very small in this desolate, windswept, raw landscape. (...) Nature is so much bigger. It might seem like a contradiction, but you feel so alive. It's very valuable when you come back to a place like L.A. and see people in their motor cars and in the shops, and no matter how tough we think life is in a big city, you really have no idea what tough is."

Chicago Tribune

"It was the adventure of a lifetime. A great chance to do something different. (...) Suddenly I saw wolf tracks about 4ft from my chosen spot. I felt very vulnerable! I was back in camp double quick. (...) I was amazed at how huge it was. And I was nervous that it might come round before it was supposed to. (...) The adult male was a huge, really powerful animal. He started to size me up. This was his territory and I was a stranger in it. It was very exciting, simply out of this world. Watching these animals, it was hard to reconcile them with the popular image of the wolf as a red-eyed slavering mankiller. The wolf is a hunter, but there's no record in North America of a healthy one ever killing a human being."

  DAILY MIRROR

"What really fascinated me about the wolf is why an animal so few people ever see or encounter should evoke such extreme hatred. My aim is to try to come face to face with a wolf in the wild and see for myself. (…) Wolves kill. They leave blood on the snow. They will always have an eerie howl. But the wolf itself is neither dangerous, evil, nor malicious. It is simply a smart animal trying to survive in tough conditions."

  EVENING CHRONICLE

"When you are filming in these savage and remote areas, surrounded by nature which is more dangerous than any wolf, it makes you feel very small – but it also makes you feel very alive. (...) I loved doing the nature film on wolves and would like to do more – I see it as a step towards conservation."

  PLAYS AND PLAYERS

REVIEWS

"Fortunately, Timothy Dalton is no 'save the whale' dilettante. In his quest to come 'face to face' with a wolf *In the Wild*, he camps out in the Arctic Circle for several days in sub-zero temperatures – and there's not a Winnebago in sight. Despite the over-the-top actorly relish with which he delivers the narration, Dalton does seem to have a genuine passion for these much-maligned creatures. (...) The only drawback is that because of his 'Bond – James Bond' associations, every time Dalton is seen driving a snow-buggy or sledge you expect some baddie in a ski-mask and black polo-neck to leap out from behind the nearest fir-tree and wrestle him off it."

  James Rapton, THE PEOPLE, 5 July 1993

"Not that Dalton is mere voice-over material: he went there, on occasion aboard a Bond-like snow-mobile. (...) For all that nature films on television have become brilliantly commonplace, for all that there is not much that jumps, flies, runs, swims or slithers that we have not now seen from every angle, this was nonetheless a smashing piece of work."

  Peter Barnard, THE TIMES, 6 July 1993

LIE DOWN WITH LIONS

1994

Lifetime Television

CAST

Marg Helgenberger (Kate Nessen), Timothy Dalton (Jack Carver), Nigel Havers (Peter Husak), Jürgen Prochnow (Marteau), Kabir Bedi (Kabir), Omar Sharif (Safar Khan), Laura Perramond (Hope), Eve Polycarpou (Zhenya), Nadim Sawalha (Kerim), Stephen Greif (Grigor), Ron Berglas (Williams), Philippe Leroy (Dolohov), Ron Donachie (Kelly), Arnaud Badem (Mousa), Paul Freeman (Dubois)

CREDITS

Director: Jim Goddard | Producers: Fabrizio Chiesa, David Evans, Geoffrey Reeve, Jim Reeve, Romain Schroeder, Karel Van Ossenbruggen | Writers: Guy Andrews, Julian Bond | Based on the novel *Lie Down with Lions* by Ken Follet | Cinematography: Eduard van der Enden | Production Design: Morley Smith | Editing: Bob Morgan | Art Direction: Damien Lanfranchi, Peter Powis | Costume Design: Raymond Hughes | Music: Carl Davis | *Running Time*: 90 mins.

THE SERIES

A two-episode miniseries (aka *RED EAGLE*).

Doctor Peter Husak introduces the American Jack Carver to his friend nurse Kate – and it is love at first sight. But when she learns, in a dramatic incident, that Jack's a CIA agent, she leaves him and marries Husak instead. The couple departs into a war area in Nagorno-Karabakh for a relief organisation. Sometime later Carver also arrives at Karabakh as he has to bring a businessman out of the country.

DALTON:

"I had read the original book, which is called *Lie Down with Lions*, some time ago and when I read the first version of the script that I saw it would seem to me that there was something out of the ordinary about this mainstream adventure story, and that was that it seemed to centre on a rather interesting love story about a woman and two men both of whom betray her. One of whom attempts anyway to redeem himself, and that seemed to me to be quite an interesting heart to a fairly popular story. (...) He [Jack] works for American intelligence, he is not a particularly, I guess at heart he is a good man he is just in a pretty shitty job and I think he has got pretty disgusted with himself and the way he is behaving and he does make an attempt to redeem himself, so there is some, you know it, there is something worth playing there."

The Making of *Lie Down with Lions*

REVIEWS

"As for Dalton, Havers and Helgenberger, they could just as well have phoned in their roles, no thanks to Guy Andrews and Julian Bond's stupifying, by-the-numbers script and Jim Goddard's lethargic direction."

Ray Loynd, VARIETY, 6 June 1994

SCARLETT

1994

CBS

CAST

Joanne Whalley (Scarlett O'Hara), Timothy Dalton (Rhett Butler), Annabeth Gish (Anne Hampton), Julie Harris (Eleanor Butler), Ann-Margret (Belle Watling), Sean Bean (Lord Richard Fenton), George Grizzard (Henry Hamilton), Jean Smart (Sally Brewton), Gary Raymond (Old Daniel O'Hara), Tina Kellegher (Mary Boyle), Rosaleen Linehan (Mrs. Fitzpatrick), Rakie Ayola (Pansy), Mark Lambert (Donnelly), Ruth McCabe (Kathleen O'Hara), Rachael Dowling (Bridie O'Hara), Julie Hamilton (Katie Scarlett), Owen Roe (Tim O'Hara), James Start (Dennis), Barbara Barrie (Pauline Robillard), Brian Bedford (Sir John Morland), Stephen Collins (Ashley Wilkes), Melissa Leo (Suellen O'Hara Benteen), Colm Meaney (Father Colum O'Hara), Elizabeth Wilson (Eulalie Robillard), Delena Kidd (Lady Morland), Ray McKinnon (Will Benteen)

CREDITS

Director: John Erman | Producers: John Erman, Robert Halmi Sr., Richard M. Rosenbloom, Art Seidel | Writer: William Hanley | Based on the book *Scarlett* by Alexandra Ripley | Cinematography: Tony Imi | Production Design: Rodger Maus | Editing: Malcolm Cooke, Keith Palmer, John W. Wheeler | Art Direction: Brian Ackland-Snow | Costume Design: Marit Allen | Music: John

Morris | *Running Time*: 90 mins.

THE SERIES

A four-episode miniseries.

A sequel to *Gone with the Wind* in which Scarlett refuses to accept Rhett's rejection and travels to Charleston to win him back. Unable to change his mind, she leaves America and establishes herself in Ireland – the land of her family – and meets the London society. In the meantime, she vows never to reveal to Rhett a secret only she knows.

DALTON:

[*Were you intimidated by the part?*] "Not by the part as given in the script. Certainly by the potential reaction to my performance in it by people who had loved Clark Gable, and I loved Clark Gable, too. Thankfully, this story was not a remake of *Gone with the Wind*, but a sequel."

  Hollywood Online

"Rhett is from Charleston, not Atlanta, and people sound completely different from the two cities. So I have had voice coaching to get the accent just right, playing a lot of tapes. There are all sorts of voice exercises to work on. I get the flavour and the pronunciation and the voice coach then makes it even more precise. Rhett was kicked out of the family home and became a riverboat gambler who got as far as Seattle, San Francisco and Britain. So you can play around a lot with that. He's sophisticated and well-travelled. The look of the man is a little easier. I toyed around with not having a moustache but then decided to go with it. The hair is parted, longer and with sideburns. I feel comfortable with the frock coats, too."

  TV GUIDE

"It's a good part. You can't be Clark Gable. You've got to play Rhett Butler and bring him back to life. It's the original great soap opera. (…) *GWTW* is a much superior piece of work. *Scarlett* is a good story but without the same literary value."

  PARADE

"It's actually about human passion. I knew essentially that it wasn't going to be cheap exploitation when I saw the script and the cast. (…) The Southern accent was deliberately subtle. At first I thought it should be strong, but then I decided against that. Rhett is wealthy, aristocratic, educated and cosmopolitan. He's well-travelled. He's left the South. In many senses he is of them, but he's separate from them. Rhett's been around. (…) Once I decided to take this role I headed straight to Margaret Mitchell and read the original book for the first time. Rhett is a pirate and a crook, a businessman and a profiteer, but he's a creation of a woman's mind, and I suppose he might be what every woman would like to see in a man. (...) Even though the characters are the same it's a completely different story. (...) Rhett's walkout on Scarlett isn't just a spat. It's the result of a seven-year failure. He couldn't make her love him, and yet he got trapped – no, he trapped himself. He was aware of what he was doing. He took a gamble and it didn't work. You always have to learn once, and then as soon as you see the way the wind blows you should know better the next time. He went into this with his eyes open, and it didn't work. I've done that in my life. (...) You know from the book what the author intended Rhett to be. You find those parts of yourself that understand him, and then you go back to the character and absorb yourself in that person. (...) Rhett needs to be fulfilled in love or to be made whole again or for the first time. You don't get a sense that he's had a fulfilling relationship before."

REUTER NEWS SERVICE

"The most complicated things have been to ride racehorses, to drive the cars, to climb the stairs with the women in the arms, to carry them through corridors and doors... Everything has been very complicated, even the simplest thing has been complicated."

EL SEMANAL

"Producers didn't want me in their films because I was too specifically identified as James Bond. That's why I went to TV to carve out a new niche. It's the reason I agreed to play Rhett Butler in *Scarlett*. It took tackling another screen icon to break the Bond mould."

CALGARY SUN

"I loved playing Rhett even though it was daunting. I don't search these parts out but if you are offered something like this you can't turn it down. I would have been a coward and felt rotten about myself if I hadn't dared to take it on. (...) Scarlett is a woman you admire but who behaves appallingly."

DAILY MIRROR

"It is our job to create it [the sexual chemistry]. (...) She [Scarlett] is very mercurial and there are a lot of qualities in her I wouldn't like."

NEWCASTLE EVENING CHRONICLE

"I don't deliberately search these parts out. As an actor, ideally you would only play new parts which nobody could draw any comparisons with. But Rhett and Bond are great parts, and you would feel rotten for the rest of your life if you didn't dare do them. (...) It was in mind to do *Scarlett* without it [moustache], to make him more different from Gable. But when you go to Rhett Butler in the books, he's described as having a moustache, and people are always talking about it – so I played him with one."

EVENING CHRONICLE (1)

"I thought that, by playing Rhett Butler, I would basically be nailing myself up on a cross. But my housekeeper said she'd never speak to me again if I didn't take the role, so I didn't have much choice."

EVENING CHRONICLE (2)

REVIEWS

"And, to answer the big question, the new Scarlett O'Hara and Rhett Butler — Joanne Whalley-Kilmer and Timothy Dalton — do as well as can be expected under the circumstances. (...) Whalley-Kilmer and the underrated Dalton have proven their talents elsewhere, but the script lets them down with these one-dimensional characters."

Tim Gray, VARIETY, 8 November 1994

"Finally, of course, there's no avoiding the almost mythic matter of Vivien Leigh and Clark Gable, the Scarlett and Rhett for ages. Ms Whalley-Kilmer and Mr Dalton are not nearly as monumental and, wisely, they don't even try. Mr Dalton's Rhett is less impetuous, more thoughtful. Physically and emotionally, the mustached actor resembles Walter Pidgeon more than Gable."

John J. O'Connor, THE NEW YORK TIMES, 11 November 1994

"Dalton sports a Gable-style mustache that for some reason only serves to draw attention to his chin, which has a cleft wide and deep enough to hide a supply of subway tokens. The actor turns himself into a cartoon of a matinee idol, all heavy-lidded and smarmy-smiled."

Ken Tucker, ENTERTAINMENT WEEKLY, 11 November 1994

"Timothy Dalton has an easier time playing Rhett. No, he's no Clark Gable, either. But as James Bond, he is accustomed to stepping into used shoes".

Jeff Jarvis, TV GUIDE, 12 November 1994

"Timothy Dalton plays Rhett for laughs, but so did Gable."

John Leonard, NEW YORK MAGAZINE, 14 November 1994

"We are introduced to the rakish Rhett (played by former 007 Timothy Dalton with a remarkably halfhearted stab at a drawl) as he sits playing cards in a bordello (run by Ann-Margret)."

    David Hiltbrand, PEOPLE, 14 November 1994

"Rhett is smarmily played by Timothy Dalton as if he doesn't give a damn about followin' in the *footsteps* of Clark Gable, the King of Hollywood."

    Maureen Paton, DAILY EXPRESS, 14 December 1994

"Joanne Whalley-Kilmer fiddle-de-dees prettily as Scarlett, Timothy Dalton wears a selection of wide-awake hat which seems, like the character of Rhett, rather too large for him and tonight, John Gielgud, makes his customary short but forceful appearance."

    Nancy Banks-Smith, THE GUARDIAN, 14 December 1994

"There's Timothy Dalton as Rhett Butler, pulling up the corners of his mouth so his laugh lines rhyme with his rake's moustache. It's a risky strategy: in making every detail remind you of Clark Gable you often see Dalton as pale shadow rather than incorrigible Southern sex beast."

    Stuart Jaffries, THE GUARDIAN, 7 December 1996

CLEOPATRA

1999

Hallmark Entertainment

CAST

Leonor Varela (Cleopatra), Timothy Dalton (Julius Caesar), Billy Zane (Marc Antony), Rupert Graves (Octavian), John Bowe (Rufio), Art Malik (Olympos), Nadim Sawalha (Mardian), Owen Teale (Grattius), Philip Quast (Cornelius), Daragh O'Malley (Ahenobarbus), Bruce Payne (Cassius), Sean Pertwee (Marcus Brutus), David Schofield (Casca), Kassandra Voyagis (Arsinoe), Indra Ové (Charmian), Josephine Amankwah (Iris), Caroline Langrishe (Calpurnia), Elisabeth Dermot Walsh (Octavia), Ralph Brown (Guevarius), James Cosmo (Agrippa), Denis Quilley (Negotiator Senator), James Saxon (Pothinus)

CREDITS

Director: Franc Roddam | Producers: Robert Halmi Jr., Robert Halmi Sr., Steve Harding, Dyson Lovell | Writers: Anton Diether, Stephen Harrigan |

Based on the book *Cleopatra* by Margaret George | Cinematography: David Connell | Production Design: Martin Hitchcock | Editing: Peter Coulson | Art Direction: Frank Walsh | Set Decoration: Judy Farr | Costume Design: Enrico Sabbatini | Music: Trevor Jones | *Running Time*: 90 mins.

THE SERIES

Dalton participates in the first episode of this two-episode miniseries.

Cleopatra seduces the Roman ruler Julius Caesar to secure the throne of Egypt. They both fell in love and have a son. However, Caesar's Roman followers and wife are not pleased by the union. In fact, as Caesar has only a daughter by his wife, he has picked Octavian as his successor and the son of Cleopatra is seen to be a threat to his future leadership. Thus Brutus and other Roman legislators plot the assassination of Caesar.

DALTON:

"I would not admire someone who wanted to dominate the world. You admire that tenacity, that ruthlessness, that ambition, that political skill--from a distance. It was important to remind the audience that he did have quite a searing ambition to be almost a god... [in a scene] by the Sphinx when he talked about not wanting to be remembered in crumbling stone, that he was going to shape the world for history to come. (...) Caesar nearly loses to Cleopatra, nearly loses his focus. He says in our movie, 'I have to go. When I'm with you, I lose myself.' Antony never has the strength to do that."

TV RATINGS REPORT

"That fascination with any woman who could change the nature of the world through love is one of the reasons for the enduring quality of the story and its great excitement and fascination. (...) A huge sense of reality. It feels real; it looks real. The soldiers have travelled. They are battle worn, they're hard, and yet there is the light, and the change of colour, and the action and the movement. You get a tremendous sense of glamour that does not rely on the Hollywood glitz. It is born out of a reality, a size, a breadth, and that is great, too. (...) It's Cecil B. DeMille, but better. (...) I'd never ridden a chariot before so the main thought is just staying on. (...) History is littered with great stories, but this is one of them. (...) We filmed in the place called Ouarzazate, across the Atlas Mountains, on the edge of the Sahara Desert. I filmed the first Bond movie... we filmed there. And the studios aren't really studios...there's no roof or anything. Nothing's got a roof. It's just like three walls and the fourth wall is open Sahara Desert. It was marvellous. I mean, it reminded me of what Hollywood might have been like in the 30's or 40's. I'm sounding silly, I know! There are childish pleasures, and this is one of the best. It was just fantastic. It was thrilling."

> The Making of *Cleopatra* [DVD]

"The script is remarkably honourable to the narration of history and the essence of the characters. Here you have a story about a woman who changes the lives of two of the greatest men in the world, because of love and because of politics. She's a woman who struggles for her nation's freedom in this male-dominated world of militaristic, almost fascistic might. Then these two men genuinely fall in love with her. (...) He [Caesar] was a man of formidable intellect and energy, a man driven by ruthless ambition, a great politician and a military genius. (...) You become more and more seduced by the richness of life in the East, all the while seeing these hopeless monuments to death from the ancient Egyptian kings who believed they would live forever."

> THE NEW YORK TIMES

"Julius Caesar was a completely surprising man. You can't ever think of a modern example. Modern men aren't like that anymore. Caesar was not only a ruthless politician and a smooth adjudicator but a military genius."

> SCRIPPS HOWARD NEWS SERVICE

"I had one of the most exciting first days on *Cleopatra* that I've had on any movie ever. They built ancient Alexandria in the desert. It started with a....fabulous 300ft barge built in the desert sand, then swept through marketplaces, and squares and streets, through bronze gates 70, 80 feet high right up to 'Cleopatra's' Palace and then they said ok now can you ride a chariot? We're going to do your entrance, so Caesar entered Alexandria with a 1000 men it was like being transformed back. (...) I mean my initial costume was wearing the armour so all I felt was god this is heavy why didn't they make that out of fibreglass? But the truth is I am glad they didn't because...surrounded by that set wearing those costumes in that armour...you can't help but transform, you do transform. I mean even wearing what you might think of is silly, you know we are all wondering around... Skirts and sandals... You know I'm walking around in a skirt but after a few minutes in the heat you realise this tunic is the most comfortable, the most easy, the most lovely thing in the world to wear. I mean you if we should all be wearing them anywhere we go that is hot in the world there terrifically comfortable and easy, and oddly... male."

> Good Morning America interview

"I actually had to learn to drive a chariot and I quickly discovered that the main thing is just to hold on for dear life!"

OK

REVIEWS

"Yet Varela also connects believably with Timothy Dalton, who makes for a charismatic and commanding Julius Caesar."

Ray Richmond, VARIETY, 20 May 1999

"Julius Caesar arrives, helps Cleopatra oust her sister and brother to become queen, and falls for her. But even when cavorting with Cleopatra, Timothy Dalton's Caesar is the essence of a buttoned-down Englishman. "

Caryn James, THE NEW YORK TIMES, 21 May 1999

"Chilean-born Leonor Varela has the exotic allure to make this Cleopatra the plausible conqueror of a virile, commanding Caesar (Timothy Dalton)."

Terry Kelleher, PEOPLE, 24 May 1999

HERCULES

2005

NBC

CAST

Paul Telfer (Hercules), Timothy Dalton (Amphitryon), Elizabeth Perkins (Alcmene), Sean Astin (Linus), Leeanna Walsman (Megara), Kristian Schmid (King Eurystheus), Kim Coates (Tiresias), Jamie Croft (Young Hercules), Luke Ford (Iphicles), Tyler Mane (Antaeus), Robert Taylor (Kiron, the Centaur), Leelee Sobieski (Deianeira), John Bach (Creon), Peter McCauley (Nestor), André de Vanny (Young Iphicles), Maria Cristina Heller (Phea)

CREDITS

Director: Roger Young | Producers: Robert Halmi Jr., Robert Halmi Sr., Jeffrey M. Hayes, Brett Popplewell | Writers: Charles Edward Pogue | Cinematography: Donald M. Morgan | Production Design: Leslie Binns | Editing: Benjamin A. Weissman | Art Direction: Nigel Evans, Mark Robins | Set Decoration: Lisa Thompson | Costume Design: Marion Boyce | Music: Patrick Williams | *Running Time*: 120 mins.

THE SERIES

Dalton participates in the first episode of this two-episode miniseries.

Alcmene, Princess of Thebes, while waiting for the return of her husband Amphitryon from war, gets cheated by Zeus and finds herself carrying the great god's child. When Hercules is born, he is rejected by his mother, envied by his brother, and loathed by Zeus's wife. However, the demigod has his allies: his foster-father Amphitryon, who exalts in the boy's potential; his faithful companion Linus; the blind oracle Tiresias; a beautiful nymph and the priestess Megara, who will become his wife.

DALTON:

"I'm cuckolded by the god I suppose I worship, which is a pretty difficult situation if you think about [laughs]. (...) He [Robert Salmi Sr.] does things well. He goes for it. He doesn't always get it right, but he's got chutzpah, panache and style. (...) I thought it was just about a strong he-man. I didn't realise it was quite a revolutionary story, too. The thing about the Jesus legend is it's all about getting into a heaven outside earth. The Hercules legend is about finding, in a sense, heaven on earth by growing to your highest fulfilment. (...) He [Amphitryon] is a perfectly decent, nice fellow. Not the sort of part I usually do. Miles outside my normal range [laughs]."

    ASSOCIATED PRESS

"In modern age we have the ability to do wonderful things with computers, we can make fantasy appear real. (...) It's not only a story of a strong man as Hercules' strength is also intellectual and emotional."

Hercules: The Myth Comes Alive [DVD]

REVIEWS

"Former 007 Timothy Dalton exudes kindness as Amphitryon, who becomes a foster father to Hercules."

Hal Boedeker, ORLANDO SENTINEL, 14 May 2005

"Timothy Dalton and Elizabeth Perkins are mutteringly awful as the parents, Perkins wearing a long puss through the whole ordeal."

Tom Shales, THE WASHINGTON POST, 16 May 2005

AGATHA CHRISTIE'S MARPLE

2006

ITV

CAST

Geraldine McEwan (Miss Marple), Timothy Dalton (Clive Trevelyan), Robert Hickson (Arthur Hopkins), Robert Hardy (Winston Churchill), Laurence Fox (James Pearson), James Murray (Charles Burnaby), Ian Hallard (Reporter), Zoe Telford (Emily Trefusis), Jeffery Kissoon (Ahmed Ghali), Mel Smith (John Enderby), Rita Tushingham (Miss Elizabeth Percehouse), James Wilby (Stanley Kirkwood), Paul Kaye (Dr. Ambrose Burt), Michael Brandon (Martin Zimmerman), Carey Mulligan, (Violet Willett), Patricia Hodge (Mrs. Evadne Willett)

CREDITS

Director: Paul Unwin | Producers: Michele Buck, Phil Clymer, Rebecca Eaton, Matthew Read, Bill Shephard, Damien Timmer | Writer: Stephen Churchett | Based on the book *The Sittaford Mystery* by Agatha Christie | Cinematography: Nicholas D. Knowland | Production Design: Rob Harris | Editing: Jon Costelloe | Set Decoration: Claire Nia Richards | Costume Design: Frances Tempest | Music: Dominik Scherrer | *Running Time*: 93 mins.

THE SERIES

Dalton participates in the episode "The Sittaford Mystery" (2x04)

The death of the presumptive future Prime Minister is predicted during a séance in a snowbound country hotel, and he is found stabbed to death in his room the next morning. In addition, a dangerous convict has escaped from Dartmoor Prison.

DALTON:

"Marple is the kind of show I normally never get a chance to be part of. If you're a boy, you always want to be in a western; and any actor I know would like to be in a horror. This mystery whodunnit sort of fits into those genres."

>   THE TELEGRAPH

"There are certain kinds of film every actor has always wanted to be in: a horror movie, a Western and an Agatha Christie mystery. You don't have to take it that seriously – you can just enjoy it. They don't represent the real Britain. There's never been a Britain like Agatha Christie's – although many wish it were like that. There's an element of wish fulfilment about her stories."

>   EXPRESS ON SUNDAY

"In many ways, I suppose, Christie's cosy, idyllic England never really existed. I suspect the whole thing is more folklore than fact."

>   THE SUN

REVIEWS

"The actors are top notch, as well. There's always been a notion with American critics that British actors are somehow better trained than American actors, although if you ask most British actors, they're equally envious of American actors' sense of immediacy. But clearly, for this type of mystery, British actors reign, and this series does an amazing job of picking both seasoned pros and fresh faces to bring the stories to life. "

>   Paul Mavis, dvdtalk.com, 5 September 2006

"Mel Smith gives a wonderfully understated performance as the man in charge of the investigation, helped by the wily Miss Marple (Geraldine McEwan). As always, the cast is A-list – here it includes Timothy Dalton, Matthew Kelly, Patricia Hodge and Rita Tushingham."

>   David Cater, THE TIMES, 25 May 2007

UNKNOWN SENDER

2008

Strike TV

CAST

Timothy Dalton (Miles) Joanne Whalley (Carolyn), Stan Freberg (radio host)

CREDITS

Director: Steven E. de Souza | Producers: Amy De Souza, Daniel De Souza, Steven E. de Souza, Kevin Rubio, Gregg Vance, Marilyn Vance | Writers: David De Souza, Steven E. de Souza | Cinematography: Edward J. Pei | Production Design: Joshua Stricklin | Editing: Daniel De Souza, Terry Kelley | Music: Adam Cohen | *Running Time*: 10 mins.

THE SERIES

Dalton participates in the web episode "If You're Seeing This Tape..." (1/9).

A philanthropist engaged in a bitter divorce prepares a video will.

DALTON:

"What we're doing here is having some fun, working with people we like and hopefully giving people who click on this, a moment of kind of intriguing entertainment."

      Strike.TV

DOCTOR WHO

2009–2010

BBC

CAST

David Tennant (The Doctor), John Simm (The Master), Bernard Cribbins (Wilfred Mott), Timothy Dalton (The Narrator / Rassilon, Lord President), Catherine Tate (Donna Noble), Jacqueline King (Sylvia Noble), Billie Piper (Rose Tyler), Camille Coduri (Jackie Tyler), John Barrowman (Captain Jack Harkness), Freema Agyeman (Martha Smith-Jones), Noel Clarke (Mickey

Smith), Elisabeth Sladen (Sarah Jane Smith), Jessica Hynes (Verity Newman), June Whitfield (Minnie Hooper), Claire Bloom (The Woman), Tommy Knight (Luke Smith), Russell Tovey (Midshipman Frame), David Harewood (Joshua Naismith), Tracy Ifeachor (Abigail Naismith), Lawry Lewin (Rossiter), Sinead Keenan (Addams), Matt Smith (The Doctor)

CREDITS

Director: Euros Lyn | Producers: Russell T. Davies, Julie Gardner, Tracie Simpson, Steven Moffat, Piers Wenger | Writers: Russell T. Davies, Steven Moffat, Robert Holmes, Sydney Newman | Cinematography: Rory Taylor | Production Design: Edward Thomas | Editing: Philip Kloss | Art Direction: Stephen Nicholas | Set Decoration: Julian Luxton | Costume Design: Louise Page | Music: Murray Gold | *Running Time*: 75 mins.

THE SERIES

Dalton participates in the Christmas'09 Special – the transition between 10th and 11th Doctors – in the episodes "The End of Time: part one" (4x17) and "The End of Time: part two" (4x18).

The Tenth Doctor, while trying to escape from a prophecy of his imminent end, is drawn into a plan by his old nemesis, the Master. The Master brings the human race under his control as part of an elaborate plan to restore the world to the Time Lords – the Master and the Doctor's people – from their downfall in the Time War.

DALTON:

"I just did a bit in *Doctor Who* last year, and I've been watching *Doctor Who* all my life, so it was a joy to be in it. The real link is that we like being a part of stories we like and want to share with others."

ENTERTAINMENT WEEKLY

"I'd seen it as a kid, but I've certainly not followed it as a fan. The last one, I saw on BBC America, and I thought everything about it was fantastic. (...) I'm not an expert. I've not studied it. But I do know that Russell [Davies]'s script is one of the most extraordinary scripts that I've ever read. It covers many genres. It's like reading five or six different movies all at once. He's blended the imaginatively outrageous with the ordinary and prosaic, and moves between them with ease."

DOCTOR WHO MAGAZINE

"I didn't see them all [episodes] but I can remember William Hartnell right at the beginning. *Doctor Who* has been part of just about everybody's life, hasn't it? It's a hell of a series. (...) The minute you open the robes you reveal the kind of person this Lord President is: he's a soldier."

DOCTOR WHO FIGURINE COLLECTION

"Having been a kid watching that, when someone rings you up in later life and says, 'We want you to come and play a Time Lord…' Well, Doctor Who's a Time Lord! Time Lords are it! So the answer is yes! I had great fun doing it. It was wonderful people to work with. (…) We struggled to find what to wear, and I saw on a rack this sort of leather thing. I don't know where it'd come from, but it looked like it'd come out of *Antony and Cleopatra*! Or, you know, some *300* movie! And I thought, 'That, actually, is gonna go great with the robe. What about that? Can we use that?' And they said, 'Oh, yeah, that's a terrific idea! We'll just put a badge on it or something.' [Laughs.] I mean, they don't make things for you with *Doctor Who*. You've got to find stuff on racks!"

A.V. Club

REVIEWS

"The centrepiece of the two-parter was the battle between the Master (John Simm) and the Doctor but it was interwoven with the Time Lords of Gallifrey, including an imposing Timothy Dalton, and two aliens wearing spiky green swimming hats."

David Stephenson, EXPRESS ON SUNDAY, 3 January 2010

"Dalton brings a lot of heavy seriousness to the role, which is just what's needed."

Mac McEntire, dvdverdict.com, 4 February 2010

CHUCK

2010—2011

NBC

CAST

Zachary Levi (Chuck Bartowski), Yvonne Strahovski (Sarah Walker), Joshua Gomez (Morgan Grimes), Timothy Dalton (Hartley Winterbottom / Alexei Volkoff / Gregory Tuttle), Linda Hamilton (Frost, Mary Bartowski), Adam Baldwin (John Casey), Ryan McPartlin (Devon Woodcomb), Sarah Lancaster (Ellie Bartowski), Mark Christopher Lawrence (Big Mike), Vik Sahay (Lester Patel), Scott Krinsky (Jeff Barnes), Bonita Friedericy (General Diane

Beckman), Lauren Cohan (Vivian Volkoff), Mekenna Melvin (Alex McHugh), Mini Anden (Carina), Mercedes Mason (Zondra), Richard Burgi (Clyde Decker)

CREDITS

Director: Robert Duncan McNeill, Peter LauerMilan, Cheylov, Zachary Levi, Allan Kroeker | Producers: Chris Fedak, McG, Robert Duncan McNeill, Josh Schwartz, Nicholas Wootton | Writers: Josh Schwartz, Chris Fedak, Nicholas Wootton | Cinematography: Buzz Feitshans IV | Production Design: Dina Lipton | Editing: Kevin Mock | Music: Tim Jones | *Running Time*: 60 mins.

THE SERIES

An average "computer-whiz-next-door" named Chuck receives an encoded e-mail from an old college friend now working for the Central Intelligence Agency (CIA). The message embeds the only remaining copy of a software program containing the United States' greatest spy secrets into Chuck's brain.

Dalton participates in the following episodes of the 4th season:

- Chuck Versus the First Fight (4x07)

- Chuck Versus the Leftovers (4x10)

- Chuck Versus the Gobbler (4x12)

- Chuck Versus the Push Mix (4x13)

- Chuck Versus the Family Volkoff (4x20)

- Chuck Versus the Cliffhanger (4x24)

DALTON:

"My name is Tuttle and he's a sort of rather ineffectual, I think, slightly run-down... sort of guy who works in the offices in one of the secret services, you know, a never-has-been. Not a never-has-been, he would be a never-was, a never did it, never made it, really. (...) First, I was asked to do this and the producers, George and Chris, sent me a whole bunch of DVDs, so I started watching the show, and I think it's terrific, really, really liked it. It was so unlike what I've experienced on TV shows, and it was totally unpredictable and dangerous and it broke the rules and it was very funny. (...) They [cast] are lovely! Everyone is great!"

  NBC Electronic Publicity Production

"I had such a good time. (...) Oh, but they were great. It was so funny, so *alive*. I mean, they were under such pressure, and so adrenalised. You'd go in the writers' room, with its pizzas all over the place and all the cups of coffee, and the walls would have scribbled ideas on whiteboards and blackboards, and you'd bang around ideas and thoughts, and you'd have to learn stuff immediately. Immediately! (...) Zach [Levi] was great, and Yvonne [Strahovski]. They were fabulous to work with. I don't think I've ever worked with a crew who could work so fast and so well and without any kind of sweat, with lots of pressure but no tension, if you understand the distinction. It was just a delight to do that. And I was given some space, which I loved, because I could take it on in a certain way. And people seemed to enjoy it, and I enjoyed it, and there we are! I was exhausted, but I was thrilled."

A.V. Club

"Within the framework of what this series is all about, my character, Tuttle, is in the spy world, but he's not an agent. He's not a trained spy. He's not someone who goes out into the field. He's more of a bureaucrat as it were, but he's called a handler. You could tell he might have wanted to be a spy, but he never made it. He wasn't good enough. He might have been a wannabe, though, or still is a wannabe."

ENTERTAINMENT WEEKLY

"It isn't very nice playing just a really nasty bad guy. You've got to find a way to show how much you're enjoying it!"

TV GUIDE

"When [executive producers] Chris Fedak and Josh Schwartz asked me to do it, they sent me a whole bunch of DVDs of the show to let me know what kind of work they were doing. I love the show; I thought it was great - it had this wonderful, anarchic quality to it. And then they told me what kind of character they had in mind for me. It was such fun to literally play one character and then absolutely turn into another character altogether! The challenge if course is that both of those characters were Volkoff. Yes, you can say he's schizophrenic - he's different all the time - but nevertheless inside every one of those parts he's played, he is the same man. So you have to tie that together. It's an interesting arc. (...) To be the main bad guy is a good role, and they've used it well."

USA TODAY

REVIEWS

"The person who plays Volkoff is a bit of a surprise, but suffice to say he does a wonderful job. (...) Linda Hamilton does a good job as Chuck mother, but the person who steals the most scenes is Timothy Dalton. As Mary's MI-

6 handler who never goes out into the field he's the perfect spy nerd, and it's hilarious to watch the one-time James Bond fumble and fold under pressure. (...) This season's guest stars Linda Hamilton and Timothy Dalton do a fantastic job and add a lot to the show."

    John Sinnott, dvdtalk.com, 7 October 2011

"Soon enough, they [Chuck and his mother] are both reunited, but it's not long until a new mission presents itself: trying to find out more about Russian arms dealer Alexei Volkoff (another example of the show's clever casting – who plays Volkoff is a terrific surprise, and there are some other great minor cameos/roles this season, as well.)"

    Aaron Beirle, dvdtalk.com, 11 October 2011

PENNY DREADFUL

2014–2016

Showtime

CAST

Eva Green (Vanessa Ives), Timothy Dalton (Sir Malcolm Murray), Josh Hartnett (Ethan Chandler), Harry Treadaway (Dr. Victor Frankenstein), Rory Kinnear (John Clare), Reeve Carney (Dorian Gray), Billie Piper (Lily / Brona), Danny Sapani (Sembene), Simon Russell Beale (Ferdinand Lyle), Helen McCrory (Madame Kali), Patti LuPone (Cut-Wife / Dr. Seward), Olivia Llewellyn (Mina Harker), Wes Studi (Kaetenay), Nicole O'Neil (Witch #1), Olivia Chenery (Witch #2), Sarah Greene (Hecate Poole), Douglas Hodge (Bartholomew Rusk), Noni Stapleton (Gladys Murray), Jack Hickey (Junior Inspector), Stephen Lord (Warren Roper), David Haig (Oscar Putney), Jonny Beauchamp (Angelique), Ruth Gemmell (Octavia Putney), Tamsin Topolski (Lavinia Putney), Graham Butler (Peter), Sebastian Croft (Boy Familiar), Hannah Tointon (Maud Gunneson), Alex Price (Proteus), Gavin Fowler (Simon), Robert Nairne (Vampire), Alun Armstrong (Vincent Brand), Olly Alexander (Fenton), Cokey Falkow (Scarman), David Warner (Professor Abraham Van Helsing), Lorcan Cranitch (Inspector Granworthy), Ronan Vibert (Sir Geoffrey Hawkes), Anna Chancellor (Claire Ives), Brian Cox (Ethan's father)

CREDITS

Directors: J.A. Bayona, James Hawes, Brian Kirk, Coky Giedroyc, Dearbhla Walsh, Damon Thomas, Kari Skogland, Paco Cabezas | Producers: Chris W. King, James Flynn, Pippa Harris, Sheila Hockin, John Logan, Sam Mendes, Morgan O'Sullivan | Writer: John Logan | Cinematography: Xavi Giménez, John Conroy, Owen McPolin, P.J. Dillon, Nigel Willoughby | Production Design: Jonathan McKinstry | Editing: Jaume Martí, Bernat Vilaplana, Michele Conroy, Christopher Donaldson, Aaron Marshall, Geoff Ashenhurst, Gareth C. Scales | Art Direction: Antonio Calvo-Dominguez, John King, Gary McGinty, Jo Riddell, Colman Corish, Conor Dennison, Adam O'Neill, Shane McEnroe | Set Decoration: Anais Chareyre, Philip Murphy, Damian Byrne | Costume Design: Gabriella Pescucci | Makeup Dept.: Sarita Allison | Music: Abel Korzeniowski | *Running Time*: 60 mins.

THE SERIES

Season 1 (8 episodes)

The enigmatic Vanessa Ives enlists the skilled gunman Ethan Chandler to do some "night work." She introduces him to Sir Malcolm Murray, father of the recently-abducted Mina Harker and the trio infiltrates a vampire nest in search of Mina. They find and kill a vicious vampire, later enlisting Victor Frankenstein to examine it.

Season 2 (10 episodes)

The mysterious Evelyn Poole and her assistants start to corner Vanessa. Because of a massacre committed in the Mariner's Inn, Ethan believes he needs to leave London. Dr Frankenstein works under Caliban's pressure to give him a bride. Sir Malcolm is despised by his neglected wife.

Season 3 (9 episodes)

All the characters are scattered around the world. A distraught Vanessa fights a severe depression with the help of a psychiatrist; Frankenstein seeks redemption with the aid of Dr Henry Jekyll; Sir Malcolm meets a mysterious man in Zanzibar; Ethan Chandler is escorted home to his father, with Hecate in tow; and the Creature sets on a journey after his memories re-appear. A new threat hangs over London in the form of Count Dracula.

DALTON:

"There is good writing on TV, and some splendid writing on TV. But it's not common. So when it's in front of you, and it's good, and you've got someone like [writer and showrunner John Logan], and someone like [director J.A. Bayona] doing the first two episodes... You've *got* to do it. You can't say no, really. You *could* — but you shouldn't. (...) [In *Penny Dreadful*] You have to have characters you believe in, characters you empathise with. You have to have truth. And then you take them on a really interesting and scary journey. We are human beings watching, and we do have to empathise. I think that's what we're doing, and I hope that's what we're doing in *Penny Dreadful*. Showing an audience that all of these people are humans. Even if they're warped, even if they've got great problems. They're human beings, and they're trying to come to terms with themselves. But that's the boring side. [Laughs] On the other hand, you could say, 'All the good-looking people! Blood! Sex! Violence!' And fortunately, we've got it all."

THE WEEK

"He's absolutely determined and he'll use any method -ANY METHOD- to get what he wants. He says, 'To save my daughter, I'd murder the world. [One character] describes Sir Malcolm as weak, foul, lustful and vainglorious; I would add to that obsessive and manipulative – and he's the good guy!"

EMPIRE MAGAZINE

"It's not just about blood and fear and mystery, it's maybe about the fear within ourselves, it's about, you know, we don't like to think about ourselves, the fears, the *shames* and the *guilts* and all that. It exists, you know, in a world where those demons – if you like – within us can be express outside of us and can be real as we you were living in an older time when you believed in the gods, or the devil or the demon, you know? It's not a horror movie, it's a drama, it's about a group of – I have to say rather warped – people, but then maybe we all are rather warped, in some way."

Flicks And The City

"It's brilliantly written. It's superbly written by John Logan. He's a fine dramatist. There's nothing simple, nothing black and white. It's complex, and yet it's sort of highbrow, but in a lowbrow wrapper. There's tremendous excitement and mystery and disturbance and terror. Yet it's always very intelligent, so you can enjoy it on any level you like. (...) You know, I do find that you generally know within about 12 or 15 pages [of a script] whether you're going to be able to put it down. This, you carry on reading. There's such fascination, mystery in it. I got drawn to the story first. Then, of course, you have to look at your character and think, 'What can I do with it? Can I bring this to fruition? Can I do what the writer, the author, is intending here? What the hell is he intending?' You get intrigued by it. You call up and say, 'Well, what happens next? I want to know what happens next.' (...) [Sir Malcolm] is an African explorer, and that could tell you something about his character, but it's also a metaphor for a man that is on a quest for the source of the Nile. The quest for the source of any river is madness, because you can't find it ever. It's water, and however small a patch of water you find, that bit of water comes from somewhere else. You gradually get this feeling that he's an extremely manipulative, obsessive, determined man, who is totally ruthless, but he's trying to save his daughter. What a fabulous combination of opposites. It's great, so the more I just got into it, the more intrigued I was and the more challenged I was by the idea of trying to bring this man to life, make him real and entertaining in a true way. (...) I don't like the idea of a series, to tell you the truth. I don't like the idea of not knowing what I'm doing. I don't like the idea of not knowing how well it is going to be written, but on this one, John promised he was going to write them all, which is great. I'm not a spring chicken anymore. I'm up there in my 60s. This is a terrific part, so I thought, 'Come on. Do it. Give it a crack.'"

    Yahoo! TV

"What I liked about the script is that it wasn't superficial. It's a big, gaudy, lurid sort of show, in which questions of evil and love and what it means to be a human being are addressed."

    THE IRISH TIMES

"I thought that was a terrific scene [*playing the Devil in 1x05*]. I really liked that scene, the evil, wicked seduction of it. It's also quite a frightening scene and she [Vanessa] is terribly vulnerable in it. (...) There's an awful lot about Sir Malcolm *not* to like, so go for that, and then try and find something that surprises you. I mean, my favourite line of mine, perhaps, in that first season was, 'To save my daughter, I would murder the world.' Because who does not understand that, that depth of emotional commitment to your own, to your blood, to your daughter? And that means that you can get away with an awful lot, when you know that he would murder the world to save his daughter."

    ASSIGNMENT X (I)

"Sir Malcolm, he's one of those men who has profited from the great advance across the globe of the British Empire. He's one of those driven, pragmatic, intelligent, greedy people who exploit the world, who's made tremendous wealth from exploiting the natives in Africa. Some go out for adventure, some go out for the glory of discovery. He does all that, but the purpose of discovery is to exploit. You don't just go and take a picture of the view! It's, 'What is there that we can take? What is there that we can steal? What is there we can own or manufacture?' And that's what he has done. Vanessa describes him as being weak, vain, lustful, vainglorious, and a few other things. I would add to that obsessive, manipulative, monstrously egotistical. (...) [The search for the Nile] It's a metaphor for his search for his daughter –

his dead daughter. A metaphor for his guilt. (...) I think the thing that distinguishes Sir Malcolm and Vanessa is that he's quite prepared to live with his guilt. (...) He's beset by the guilt of his children's deaths, to which – certainly to his son's – he powerfully contributed. But as he also says himself, it's a bit false, because he's not a good person. He's *not* a good person! But he is a realistic person, I think. He's a human being. Who isn't flawed? There's no black and white. Everyone's flawed."

THE ART AND MAKING OF PENNY DREADFUL

"I've known people, all gone now. I've known men like Sir Malcolm. Motherf– ing hard. Sons of bitches who would [finger snap] kill at the drop of a hat. I don't mean anybody in general, but you know? Men from the army or in the street. When it came to it, they'd think nothing of violence. But they absolutely loved their family. (...) His daughter's [Mina] gone. He's got a lot of pieces to pick up. He's obviously in a very vulnerable state. And as Vanessa has said to him in that terrific scene when she comes back a full-grown woman and they embark on this course together, with that wonderful relationship of repulsion and attraction – which I loved, a wonderful dynamic between Vanessa and Malcolm – she said 'When this is over you will stay and I will go on'. (...) He allows his heart to come to the fore. And you might recognise who it comes to the fore with. He goes down a very, very... well, the path is the stuff of myths! Think of the Sirens, think of the Nemean Lion! He gets taken to a place where he and his sense of self and tough ability to deal with his crimes, his sins and his guilt, are severely tested. (...) I wouldn't really call *Penny Dreadful* a horror show. (...) When I think of horror, I think of something some people aren't going to like or particularly want to see. Something that just exploits fear and gore. But when I think of the book *Frankenstein*, I'm looking at... it's unbelievable... it's about a half-human who's desperate to became human."

FAMOUS MONSTERS

"It's actually a really difficult thing to describe. It's a bit like saying what Moby Dick's about; a captain chasing a whale. But if you just said that you'd miss the entire point. When I read *Penny Dreadful* I was thrilled. It was involving, disturbing, exciting and brilliantly written. On one level it's exciting; there's blood, sex, violence, mystery, fear, psychological terror and a lot of very good-looking people. On another level it's quite a highbrow story about guilt and redemption. (...) The story is, in a way, framed by the time it's played in, which is that late Victorian, height of industrial revolution period when science was really challenging religion and ancient mythology. The world of *Penny Dreadful* encompasses both so your mythological or religious demons, your devil or your gods, can exist side by side with your scientific, psychological, psychotic demons. Sir Malcolm is an explorer and an obsessive and determined man on a quest to find his daughter, a quest of extreme difficulty and danger that needs courage. (...) I don't think Malcolm is just using a figure of speech when he says to save his daughter he would murder the world. He means he would kill our leading lady. He would sacrifice her to save his daughter. Interestingly she describes him as weak, foul, lustful and vainglorious. You are getting rich characters here. (...) We have got brilliant actors coming in, just look at Simon Russell Beale and Helen McCrory. As you go down the list they are marvellous people and it's thrilling they're doing this because it's a great show. (...) There's a fight at the beginning of episode one. You need action. It is a real element of life and a necessity if you're on a dangerous quest. Very good people choreograph these things and then actors come along and mess it up, which actually gives the added texture of realness. (...) It's wonderful writing and I think that's what captured all the cast. Most actors that I know have always wanted to be in a horror film, most male actors have wanted to be in an American Western since they were boys, and I think you could go further with lots of other genres too. This isn't a horror movie but it does have those aspects and they are thrilling because it's actually disturbingly well written. Everything has a kickback to us as individuals. We are all complex and we have our strengths and weaknesses, our gods and demons within us, and often it's the demons that drive us rather than the good."

EXPRESS ON SUNDAY

"He and Vanessa were the backbone for Season One, that quest to rescue his daughter, and he fails. Not only has he lost his daughter, he is a man with a rather monstrous ego! It hurts him in lots of ways, and he is left picking up the pieces. A vulnerable man makes mistakes, and he meets [Evelyn]. She's a consolation for him, and that has disastrous consequences! A very bad choice! A terrible choice!"

SCIFI NOW

"It represents a big opening up of the show [season 3]. We've got a lot of new characters coming in and we've got a lot of new locations, like the American West. So the whole show has opened up. There's many more stories now. There's lots of new characters, interesting characters. It's like a tree where the branches keep growing and growing and growing. (...) On the one hand, it's really great because you've got different locations, different things for the audience to see and new storylines. On the other hand, if they don't all work, it's going to be a drag. And I don't know, because I've not seen it. Theoretically I think it's a good thing. There may be more narrative now than psychological complexity, but I think maybe one does have to live with the fact that you get the psychological complexity in season one, you know the people and then you just perhaps have to let them loose on their stories. (...) But Malcolm, I think, is difficult to write. You know, he's relatively well-adjusted, he can cope. I'm saying this to John Logan right at the beginning, and he said, 'No, no, it's all right. We've got some good storylines.' He didn't seem to have a problem with Malcolm's coping mechanism. (...) He's been a bit melancholy, romantic and all the rest of it. And then all of a sudden, turns up the strangest person you can imagine in Zanzibar: An Apache American Indian who wants Sir Malcolm to come with him. And just as Sir Malcolm is bemoaning the lack of quests, the lack of challenges, the lack of glorious journeys, this American strange shaman or whoever he might be is asking him to come to America. So I basically tag along behind Wes Studi, who is playing an Apache American Indian although he himself is, in fact, a Cherokee American Indian. And he's got something to do with Ethan, but we don't know what."

    EMPIRE

"Well, the story ended. I know a lot of people didn't think so, and there was a lot of sadness that it did end. It really rather shocked me how people can fool themselves. I used to look occasionally on the Internet, and because there was a sort of a leader, and a group of disparate people, everyone started talking about *The League Of Extraordinary Gentlemen*, thinking that it was this team of people that were going out and solving the world's problems and fighting evil and all that, and that was absolutely nothing to do with it. Those characters were only introduced in Episode 1 because they were the characters that were going to be followed throughout the series, not because they were going to league of whatever it was. (...) But the real story was about this young woman [Vanessa Ives] who, because she saw her mother having intercourse with a man [Sir Malcolm Murray] that wasn't her father, in fact, a man that she probably idolized, and found it erotic, thought it was evil, and could never have an orgasm without thinking she'd been taken by the Devil, an incubus. And when she therefore can't be cured, and loses her life, the main thrust of the story is over. And that's what happened. I am not saying it wasn't because of other reasons as well, but that was the main reason."

    ASSIGNMENT X (II)

REVIEWS

"The better news, for now, is the acting. In addition to Treadaway's thoughtful take on Dr Frankenstein, both Dalton and Green are engaging as the lead characters."

Hank Stuever, THE WASHINGTON POST, 19 May 2014

"In the face of the onslaught, I thought the show's leads, Eva Green as imperious occultist Vanessa Ives and Timothy Dalton as whiskery African explorer Sir Malcolm Murray stood up very well."

Andrew Billen, THE TIMES, 21 May 2014

"Another former Bond star, Timothy Dalton, convinces as male lead Sir Malcolm Murray, an aristocrat desperate to track down his daughter, who he believes has been abducted by a vampire."

Colin Robertson, THE SUN, 21 May 2014

"Josh Hartnett is rather good as a wirey proto-cowboy and gun-for-hire, and Timothy Dalton is splendidly growly and grumpy as a monster-hunter called Sir Malcolm, although it is essentially an impersonation of Arthur Conan Doyle's Professor Challenger."

Mark Smith, THE SUNDAY HERALD, 24 May 2014

"Anything featuring Dorian Gray, the wild west, and actors Eva Green and Timothy Dalton is gamey enough for my delighted palate: a winner. Expect a cult following soon."

Euan Ferguson, THE OBSERVER, 25 May 2014

"The scenes involving Dalton and Eva Green as the mysterious psychic Vanessa possessed a consistent poetry, just as Rory Kinnear's tragic, lonely monster gave a soul to Dr Frankenstein's creation."

Brian Lowry, VARIETY, 29 June 2014

"Throughout *Penny Dreadful*'s short run, their [Vanessa and Sir Malcolm] relationship has been a series highlight. Their tumultuous past keeps them from respecting one another, but at the same time their pain and drive to find Mina keep then united. It helps that Green and Dalton are so fantastic in their scenes together."

Eric Eidelstein, indiewire.com, 30 June 2014

"The cast is deeply impressive. Dalton is, obviously, The Man — stern, overbearing and sort of a dick, but exactly the kind of Victorian Alpha Male that anyone would follow into a vampire nest."

David Johnson, dvdverdict.com, 11 October 2014

"Eva Green was bewitchingly quiet and serious as Vanessa, while Timothy Dalton was on marvellous whiskery form as the magisterial Sir Malcolm."

Charlotte Runcie, THE TELEGRAPH, 5 May 2015

"Writer John Logan's dialogue is also terrific fun, with huge chunks of exposition immeasurably enlivened by his flamboyant wordplay, delivered by actors such as Green, McCrory and Timothy Dalton who make it sing with apparent ease. Although nothing matched Dalton's delicious employment of the word 'chicanery' last year."

Phelim O'Neill, THE GUARDIAN, 7 July 2015

DOOM PATROL

2019–2020

DC Universe

CAST

Diane Guerrero (Crazy Jane), April Bowlby (Elasti-Girl), Alan Tudyk (Mr Nobody / Eric Morden), Matt Bomer (Larry Trainor), Brendan Fraser (Cliff Steele), Timothy Dalton (Niles Caulder "Chief"), Riley Shanahan (Robotman), Matthew Zuk (Negative Man), Joivan Wade (Cyborg), Phil Morris (Silas Stone), Julie McNiven (Sheryl Trainor), Kyle Clements (John Bowers), Jon Briddell (Darren Jones), Bethany Anne Lind (Clara Steele), Devan Long (Flex Mentallo), Alec Mapa (Animal-Vegetable-Mineral Man), Curtis Armstrong (Ezekiel the Cockroach), Julian Richings (Heinrich Von Fuchs) // Abigail Shapiro (Dorothy), Karen Obilom (Roni Evers), Mark Sheppard (Willoughby Kipling), Lex Lang (Candlemaker), Jackie Goldston (The Secretary), Hannah Alline (Pretty Polly), Stephanie Czajkowski (Hammerhead)

CREDITS

Directors: Dermott Downs, Carol Banker, Rob Hardy, Harry Jierjian, Chris Manley, Stefan Pleszczynski, Salli Richardson-Whitfield, Rebecca Rodriguez, T.J. Scott, Rachel Talalay, Glen Winter, Wayne Yip // Jessica Lowrey, Omar Madha, Samira Radsi, Amanda Row, Kristin Windell | Producers: Greg Berlanti, Jeremy Carver, Geoff Johns, Sarah Schechter, Gideon Amir | Writers: Jeremy Carver, Arnold Drake, Tom Farrell, Bob Haney, Burno Premiani | Cinematography: Magdalena Górka, Scott Winig, Chris Manley | Production Design: Graham 'Grace' Walker | Editing:

Brian Wessel, Sara Mineo, Marc Pattavina | Music: Kevin Kiner, Clint Mansell | *Running Time*: 60 mins.

THE SERIES

Season 1 (15 episodes)

A group of outcasts, of different periods, are rescued from a certain death by The Chief, a scientific who gathers them in an isolated mansion. These people now possess a sort of superpowers but they don't know how to control them. When the Chief is kidnapped by Mr Nobody, a villain who wants to destroy the world, the Doom Patrol will have to learn how to stop him and save the world (not always with good results).

Season 2 (9 episodes)

After discovering the origins of their accidents, the Patrol is angry with The Chief. Meanwhile, The Chief takes care of his special daughter, Dorothy. And while each member of the Patrol deals with their personal and familiar problems, Dorothy inadvertently puts the world in danger again.

Dalton participates in the following episodes of the 1st & 2nd seasons:

1x01 Pilot	2x01 Fun Size Patrol
1x02 Donkey Patrol	2x02 Tyme Patrol
1x03 Puppet Patrol	2x03 Pain Patrol
1x05 Paw Patrol	2x04 Sex Patrol
1x06 Doom Patrol Patrol	2x05 Finger Patrol
1x07 Therapy Patrol	2x06 Space Patrol
1x09 Jane Patrol	2x07 Dumb Patrol
1x10 Hair Patrol	2x08 Dad Patrol
1x15 Ezekiel Patrol	2x09 Wax Patrol

DALTON:

"All the characters in our show are hopeless. I mean, even the Chief is pretty hopeless a lot of the time. And that's very appealing. It was appealing to me, anyway. I hope I'm right in thinking they're a fairly unique bunch of people. (…) I suppose the first thing you think of when you see Chief in a wheel-chair is X-Men. But you don't want to do that. If you're thinking of the tough, heavy lead. I think he's much more vulnerable than that, and he's got weaknesses. It's lovely to think of him being a coward. He's scared, So, I'm looking at that side of things. And we'll let control and authority take care of itself. (…) I had an idea of what kind of man [the Chief] was and what he was doing, but he was about, in the broad sense. But no, not in a specific day-by-day sense. (…) I love to work with the writers. On movies, they don't like writers. But on TV, you get writers. (…) We work under torturous circumstances! But we're still getting some good work done. And we're doing less and less each week, probably. In order to maintain quality, but it's tough. Simple as that. If it gets worse, we'll revolt! We'll have a peasant's revolt."

SFX

"I love the fact that he [The Chief]'s such a coward, which wasn't as apparent," he said. "I don't know whether I put that into it or if it was already there, but I like that. He's certainly not two-dimensional; he's not like a comic character, is he? That's one of the things that makes it special. I mean, there is an insane logic that works its way through it, if you want to be bothered with trying to understand that. Otherwise, just go with the flow! Don't try to make it fit or be logical. It's fantastic, and it's wonderful. (…) The whole nature and the set-up is completely different [to X-Men]. Those people were dangerous people. I mean, they grow knives and slash people, and ours don't. Ours are dangerous to themselves. Ours are a group of complete screw-ups. They're messed up people that Caulder is shaping, helping, and mentoring. (…) He [The Chief] does not like Mr. Nobody. If you've read the comic book, I am assured that there has been a previous war, as it were, where everyone got destroyed. (…) I think there might be more than one [ex-wife]. I say 'might be' because it's a question of whether you're truly married, or whether your marriage is a figment of someone else's imagination (…).

[Regarding doing a project with lesser-known characters] I would say it's much better to have no preconceived notions."

KSiteTV

"They call him the Chief, yeah. I suppose, yes. He's looked after them. They're just a group of very complex individuals, very self-destructive, and very vulnerable, but we're all coming together into my domain, as it were. I look after them, I'm a father figure to them, and a mentor, maybe. (…) I did a terrible thing to him [Mr Nobody] – [laughs] depends how you look at it. Anyway, he is an absolute enemy, an absolute enemy. He's after me for revenge, and he won't stop. (…) Well, in himself, he [The Chief]'s very interesting. I've been calling him an explorer, because he is an explorer – he's an explorer of the mind, he's an explorer of the world, he's an explorer of science. As an individual, he's fantastic. His aims might not be so fantastic, or they'd be open to question, perhaps, but he rescues and saves these people. (…) I think you need to know some things [about the character]. You certainly need some parameters. I would certainly say that would be the case. So I do have certain parameters that I know are within the character of the man. But someone else might say, 'No, no, no, you could just play the scene, play it as it is, because all the scenes are structured so it'll all work out in the end as we want it to work out in the end.' But no, you should know what's happening. And we have a wonderful show runner, Jeremy Carver, who has got a fantastic emotional and intellectual grip on the story, and is terrific to work with. (…) When I read it [*Doom Patrol*], I'd never read anything like it ever before. It's completely, sanely insane, and wonderful, and hugely imaginative. It's based on a cartoon. I say 'cartoon,' you will probably say 'comic.' You fit the style into what you're doing, really, but it is people. It's people, not pictures. (…) It is pretty much the strangest-looking thing I've ever seen that we're doing, but when you're doing it, we have scenes to play, relationships to create, vulnerabilities to expose, so it's just like playing a scene anywhere, with anybody, in rather bizarre surroundings sometimes."

Assignment X

"In many ways he's a phony father figure. Maybe he's fallen in love with his own monstrous creations, in an egotistical way. Certainly by the end of the first season I think he's feeling a very heavy amount of guilt and wants to try to make amends. But when you think of what he's done — how he's ruined those lives, how he's turned them into screwed-up lost souls — it's a pretty terrible thing he's done."

Chicago Tribune

"I see him [The Chief] as a man in a certain set of circumstances, I think. One's experience of life tells you we are capable of doing great good, and sometimes doing bad. He's doing this because of his daughter, but what he does is horrendous. I mean, it's egotistical and perhaps sort of obsessive and maniacal. He destroys those lives. He takes them and turns them into shadows of their — well, not even shadows of their former selves. He turns them into tragic creatures, who were failures. It's unforgivable, really. But, I suppose, at the same time, they are now his creations and he starts to feel a kind of responsibility for them. Maybe that's egotism too. I don't know. Essentially, what has been driving this has been what he sees as his need to protect his daughter, his need to find a means of being able to protect his daughter, who he knows is someone he loves to death. She's his daughter, but she's also an extraordinarily dangerous creature. It's obviously a conflict, but we all carry conflicts within us. So he's still the same man, it's just that more about him is being revealed.

What about Chief do you relate to personally?

Well, I know what it's like to be a parent. Apart from that, nothing. Nothing much else at all. I like to think of myself as being curious, but then most of us are curious. I mean, in reality, I've got my legs. Hard to see sometimes, of course. Not a lot. But he's a human being. It doesn't get more personal. Yeah, he's a human being. I can find what I believe are all the necessary qualities that he has. I can find them in myself, because we are all made up of many complex emotions and feelings. Our job is to tap into those, even if they are diluted. We've got to tap into what makes a character work and find that in yourself. If you can't find it, you have to be good at pretending it.

Do you have a favorite thing about season two?

I find it very moving. Maybe more moving emotionally than season one. Or maybe that's just me looking at things in a different way. I mean, I think this show is unique. It's not a show you can easily talk about because it continually springs surprises on you. I think that's one of the glorious things about the show. It's splendid in its imagination. It's imagination run riot. It's imagination given no boundaries. You can go and play in the playground of imagination — I think I stole that phrase. Yet it is totally human. I mean, it's odd to say that, because it's instinctually human. You think of these people, even if they're made of steel, they're human. Even if they're surviving in a way that no one could have ever survived from radiation, they're human, they're real. Real people don't dissolve into a blob when they get stressed. These people do and we understand it. We understand it on a human level. I was just thinking that, when we do comic books, we start with reality and humanity and life, and then stretch it with fantasy out into being a fantastical event that we look at and enjoy. I think in this it brings much more enjoyment because we've taken the fantasy comic and actually brought it back to our world, to our humanity. It's filled it and it has been enriched by that. I don't think there's a character in the show that you can't identify with in some way as being human, yet they're not human at all. So it comes for everything. We've somehow been able to combine a genuine, understandable humanity with a totally absurd, weird fantastical series of events that these characters come across in their lives. It all works together. I love the show. I've never seen anything or been in anything like it.

(...) I'm happy, very happy about this show in a different kind of a way than I'd be happy about another show, because this is a kind of a show I've never done before. It's a kind of a show that I've not seen before. When I say it's unique, I mean, I truly mean that. It's just such a delight to watch it on the screen and think, 'I was part of this'."

LOOPER

"After I shot my very first scene for the show, a crew member said, 'I wouldn't trust you an inch!' But it's essential to play the bad guy as a joy to watch. You have to give him a twinkle. 'He's behind you!'

(...) On one level, you could call him [The Chief] an absolutely ruthless, self-serving individual. But then, whatever he's done, he does love these people. I mean, on another level, he loves them because he made them. And you have to remember that he might also say terrible things to deflect the bad guys. He loves his terribly, terribly dangerous daughter. He loves her enough to give up what you see he gives up in the second series.

(...) When I was with Pisay Pao, who plays Niles's daughter's mother, we had meetings and legal contracts about what we should and shouldn't do, what we didn't want to do physically. I got really pissed off with it all. I felt initially that it didn't need contracts, because I was determined to make sure she was OK and I was OK. And actually I was wrong to be irritated. Because it was in our favour. Anything we said we didn't want to do – about sex and love and bodies – wasn't done. It's better these days."

THE INDEPENDENT

"I just got a call and they said that they had been sending a script so I got a script and it is quite just like nothing else I have ever read in my entire life. It had been shockingly bizarre and intriguing and eccentric and fascinating and surprising and funny outpourings of these real emotion and sense that it was magnificent. What I had been studying was magnificent, the question was going to be in a position to perform it? I presume they've.

(...) There's still the identical wacky insanity, there's still that inventive absurdity. I believe somewhere along the line, and that I think that it's wonderful, the showrunner mentioned to his authors' picture, envision beyond creativity and we can put it inside this series'. However, I believe today in the next season, we're currently delving deeper into the mechanisms of people's lifestyles and the way they relate to one another and what's happening to these. We delve deeper in the risks to their presence, the dangers of collapse. It's in 1 sense darker but it's a great deal more moving, it is far more emotional and I believe you find the development of those people starting to take accountability and start to develop'. You cannot speak about this show just like you could discuss another show as it always disturbs you but it is really excellent. I believe that it's a much better season. It is deeper and it is wealthier and that I believe you are likely to feel for everyone and learn more about everybody."

BINGE

REVIEWS

"They're each victims of tragic origins that allow them to find their way into the company of Niles Caulder AKA the Chief, who's played to perfection by Timothy Dalton. Actually, one could describe him as the Charles Xavier of the piece because he's the one who has a comparable analog. I've long thought Dalton to be an underrated James Bond, so I'm delighted to see him here."

Eric Joseph, WE GOT THIS COVERED, 11 February 2019

"Of more emotional consequence is Brendan Fraser as Cliff Steele, a philandering race car driver who, after a 1988 accident, becomes a brain somehow integrated with a robotic body (played by Riley Shanahan, accompanied by Fraser's voice) by wheelchair-bound Dr Niles Caulder (Timothy Dalton, acting with a twinkle), a genius who has turned his rural mansion into a halfway house for individuals with special gifts or curses."

Daniel Fienberg, HOLLYWOOD REPORTER, 14 February 2019

"Dalton brings some extra gravitas to the character that at the same time softens him and complicates him. He seems nicer, but also more slippery. It's immediately clear that he's somewhat of a mad scientist, and that the line between him and the Nazi doctor that turned Tudyk's character, Eric Morden, into Mr. Nobody is a blurry one, and I look forward to seeing how his relationship with the team unfolds."

Eric Frederiksen, BATMAN NEWS, 14 February 2019

"Bolstered by Fraser's easy charm and some knockout acting by Dalton, *Doom Patrol* stakes its claim as DC's best streaming option—simply because it understands and subverts expectations with its unique mix: It's not just funny, it's not just sweet, and it isn't afraid to push the boundaries on either."

Jacob Oller, PASTE, 14 February 2019

"As Dr. Niles Caulder, Timothy Dalton seems prepared to show up for a few minutes every couple of episodes before vanishing back to the sixth season of *Penny Dreadful* of my dreams. This decision minimizes the characters a bit, but that's part of the joke."

    Eric Thurm, POLYGON, 15 February 2019

"Of more emotional consequence is Brendan Fraser as Cliff Steele, a philandering race car driver who, after a 1988 accident, becomes a brain somehow integrated with a robotic body (played by Riley Shanahan, accompanied by Fraser's voice) by wheelchair-bound Dr. Niles Caulder (Timothy Dalton, acting with a twinkle), a genius who has turned his rural mansion into a halfway house for individuals with special gifts or curses."

    Daniel Fienberg, THE HOLLYWOOD REPORTER, 15 February 2019

"Dalton is doing a nice job straddling that line between loving 'father' and a crazed scientist who may not be that far removed from the ones Caulder's running from."

    Ray Flock, BLEEDING COOL, 16 February 2019

"Timothy Dalton also delivers a similarly surprising performance as Dr Niles Caulder –despite what comic readers already know about the manipulative mentor, you can't help but be seduced by Dalton's performance, sort of a dark mirror image of the trustworthy idealism of a Charles Xavier."

    David Pepose, NEWSARAMA, 18 February 2019

"Dalton gets a lot to do this week, showing different sides of his character, and reminding us why he's so good in this show. The scene between him and Tudyk crackles as these two actors appear to be having great fun with their characters, and with one another. Dalton's Chief is so charming and mischievous and it plays perfectly against Nobody's meta-arrogance and (limited) omniscience. I want more of the Chief and his frenemy/drinking buddy Kipling (Dalton and Sheppard play perfectly off one another, and the history hinted at between them is believable)."

    Aron Sagers, DEN OF GEEK, 16 March 2019

"Timothy Dalton carried most of the episode by himself, a feat not many people could do and just shows what a treasure he is for this show."

    Jacoby Bancroft, HIDDEN REMOTE, 19 April 2019

"However, the MVP of this episode is unquestionably Timothy Dalton, who finally gets a spotlight in the series and is tasked with selling some of the strangest scenes of the actor's long career. I never thought I'd be reviewing a series where Timothy Dalton played a scientist romancing a neanderthal woman, but here we are. To his credit, Dalton never gives the material anything less than the utmost gravity and earnestness. He's truly incredible in this episode. Niles begins the episode as a wide-eyed explorer and shows a kind of honesty and vulnerability we haven't quite seen from the Chief. By the time the episode ends, we begin to see what would make a man like Niles Caulder devote his life to gathering the misfits of the world. Through it all, Dalton maintains a sly gleam in his eyes. It's a heck of a performance, but it's still very subtle, which helps to balance out some of the episode's more out-there aspects."

  Nathan Simmons, AIPT!, 20 April 2019

"To Dalton's credit, he plays Niles Caulder during these moments as a man whose mind is spinning. You can almost see the wheels turning behind his eyes. All in all, the acting throughout this episode elevates an already-excellent script."

  Nathan Simmons, AIPT!, 19 May 2019

"As much as we might want to hate Caulder for what he's done, it quickly becomes impossible thanks to Timothy Dalton's emotionally rich performance. How can you hate a person who so clearly hates themselves?"

  Jesee Schedeen, IGN, 24 May 2019

"Dalton brings an almost unfair level of gravitas to this endlessly silly show and Fraser continues to impress with his voice work, both funny and fearsome and peppered with enough 'fucks' to power a whole season of *Deadwood*."

  Vinnie Mancuso, COLLIDER, 20 June 2020

"Timothy Dalton manages this particularly nicely, explaining the origins of the clock-faced Physician Tyme with absolute seriousness as Tyme's story will get more and more ridiculous with each sentence."

  Craig Smith, CHECKERSAGA, 21 June 2020

"Dalton conveys genuine regret as The Chief tries to make amends, but he remains a desperate man."

  Aaron Seger, DEEN OF GEEK, 25 June 2020

"Timothy Dalton's performance as Caulder shifts between being heartbreaking in moments when the scientist is lamenting his lifetime of setbacks and losses, and then outright campy in moments where the show veers back into absurd territory — which it thankfully still does quite often."

    Charles Pulliam-Moore, GIZMODO, 2 July 2020

"Timothy Dalton plays Niles with a level of disingenuousness that he otherwise doesn't give to the character."

    LaToya Ferguson, VULTURE, 9 July 2020

THEATRE

TIGER AT THE GATES	157
OUT OF THE FRYING PAN	157
ARMS AND THE MAN	158
BILLY LIAR	158
CORIOLANUS	159
TROILUS AND CRESSIDA	160
THE BACCHAE	162
LITTLE MALCOLM AND HIS STRUGGLE AGAINST THE EUNUCHS	162
RICHARD II	164
AS YOU LIKE IT	165
HADRIAN THE SEVENTH	167
SAINT JOAN	168
THE DOCTOR'S DILEMMA	169
THE PROMISE	170
WAR AND PEACE	170
THE THREE PRINCES [TV]	171
THE MERCHANT OF VENICE	172
HENRY V	172
THE ROYAL HUNT OF THE SUN	173
A GAME CALLED ARTHUR	175
FIVE FINGER EXERCISE [TV]	176
MACBETH	177
CANDIDA [TV]	178
THE SAMARITAN	180
KING LEAR	181
LOVE'S LABOUR'S LOST	183
ROMEO AND JULIET	184

LOVE'S LABOUR'S LOST 186

HENRY IV, parts I & II..187

HENRY V..190

A KIND OF BONUS [radio] 193

THE HAPPIEST DAYS OF YOUR LIFE? 193

THE VORTEX [radio] 194

THE VORTEX 195

WHITE LIARS & BLACK COMEDY 197

THE LUNATIC, THE LOVER AND THE POET............................199

SHAKESPEARE'S ROME [Julius Caesar + Antony and Cleopatra] 200

HENRY IV, part I...202

ANTONY AND CLEOPATRA [TV] 205

UNCLE VANYA [radio]...206

THE TAMING OF THE SHREW 207

ANTONY AND CLEOPATRA...210

A TOUCH OF A POET...213

SAVE THE ROSE 218

LOVE LETTERS 219

PETER AND THE WOLF 220

STAR CROSSED LOVERS 221

HIS DARK MATERIALS...222

THE LION IN WINTER CONCERT 227

JOHN BARRY: THE MEMORIAL CONCERT 227

THE STORY OF OUR YOUTH 228

TIGER AT THE GATES

1963

The Herbert Strutt School (Belper)

CAST

Timothy Dalton (Paris), Jeanne Crane, ...

CREDITS

Author: Jean Giraudoux

THE PLAY

After returning from battle as a peacemaker, Hector tries to convince Ulysses and the citizens about the insanity of war. They all agree that the Trojan War shall not take place. But the poets need a war for their elegies; the king, because it is custom; the lawyer, because of his honour; and others, for various mean reasons. And so, in spite of all logic, the war erupts.

OUT OF THE FRYING PAN

1963

Park Secondary School (Belper) & Wirksworth

CAST

Belper Players: Judith Goodall (Princess Yasmeen), Timothy Dalton (servant), Alistair Hague, Jack Dark, Jeanne Crane

CREDITS

Authors: several authors, translators, and scholars

THE PLAY

A skit based on one of the stories from the *Thousand Nights and One Nights*. Three Princes compete for the hand of Yasmeen, the daughter of the Caliph of Bagdad. They have to fulfil the task of going to the ends of the world and back, and the one who comes back with the thing judged to be the most fantastic shall marry Yasmeen.

ARMS AND THE MAN

1964

–

CAST

Belper Players: Timothy Dalton (Sergius), Jeanne Crane, ...

CREDITS

Author: George Bernard Shaw

THE PLAY

Raina Petkoff is a young Bulgarian woman engaged to Sergius Saranoff, one of the heroes of the 1885 Serbo-Bulgarian war, whom she idolises. One night, a Swiss mercenary soldier in the Serbian army, Captain Bluntschli, climbs in through her bedroom balcony window and threatens to shoot Raina if she gives the alarm.

BILLY LIAR

1964

–

CAST

Belper Players: Timothy Dalton (Billy Fisher), Margaret Pooley, Jeanne Crane

CREDITS

Author: Keith Waterhouse & Willis Hall

THE PLAY

A teenager from a North Country town, Billy Fisher, is an incurable, idle and dishonest liar, who to escape from his dull job imagines himself in many different situations, so truth and fiction become mixed. His family is unable to understand or control him, realising that he is good for nothing. He is also simultaneously engaged to three girls.

CORIOLANUS

August 19th, 1964

Queen's Theatre (London) // Ellen Terry Theatre (Tenterden, Kent)

CAST

National Youth Theatre: John Nightingale (Coriolanus), Mary Grimes (Volumnia), Timothy Dalton (Tullus Aufidius), David Stockton (Menenius Agrippa), Timothy Block (Cominius), Charlotte Womersley (Virgilia), Derek Seaton (Sicinius Velutus), Elizabeth Holmes (Valeria), Leslie Robarts (Junius Brutus), Mark Powell (Young Martius), Timothy Meats (Titus Lartius) // Robert Davies (Tullus Aufidius), Clive Emsley (Cominius), David Suchet, Nicholas Gibson & Simon Taylor (Volscian Senators), Timothy Dalton, Alan McTeer & David Haddy (serving men to Aufidius)

CREDITS

Director: Michael Croft | Author: William Shakespeare | Associate Director: Geoffrey Reeves | Art Direction: Barry Newberry, Christopher Lawrence

THE PLAY

The production is set in the period just before World War I, drawing parallels between the militant nationalism of Coriolanus and the doctrines of the Kaiser in the Second Reich. Rome is in a mutinous mood. The citizens are protesting about their rulers' incompetence and the shortage of food. A popular senator, Menenius Agrippa, has just managed to calm them when the arrogant and passionate young general, Coriolanus, arouses their emotions again.

DALTON:

"He [Peter Dews] and Michael Croft were my great *teachers*, and I was immensely lucky."

THE TIMES

REVIEWS

"Michael Croft has nursed this National Youth Theatre through good seasons and bad, but this *Coriolanus* must surely qualify as the best thing the NYT has yet given us. No excuses need be offered for the tender ages of the cast. This production, indeed, is superior in every respect to the Mermaid's *Macbeth*, the Joan Littlewood *Henry IV* and even Sir Tyrone Guthrie's *Coriolanus* at Nottingham last year. (...) For most of the evening I was propelled along by the sheer robustness of the offering, and found it possible to forget for long periods that these brave fellows were children only yesterday."

    Herbert Kretzmer, DAILY EXPRESS, 19 August 1964

"This young company gives a mature performance, and, remembering they are all under 21, are astonishingly good."

    Arthur Thirkell, DAILY MIRROR, 19 August 1964

"Admitting that the aim is not to nurse future West End prodigies, but to afford the maximum enjoyment to a crowd of young amateur actors, the set pieces and crowd scenes are effective, if unspontaneous."

    THE TIMES, 19 August 1964

"I like the production best for its freshness, good speaking, and sustained level of effective acting."

    R.B.M., THE STAGE, 20 August 1964

TROILUS AND CRESSIDA

September 13th, 1965 // September 25th, 1966 [TV]

National Theatre (London) & Empire Theatre (Sunderland) // BBC [filmed at the Belgrade Theatre (Coventry)]

CAST

Andrew Murray (Troilus), Charlotte Womersley (Cressida), Kenneth Cranham (Thersites), David Stockton (Pandarus), Derek Seaton (Ulysses), Dennis Marks (Achilles), Haydn Biddle (Ajax), Ian Woolridge (Menelaus), Leslie Robarts (Agamemnon), Mary Payne (Helen), Norman Eschle (Aeneas), Richard Godden (Priam), Tim Haunton (Prologue), Timothy Block (Hector), Timothy Dalton (Diomedes)

CREDITS

Directors: Paul Hill & Michael Croft (stage directors) / Bernard Hepton (TV director) | Author: William Shakespeare | Producers: Michael Bakewell, Michael Croft, Paul Hill | Costumes: John Bright | Art Direction: John Buglir

THE PLAY

The Greek king, Agamemnon, and his brother Menelaus, together with their counsellors, Ulysses, and Nestor, are camped outside the Trojan walls while their great military hero, Achilles, is in his tent, refusing to fight. Inside Troy, King Priam argues with his older sons, Hector and Paris. Their priestess sister, Cassandra, prophesies destruction for all while their younger brother, Troilus, is not paying attention to the conflict as he has met and fallen in love with Cressida.

REVIEWS

"It would be unfairly patronising to suggest that when we are disappointed by Youth Theatre actors, it is because they have failed to make effects that are beyond their powers. (...) It is therefore a pity that, instead of suggesting that Troilus has awakened appetites beyond her [Cressida's] control, she turns to Tim Dalton's superciliously savage Diomedes for no reason than light-mindedness."

> THE TIMES, 14 September 1965

"Oh to be in Moscow, now the National Youth Theatre's here Michael Croft's excellent enterprise drawn from amateur actors of many schools is this week giving a vociferous, lively, and enthusiastic production of *Troilus and Cressida* which does not overtax their skill too badly. (...) In its last stages the play did, in fact, take over to a certain extent."

> Philip Hope-Wallace, THE GUARDIAN, 14 September 1965

"A week ago *Antony and Cleopatra* proved beyond the National Youth Theatre's capabilities but last night *Troilus and Cressida* was more suited to the company's talent."

> A.B., DAILY EXPRESS, 14 September 1965

"Tim Dalton is a serious young man who hopes to become a professional actor."

> SUNDERLAND ECHO, September 1965

"The production was an excellent example of the team-work which is now legend among these enterprising and enthusiastic young people. (...) Delivery was clear and unaffected. (...) The most important point of all is that we have the National Youth Theatre and when we consider that only a small percentage of these youngsters will actually become professional actors, it is to Michael Croft we must pay homage."

> Margaret Campbell, THE STAGE, 29 September 1966

THE BACCHAE

June 18th, 1966

Vanbrugh Theatre (London)

CAST

Royal Academy of Dramatic Art: Robert Oates (Dionysus), Hayward Morse (Pentheus), Sally Faulkner (Agave), Timothy Dalton (herdsman), Murray Noble (messenger), Christopher Heywood (Cadmus), Rudolph Willrich (Teresias)

CREDITS

Director: Hugh Morrison | Author: Euripides | Translation: Philip Vellacott | Scenic director: Rovertos Saragas | Music: Richard Newson

THE PLAY

Dionysus arrives in Thebes and proclaims that he has come to avenge his rejection by the people of the city. Then he disappears to join his ecstatic worshippers, the Bacchae, at the mountains. When Pentheus tries to have Dionysos arrested, the prophet Teiresias advises him to accept the god, but Pentheus sends his guards anyway.

REVIEWS

"Timothy Dalton brought a variety of thought and feeling into the long speech of the Herdsman."

    H.G.M., THE STAGE, 23 June 1966

LITTLE MALCOLM AND HIS STRUGGLE AGAINST THE EUNUCHS

August 30th, 1966

Royal Court Theatre (London)

CAST

National Youth Theatre: Timothy Dalton (Malcolm Scrawdyke), Barrie Rutter (Dennis Charles Nipple), Anthony May (John 'Wick' Bladgen), Malcolm Storry (Irwin Ingham), Diana Porter (Ann Gedge)

CREDITS

Director: Michael Croft | Author: David Halliwell | Designer: Christopher Lawrence | Lighting: Brian Croft | Lighting Assistant: John Brown | Wardrobe: Susan Fournel | Sound: Charles Baxter

THE PLAY

In a small flat in the freezing Huddersfield winter, Malcolm Scrawdyke and his fellow art students smoke and rehearse their revolutionary attack against authority. According to Malcolm, the choice is simple: 'Freedom or serfdom'. They have established a manifesto, the 'Party of Dynamic Erection', which begins with a surreal offensive upon the eunuchs (the morons).

REVIEWS

"If the process from the climax, when talk stops and action for a moment takes brutal control, was hesitant, the hesitation is the author's, and Mr Timothy Dalton's Malcolm does not lose his remarkable sure grip on the complex, demanding role."

      THE TIMES, 13 September 1966

"Timothy Dalton, who plays Malcolm, has made this weakness a little too obvious. It is revealed mostly in the soliloquies that break up the action from time to time, but Mr Dalton allows Malcolm's emotions to master him even when the other members of the movement are there. (...) What he has done is to take too literally the words that Malcolm speaks. Malcolm is in love with words and he is capable of expressing emotions that he does not wholly feel. With his theatrical gestures, Mr Dalton has made him less of a politician than an actor. None the less, it is a vastly promising performance, and this boy's mobile face and dark good looks could take him far."

      B.A. Young, FINANCIAL TIMES, 13 September 1966

"As Malcolm, the art student over-compensating for his inadequacies with grandiose dreams of power, Timothy Dalton doesn't quite manage the manic intensity the part requires, but the scenes when the four-man 'Party of Dynamic Insurrection' [sic] acts outs its fantasies in a grubby bedsitting room are hilarious."

      Ian Christie, DAILY EXPRESS, 13 September 1966

"Not surprisingly, Timothy Dalton – as the would-be Fuhrer, Malcolm Scrawdyke – did not repeat John Hurt's triumph: the role is taxingly staccato and protracted, with immense temptations to self-indulgence. But he handled it with an intelligent control and power, notable in so inexperienced an actor, and he was closely matched by Anthony May, Malcolm Storry and Barrie Rutter."

Richard Findlater, THE OBSERVER, 18 September 1966

"As the fanatical Malcolm, Timothy Dalton tempered the character's obsessive hatred with a little too much personal charm but that was my only quarrel with a technically skilful and beautifully-sustaining performance."

Michael Billington, PLAYS AND PLAYERS, November 1966

"As Malcolm, the art student over-compensating for his inadequacies with grandiose dreams of power, Timothy Dalton doesn't quite manage the manic intensity the part requires, but the scenes when the four-man 'Party of Dynamic Insurrection' acts out its fantasies in a grubby bed-sitting room are hilarious."

Ian Christie, DAILY EXPRESS, 13 November 1966

RICHARD II

March 15th, 1967

Birmingham Repertory Theatre

CAST

Birmingham Repertory Company: Henry Knowles (King Richard II), Oliver Ford (John of Gaunt/Earl of Salisbury/Keeper), Brian Cox (Henry Bolingbroke), Peter Brookes (Thomas Mowbray/Bishop of Carlisle), Alison Key (Duchess of Gloster), Paul Robert (Lord Marshal/Sir Stephen Scrope), Roy Herrick (Duke of Aumerle), David Fennell (Herald to Bolingbroke/Servant to York/Welsh Captain/Servant to Gardener), Timothy Dalton (Herald to Mowbray/Hotspur), Richard Franklin (Sir Henry Greene/Sir Piers of Exton), Colin Farrell (Sir John Bushy/Gardener), David Stockton (Sir John Bagot/Servant to Exton), Stephen Hancock (Edmund of Langley), Ann Penfold (Queen Isabel), Graham Weston (Henry Percy), Paul Chapman (Lord Ross), Kiffer Weisselberg (Lord Willoughby), Anthony King (Lord

Berkeley/Servant to Gardener), Charlotte Howard & Alison Key (Ladies Attendant on the Queen) / Anthony McEwan, Chris Daniels, David Somers & Jonathan Mallard (Guards/Soldiers/Servants)

CREDITS

Director: Peter Dews | Author: William Shakespeare | Designer: Trevor Pitt

THE PLAY

Henry Bolingbroke, son of the great Duke of Lancaster, accuses Thomas Mowbray, Duke of Norfolk, of being involved in the recent death of the King's uncle, the Duke of Gloucester. The challenge is to be answered by a tournament at King Richard's court in Coventry, but the uncertain Richard stops the contest before it starts. He banishes Mowbray for life and, responding to Lancaster's pleas, he commutes Bolingbroke's exile to six years.

REVIEWS

"The opening play was Richard II, presented with an elaborate set that keeps the players moving as much vertically as they do horizontally, despite the sacrifice of a row of stalls to make room for an apron stage."

THE STAGE, 6 April 1967

AS YOU LIKE IT

March 21st / June 13th, 1967

Birmingham Repertory Theatre / Vaudeville Theatre (London)

CAST

Birmingham Repertory Company: Brian Cox (Orlando), Deborah Stanford (Rosalind), Colin Farrell (Touchstone), Charlotte Howard (Audrey), Alison Key (Celia), Graham Western (Charles), Richard Franklin (Corin), Oliver Ford Davis (Duke/Frederick), David Stockton (Adam), Paul Chapman (Jaques), David Fennell (Dennis), Jane Sandbrook (Lady), Paul Robert (Lord), Timothy Dalton (Oliver), Ann Penfold (Phebe), Roy Herrick (Silvius), Jim Duckett (William/Le Beau), Anthony King (Amiens/Sir Oliver Martext)

CREDITS

Director: Peter Dews | Author: William Shakespeare | Designer: Pamela

Howard | Songs: Colin Farell | Costumes: June Callear, Margaret Gillham and Michael Kennedy | Lighting: Michael Northen

THE PLAY

Orlando, the youngest son of Sir Roland de Boys, is ill-treated by his brother Oliver. When he responds to the challenge issued by the Duke's wrestler, Oliver tells the fighter to injure Orlando for real. The Duke's daughter, Celia, and her cousin, Rosalind, watch the match, and Rosalind falls in love with Orlando. Orlando wins, but the Duke gets angry when he discovers that Orlando is the son of his old enemy.

DALTON:

"He [Peter Dews] and Michael Croft were my great *teachers*, and I was immensely lucky; in my first year out of drama school I got that Birmingham season, a transfer to the Vaudeville in As You Like It (...)."

> THE TIMES

REVIEWS

"*As You Like It* has presented a particular challenge to Peter Dews, who has introduced a new note into the fashion of producing Shakespeare in modern dress. Pamela Howard's designs transpose the romance to a never-never land with motley costumes reminiscent of Carnaby Street and past-board sets that echo the more advanced greetings cards."

> THE STAGE, 6 April 1967

"Until the first interval I had hoped that the evening would turn out an unqualified triumph. I can think of few occasions on which a Shakespearian director has discovered so much novelty by paying strict attention to the sense of the text. (...) Another happy first act innovation is the setting of Duke Frederick's court. Peter Dews has placed it in a richly philistine never-never land combining the manners of Prussia and the British hunting counties. Brother Oliver is a loutish scarlet dandy."

> Irving Wardle, THE TIMES, 14 June 1967

"A return at the close of the production of the good humour and invention of the first act, light up the evening again, and there is a spirited curtain."

> R.B.M., THE STAGE, 15 June 1967

"He [Peter Dew] has had the wit to realise that the contemporary version of pastoral is the fancy dress of King's Road and Carnaby Street: that those braided tunics and flowered dolly-smocks, designed for no real weather or public occasion one can imagine in Britain, belong to an imaginary Ruritania or Arcadia of youth, an androgynous, perpetually sunlit Arden of huge paper blossoms. (...) The test of such gimmicks is how much life they give or take from the text."

Ronald Bryden, THE OBSERVER, 18 June 1967

HADRIAN THE SEVENTH

May 9th, 1967

Birmingham Repertory Theatre

CAST

Birmingham Repertory Theatre Company: Peggy Aitchison (Agnes), Peter Brookes (Cardinal Ragna), Paul Chapman (Bailiff/Dr. Courtleigh), Brian Cox (Jeremiah Sant), Colin Farrell (Father St. Albans), Oliver Ford (Bailiff/Dr. Talacryn), Richard Franklin (The Cardinal-Archdeacon), Stephen Hancock (Rector), Henry Knowles (George Arthur Rose), Gabrielle Laye (Mrs. Crowe), Alec McCowen (Fr. William Rolfe), Kiffer Weisselberg (Cardinal Berstein) / Andrew Betts, Robert Bissell, Andrew Brettell, Timothy Dalton, Chris Daniels, David Fennell, Roy Herrick, Anthony King, Jonathan Mallard, Paul Robert, David Stockton & Graham Weston (Cardinals/Papal Guards/Chamberlains/Acolytes)

CREDITS

Director: Peter Dews | Author: Peter Luke | Designer: Tim Goodchild | Costumes: June Callear, Margaret Gillham | Lighting: Alan Russell | Based on *Hadrian the Seventh* by Fr. Rolfe

THE PLAY

Two priests suddenly give Holy Orders on a man who was expelled from the seminary for lack of true vocation. He is soon in Rome to attend a conclave, and he gets elected as the new pope: Hadrian VII. Then, he decides to sell Vatican art treasures to finance feeding the world's poor. He also entertains old friends like his landlady and new ones like a seminarian until an assassin puts an end to Hadrian VII.

REVIEWS

"Relieved of its shaky superstructure and with some tightening up in the second act, the play would be well worth a London transfer."

Irving Wardle, THE TIMES, 10 May 1967

"The play has its weaknesses – some facile and elementary plotting, some minor comedy – but we shall remember the extraordinary skill of the central scenes and the response of Mr McCowen and Mr Dews (and the Repertory cast loyally with them) to every fresh demand."

J.C. Trewin, THE BIRMINGHAM POST, 10 May 1967

"The Birmingham Rep has pulled off a magnificent triumph – it was made a pearl out of an oyster. It is only afterwards that one realises that it is of the cultured, rather the natural variety."

Gareth Lloyd Evans, THE GUARDIAN, 10 May 1967

"It's a superb part for him [Alec McCowen], seized with enormous skill and charm, but he'd be helped by an adaptation which admitted more of the book's feline preposterousness, and a tighter pace to Peter Dew's production."

Ronald Bryden, THE OBSERVER, 14 May 1967

"The play of *Hadrian the Seventh*, however absorbing to initiates, may appear to others a tall story stretched beyond belief. (...) Some comedy, too, is trite. Still, one has to admire the piece for the fine theatrical decision of its central scene: the choosing of the Pope is masterly, both as it is directed by Peter Dews."

J.C. Trewin, ILLUSTRATED LONDON NEWS, 20 May 1967

SAINT JOAN

April 9th, 1968

Birmingham Repertory Theatre

CAST

Birmingham Repertory Theatre Company: Philip Anthony (De Stogumber), Anna Calder-Marshall (Joan), Paul Chapman (Earl of Warwick), Maurice Colbourne (La Hire), Anthony Corlan (Bluebeard), Timothy Dalton (Dunois), Keith Drinkel (The Dauphin), Dennis Edwards (Archbishop of Rheims), Thomas Fahy (Dunois' page), Laurence Foster (Executioner), Richard Franklin (D'Estivet), Michael Gambon (Bishop of Beauvais), Philip Garston-

Jones (De la Tremouille), Paul Henry (English soldier), Hugh Janes (court page/executioner's assistant), Anthony King (De Poulengey/clerical gentleman), Brian Lawson (Robert de Baudricourt), Jonathan Mallard (Steward), Jeremy Mason (De Courcelles), Hayward Morse (Brother Martin Ladvenu), Geoffrey Rose (The Inquisitor), Jane Sandbrook (Duchess de la Tremouille), David Smith (Warwick's page) / Domini Blythe, Alan Faulkner, Jeffrey Holland, Clinton Morris, Jane Stonehouse, Ian Yardley (assessors, courtiers, guards)

CREDITS

Director: James Cellan Jones | Author: George B. Shaw | Designer: Gordon Melhuish | Lighting: Alan Russell

THE PLAY

The life and death of Joan of Arc from the time she appears to her regional governor and her visit to the Dauphin, going through the siege of Orleans, the coronation of King Charles at Rheims to Joan's trial and her death at stake.

REVIEWS

"Some of the other playing fails to do more than indicate the general quality of the parts; we must be content with diagrams. Never mind: it remains a great play by the standards of the 20th-century theatre, and already we accept its flaws as we do the cracks upon the surface of an old master."

J.C. Trewin, THE BIRMINGHAM POST, 10 Abril 1968

THE DOCTOR'S DILEMMA

May 27th, 1968

SW English Tour

CAST

Birmingham Repertory Theatre Company: Keith Drinkel, Jane Bond (Mrs. Dubedat), Timothy Dalton (Dubedat), Philip Anthony (Sir Ralph Bloomfield Bonington), Hugh Janes, John Lynch, Jonathan Mallard, Hayward Morse, Jane Sandbrook

CREDITS

Director: Martin Kinch | Author: G.B. Shaw

THE PLAY

Doctor Sir Colenso Ridgeon has developed a revolutionary new cure for tuberculosis. However, with limited staff and resources, he can only treat ten patients at a time. From a selection of fifty patients, he will have to select ten, the ones he believes he can cure and the ones who are most worthy of being saved.

THE PROMISE

May 30th,1968

SW English Tour

CAST

Birmingham Repertory Theatre Company: Jane Bond (Lika), Timothy Dalton (Marat), Keith Drinkel (Leonidik)

CREDITS

Director: Derrick Goodwin | Author: Aleksei Arbuzov

THE PLAY

Set in the Soviet Union during and after World War II it is the story of two men and a woman they both love, exploring the possibility that they both can continue to love the same woman and remain friends.

WAR AND PEACE

September 17th,1968

Belgrade Theatre (Coventry)

CAST

Timothy Dalton (Prince Andrei), John Rowe (Pierre), Paul Howes (narrator), John McKelvey (Old Prince), Celestine Randall (Natasha), Alan David (Kusmich), Alison Jing, Margaret Diamond, Peter Needham

CREDITS

Director: Roger Redfarn | Author: Leo Tolstoy | Adaptation: Alfred Neumann, Erwin Piscattor, Guntram Prufer | Translation: Robert David Macdonald | Setting: Ken Calder | Lighting: Barry Griffiths

THE PLAY

Set on Napoleon's invasion of Russia in 1812, it follows three main characters: Pierre, an illegitimate son of a count who fights for his inheritance and yearns for spiritual achievement; Prince Andrei, who leaves his family behind to fight in the war; and Natasha, the beautiful young daughter of a nobleman who attracts both men.

REVIEW

"Great credit must go to the actors for their splendid efforts. Outstanding was Timothy Dalton as Prince Andrei, first torn one way and then another with his ideals."

        L.C., COVENTRY EVENING TELEGRAPH, 18 September 1968

"Outstanding in their demanding roles in the large cast are Timothy Dalton as Andrei (…). Anyone who calls himself a theatre-goer should sit at least once through this production – or be dispatched to the nearest battlefield."

        THE BIRMINGHAM POST, 19 September 1968

"Celestine Randall, John McKelvey, Timothy Dalton and John Rowe are highly competent, but cannot develop. Why? Because this is just not Theatre."

        THE STAGE, 3 October 1968

THE THREE PRINCES [TV]

December 28th, 1968

BBC2

CAST

Isla Blair (Jasmine), Timothy Dalton (Ahmed), Peter Jeffrey, Roy Kinnear, Kenneth MacKintosh, William Hobbs, Frederick Pyne, Frank Wylie, Gordon Gostelow, Cleo Laine, Neil Fitzpatrick, Roderick Horn, Oliver Cotton, Louise

Breslin, William Hoyland, Roy Pearce, Gavin Richards, Roger Kemp, Marc Gebhard

CREDITS

Directors: Mark Cullingham and Kenneth MacKintosh | Author: Rex Tucker

THE PLAY

A skit based on one of the stories from the *Thousand Nights and One Nights*. Three Princes compete for the hand of Yasmeen, the daughter of the Caliph of Bagdad. They have to fulfil the task of going to the ends of the world and back, and the one who comes back with the thing judged to be the most fantastic shall marry Yasmeen.

THE MERCHANT OF VENICE

March 11th, 1969

Newcastle Playhouse (Newcastle) / Brighton

CAST

Robert Flemying, Polly Adams (Portia), Christopher Bidmead, Timothy Dalton (Lorenzo), Janet Waldron (Nerissa)

CREDITS

Director: John Russell Brown

THE PLAY

[Staged in Victorian dress] Antonio, a young merchant, obtains a loan from Shylock on behalf of his friend Bassanio who requires the money to woo a wealthy heiress, Portia. Shylock agrees to lend the money on condition of claiming a pound of Antonio's flesh in case of default of payment.

HENRY V

September 23rd / October 5th, 1969

Theatre Royal (Bath) / New Wimbledon Theatre (London)

CAST

Lyric Hammersmith Company: James Fox (Henry V), Timothy Dalton (Chorus), David Austin (Sir Thomas/John Bates), Peter Gidwin (Earl of Cambridge), Rio Fanning (Pistol), Michael Gwilym (Nym/Michael Williams), David Neal (Montjoy), Sylvester Morand (Lord Scroop/Monsieur Le Fer), Terence Knapp (The Dauphin/Duke of Burgundy), Jill Dixon (Katherine), Anne Kidd (Queen of France), Phillada Sewell (Hostess/Alice), Paul Cresswell (Alexander Court), Colin Farrell (Archbishop of Canterbury/Captain Fluellen), Bernard Hopkins (Bardoplh/Duke of Orleans), Walter McMonagle (Bishop of Ely/Captain Macmorris), Malcolm Mackintosh (Boy), Michael Keating (Captain Gower), Robert Lankesheer (Charles VI), Ian White (Constable of France), Louis Haslar (Duke of Exeter), Christopher Mathews (Duke of Gloucester), Stephen Bradley (Earl of Warwick/Sir Thomas Erpingham), Alan Mitchell (Earl of Westmoreland)

CREDITS

Director: Michael Meacham | Author: William Shakespeare | Designer: Robin Pidcock

THE PLAY

King Henry V, after succeeding his father, is determined to prove his right to rule, including over France. An ambassador arrives from the French Dauphin with a provocative gift of tennis balls. Henry responds by preparing to invade France. Three of the king's friends are discovered to be plotting against him, and he condemns them to death. Pistol, Nym, and Bardolph, the companions of Henry's dissolute days in London, join the king's forces and set off for the wars. Also, the news of Sir John Falstaff's death arrives.

THE ROYAL HUNT OF THE SUN

November 4th, 1969

Belgrade Theatre (Coventry)

CAST

Timothy Dalton (Atahuallpa), David Blake Kelly (Pizarro), William Redmond (narrator), John Rhys-Davies (De Soto), Paul Howes (Estete), Aharon Ipale, Walter McMonagle, Paul Large (page), Julian Forbes, Peter Attard (Rodas), Michael Scholes, Anthony Falkingham, John Dommett, Simon Barratt, Bill

Henderson, Leigh Lawson, Jeffrey Holland, Donald Barclay, James Duggan, Stephen Smith, Kevork Malikyan, Roger Hill, Eve Karpf, Sheila Ferris, Deborah Black, Sue Bloodworth, Lynne Butler, Dianna Clamp, Lynne Dickens, Jan Feltham, Geraldine Frewin, June Grashion, Lindsay Marshall, Maureen Poole, Janet Perkins, Janet Wantling, Peter Brookes, Robin Carr, Phillip McInnerny, Michael Strobe

CREDITS

Director: Warren Jenkins | Author: Peter Shaffer | Choreography: Stewart Hopps | Sets and costumes: Terry Parsons | Lighting: Barry Griffiths

THE PLAY

A Spanish expedition under Pizarro command arrives at the land of the Incas. The Inca God is a sun god, ruler of the riches and people of Peru and thought to be immortal. However, the Spaniards have come in conquest rather than in veneration. There is misunderstanding, confusion, and the Spaniards kill 3000 unarmed Incas taking his sun god captive.

DALTON:

"I have never moved as I am moving as Atahuallpa, for instance. I have never danced or anything, really. I used to be good a football at school. I ache all over – but it is all something new I am learning…"

> COVENTRY EVENING TELEGRAPH

REVIEWS

"Timothy Dalton (who played King Louis in the film *The Lion in Winter*) has the unenviable task of playing Atahuallpa, the role in which Robert Stephens gave one of the great performances of the decade. Beginning with great dignity he became a creature, beautiful, alien and exotic, a remarkable performance."

> THE BIRMINGHAM POST, 5 November 1969

"Timothy Dalton gives on the most remarkable performances I have seen on any stage. As Atahuallpa, Sovereign Inca of Peru, his words are few – but he projects a degree of 'presence' which would overshadow a lesser production. There is a kind of animal look about his movements – and an animal expressiveness in his clipped-monotone 'Inca dialect'."

> R.E.W., COVENTRY EVENING TELEGRAPH, 5 November 1969

"What stands out in Warren Jenkin's production of *The Royal Hunt of the Sun* at the Belgrade is its sense of unity and the near ensemble playing of its large cast. (…) Timothy Dalton exploits every ounce of theatricality which is legitimately his as Atahuallpa; a man made mystical by his own intensity of belief."

THE STAGE, 20 November 1969

A GAME CALLED ARTHUR

November 19th, 1970 // February 23rd, 1971

Traverse Theatre (Edinburgh) // Royal Court Upstairs (London)

CAST

Timothy Dalton (Arthur), Judy Loe (Sally), Edward Jewesbury (Mr Lumsden)

CREDITS

Director: Michael Rudman | Author: David Snodin | Lighting: Nick Heppel

THE PLAY

Arthur is a twenty-something young man, lonely and naïve, and still a virgin as far as women are concerned, but helplessly in love with a young Spanish waiter. Tonight he has a promising date with a young actress who takes pity on him. But Arthurs' father appears unexpectedly to stay.

DALTON:

"I play a 24-year-old virgin – he couldn't make it. He's looking for beauty. It's very funny and very sad. He's looking for the ideal in life, in women, and this trendy bird comes to him on a bet and he loves her and he's so happy... He is looking for beauty and truth. The good thing about it is that you've been through some aspect of it yourself."

NEW YORK POST SATURDAY

REVIEWS

"As Arthur, Timothy Dalton conveys the edgy excitement of the young man struggling to learn the truth about himself in a phantasy situation made alarmingly real by the arrival of his very willing girl-friend."

THE STAGE, 26 November 1970

"There are too many loose ends and blank spaces. To make matters worse, Timothy Dalton, who plays the part, speaks Arthur's extremely naïve lines as if they should be taken seriously, whereas, as I see it, the naïveté is a fundamental thing in his character. I visualise him as very likeable but almost stupidity simple."

   B.A. Young, FINANCIAL TIMES, 24 February 1971

"He [Arthur] puts his foot in it so often and so crassly that you practically sweat with embarrassment; helped out by Timothy Dalton's performance which endows Arthur with a gangling mixture of hangdog ingratiation and smug offensiveness guaranteed to make him a joke outsider in any group."

   Irving Wardle, THE TIMES, 24 February 1971

"Timothy Dalton finds the right softness of voice and manner for Arthur, and Edward Jewesbury makes a convincing and pitiful bereaved father. Michael Rudman's direction favours Judy Loe rather less than the men."

   M.M., THE STAGE, 4 March 1971

FIVE FINGER EXERCISE [TV]

December 24th, 1970

BBC

CAST

Margaret Lockwood (Louise Harrington), Paul Rogers (Stanley Harrington), Timothy Dalton (Clive Harrington), Gary Bond (Walter Langer), Sally Thomsett (Pamela Harrington)

CREDITS

Director: John Gorrie | Author: Peter Shaffer Producer: Cedric Messina | Designer: Peter Seddon | Lighting: John Treays | Script Editor: Rosemary Hill | *Running Time*: 120 mins.

THE PLAY

Included in *Play of the Month* series (6x04).

The prosperous Harringtons are at war. The husband and the wife fight each other, as well as the son and the daughter. When a music teacher comes in, things begin to change, until other things start to threaten the peace.

DALTON:

"I always choose and accept parts that are rather difficult. Things like Marchbanks, or Clive in *Five Finger Exercise*, parts I wouldn't be automatically associated with."

PLAYS AND PLAYERS

REVIEWS

"*Five Finger Exercise* (BBC-1) and *Whom God Hath Joined* (BBC2) were presumably slotted into the Christmas schedules by someone for whom family festivals mean a good deal of muffled sobbing behind slammed doors. *Five Finger Exercise* had all the jolly domesticity of Elsinore. On television it looked a little stagey. A goodly number of doors were banged, sofas sobbed on, and breakfast rejected. They pivotal and slightly improbable figure of family tutor, who eventually tried to gas himself, reminded me of all those advertisements for nannies offering 'a happy home'. It had nevertheless a certain scalpel accuracy."

Nance Banks-Smith, THE GUARDIAN, 28 December 1970

MACBETH

January 29th,1971

Kennedy Theater (Hawaii)

CAST

Timothy Dalton (Macbeth), Genevieve Nelson & Juliet Plachcinska (Lady Macbeth), Don Lev (Duncan), Michael Kolba (Malcolm), Timothy Robinson (Donalbain), Michael Medeiros (Banquo), Mel Cobb (Macduff), Stephen Matthews (Lennox), Gary Francis (Ross), Paul Cornwall (Angus), John Myers (Caithness), Steve Kurtz (Fleance), William Miretti (Old Siward), William Witter (Young Siward), Dan Maloney (Seyton), Gilbert Schaeffer (Son of Macduff), Christopher Parsons (Doctor), Gerald Goulet (Porter), Hal Finlay (An old man), James Benton (A murderer), William Soares (A second murderer), Craig Emberson (A wounded captain), Alan Zimmerman (A messenger), Rod Pinks (A second messenger), Marcia Merkle, Sandra Puerta & Anton Haas (The weird sisters), Min Soo Ahn (Hecate), Valerie Charles (Gentlewoman), Sun Hi Shin, Bonita Strothman & Nancy Ward (Ladies in waiting), Erica Galper (Lady Macduff)

CREDITS

Director: Terence Knapp | Author: William Shakespeare | Designer: Richard Mason

THE PLAY

King Duncan's generals, Macbeth and Banquo, meet three strange women on a bleak Scottish moorland on their way home from crushing a revolt. The women prophesy that Macbeth will be given the title of Thane of Cawdor and then become King of Scotland, while Banquo's heirs shall be kings. Duncan creates Macbeth Thane of Cawdor in thanks for his success in the recent battles and then decides to make a brief visit to Macbeth's castle.

DALTON:

"In Hawaii, we were allowed to draw our performances out of our own personalities. What people can bring of themselves, and out of what they understand, and how they react to life – is the most special thing. Because it's personal, peculiar and idiosyncratic."

>PLAYS AND PLAYERS

"It's a great role and a very challenging role. Many fine actors have come to grief having a go at *Macbeth*. Years ago for a short while I was an associate professor at the University of Hawaii and worked with the students on a production of *Macbeth*. It is a great play."

>Showtime Chat

CANDIDA [TV]

February 21st, 1971

BBC

CAST

George Baker (Morell), Jeremy Bulloch (Lexy), Timothy Dalton (Marchbanks), Geraldine McEwan (Candida), Priscilla Morgan (Prossy), Clive Revill (Burgess)

CREDITS

Director: Alan Cooke | Author: George Bernard Shaw | Producer: Cedric

Messina | Production Design: Fanny Taylor | Costume Design: Robin Fraser-Paye | Lighting: Robert Wright | Script Editor: Rosemary Hill | *Running Time*: 120 mins.

THE PLAY

Included in *Play of the Month* series (6x06).

Candida is the wife of a famous clergyman, the Reverend James Mavor Morell. Morell is a Christian Socialist, popular in the Church of England, but Candida is responsible for much of his success. Candida returns home briefly from a trip to London with Eugene Marchbanks, a young poet who wants to rescue her from what he considers to be her dull family life.

DALTON:

"I always choose and accept parts that are rather difficult. Things like Marchbanks, or Clive in *Five Finger Exercise*, parts I wouldn't be automatically associated with."

    PLAYS AND PLAYERS

REVIEWS

"She [Geraldine McEwan] was backed with two well-drawn performances from George Baker as the parson and Timothy Dalton as the confused, heart-torn poet."

    James Thomas, DAILY EXPRESS, 22 February 1971

"By contrast, if the play is to keep its surprises the poet must be outwardly delicate. But Timothy Dalton's Marchbanks was lusty young man working hard for a pale cast of thought."

    Leonard Buckley, THE TIMES, 22 February 1971

"Geraldine McEwan's' Candida was faultless. She captured the combination of strength, pity and intelligence which made her so superior to both the men who loved her – her smug, confident husband, the Rev. James Morell (George Baker), to whom she had been a good wife and mother; and the young poet, Eugene Marchbanks (Timothy Dalton), unloved, childlike and utterly devoted to her."

    Terry Metcalf, THE BIRMINGHAM POST, 22 February 1971

"It was this credibility that was lacking in the Marchbanks of Timothy Dalton, a part played with considerable technical skill and understanding but often out of tune with the mood set by Candida herself."

    Patrick Campbell, THE STAGE, 25 February 1971

THE SAMARITAN

April 19th / September 22nd, 1971

Victoria Theatre (Stoke-on-Trent) / Shaw Theatre (London)

CAST

Timothy Dalton (Bob), Richard Moore (Godfrey), David Cook (Denny), Myra Francis (a volunteer), Alex Leppard (a man)

CREDITS

Director: Ron Daniels | Author: Peter Terson, with Michael Butler | Designer: Christopher Lawrence | Lighting: Brian Croft

THE PLAY

Bob is a bluff Yorkshireman who has just arrived in London to share a flat. Full with demons of his own, he soon destabilises the relationships in the flat. A psychological game with dark and subtly-revealing twists draws out the truth about the mysterious man from the north.

DALTON:

"When I think a part is like myself I've got nothing to hold on to. Bob in *The Samaritan* – now he was a very particular kind of person whom I had to go out and find."

>PLAYS AND PLAYERS

REVIEWS

"There are impeccable performances from Timothy Dalton as the talkative exhibitionist, Richard Moore as the good Samaritan and David Cook as the taciturn gambler."

>Michael Billington, THE TIMES, 24 September 1971

"Timothy Dalton, overwhelmed by his part, is dangerously monotonous."

>J.C. Trewin, THE BIRMINGHAM POST, 24 September 1971

"Timothy Dalton gives one of his better performances as Bob, and there is appropriately soft-pedal direction from Ron Daniels, yet the triplicate relationship is too pat to encompass the tricky heartfelt theme."

Helen Dawson, THE OBSERVER, 26 September 1971

"The take-home impression (along with memories of excellent performances by Timothy Dalton, Richard Moore and David Cook) is not of a work honed and polished until the author got it just right, but of a writer who gave up in an apparent cul-de-sac when the way out was just around the corner."

Kenneth Hurren, THE SPECTATOR, 1 October 1971

KING LEAR

March 7th* / March 20th / June 5th**, 1972

Royal Lyceum (Edinburgh) / Ashcroft Theatre* (Croydon) / Australian tour: Adelaide, Sydney, Her Majesty's Theatre (Melbourne) / Cardiff / Newcastle / Aldwych Theatre** (London)

CAST

Prospect Theatre Company: Timothy West (King Lear), Christopher Burgess (Duke of Albany), Ronald Smerczak (Duke of Burgundy), Jill Dixon (Cordelia), Ralph Watson (Duke of Cornwall), Timothy Dalton (Edgar), Mark Jones (Edmund), Ronnie Stevens (Fool), James Snell (King of France/Curan), John Bailey (Earl of Gloucester), Sheila Ballantine (Goneril), Trevor Martin (Earl of Kent), Michael Graham Cox (Oswald), Vivienne Martin (Regan), Henry Moxon (Knight), Michael Percival (Gentleman)

CREDITS

Director: Toby Robertson | Author: William Shakespeare | Associate Director: Kenny McBain | Designer: Robin Archer | Composer: Carl Davis | Lighting: Michael Outhwaite | Fights: Colin Fisher

THE PLAY

Old King Lear has decided to abdicate and divide his kingdom among his three daughters. Each will receive a portion of his domain according to how much they love him. Goneril and Regan speak eloquently and receive their share but Cordelia, the youngest, only can declare that she loves him according to a daughter's duty to a father. Lear is enraged and disowns her. Meanwhile, Edmund, the illegitimate son of the Earl of Gloucester plots against his brother Edgar.

DALTON:

"Nobody should ever play Edgar. Edgar's a bum part really. There are only two parts to play in Lear – one is Edmund the other is the King. But Edgar is in a lot of the best scenes and he can watch everybody else work. I always choose and accept parts that are rather difficult. (...) He's often played as a naive, book-reading stooge. But this makes the mad scene on the heath seem completely out of Edgar's normal character. His madness is seen as a series of acts. I never saw the part like that. Edgar goes through a very continuous journey. All he talks about on the heath is how the beggars, outcasts, and turley-gods live. Nobody knows how long he has been on the heath just think, for instance of the vagrants down at Waterloo station. You still see people sleeping in newspapers in 1972 – and that's pretty rough! But in Edgar's time a vagrant's life would have been unspeakable, awful. Any member of the aristocracy, like Edgar, who pretended to be a beggar would have had a traumatic shock. If I tried to live like a meths drinker today, it would be terrible. But for Edgar doing that *then* he would have gone a bit potty. He's chased, hunted, living on rats and, if we believe what he says old vermin. It would drive anybody bitter, angry, and mad. I could see that reaction very clearly – and it can't be a pretended madness. It's real."

PLAYS AND PLAYERS

REVIEWS

"Timothy Dalton gives a strong and beautifully balanced presentation of Edgar, Gloucester's son."

W.L. Hoffman, THE CANBERRA TIMES, 25 March 1972

"Timothy [Dalton]'s Edgar was somehow rather restrained, there was a feeling that he had stores of emotion in reserve, was waiting to use them, but never got the opportunity."

Phil Penfold, EVENING CHRONICLE, 31 May 1972

"There is an unsentimental Fool from Ronnie Stevens, and in the hovel Timothy Dalton's Edgar offers a frenzy which, in its sense of fantasy, draws us towards a perception of Lear's madness."

Charles Lewsen, THE TIMES, 8 June 1972

LOVE'S LABOUR'S LOST

February 29th / March 7th / March 20th / June 7th*, 1972

Royal Lyceum (Edinburgh) / Ashcroft Theatre (Croydon) / Australian tour: Adelaide, Sydney, Her Majesty's Theatre (Melbourne) / Cardiff / Newcastle / Aldwych Theatre* (London)

CAST

Prospect Theatre Company: Mark Jones (King of Navarre), Prunella Scales (Princess of France), Delia Lindsay (Rosaline), John Bailey (Armado), Christopher Burgess (Longaville), Timothy Dalton (Berowne), Henry Moxon (Boyet), Ian Sharp (Moth), James Snell (Marcade), Jill Dixon (Katharine), Michael Graham Cox (Costard), Michael Percival (Dumaine), Richard Ommanney (Attendant), Ronald Smerczak (Attendant), Ronnie Stevens (Sir Nathaniel), Sheila Ballantine (Maria), Terence Hillyer (Attendant), Tim Barker (Attendant), Timothy West (Holofernes), Trevor Martin (Dull), Vivienne Martin (Jaquenetta), Sally Mates (cousin), Ralph Watson (A Forester),

CREDITS

Director: Tony Roberston | Author: William Shakespeare | Associate Director: Kenny McBain | Designer: Robin Archer | Music: Carl Davis | Lighting: Michael Outhwaite | Dances: Virginia Mason | Wardrobe: Angela McIntosh

THE PLAY

King Ferdinand of Navarre decides to have a three-year period of study and contemplation at his court. To avoid distraction, he imposes a ban on women, who will not be allowed within a mile of the court. Berowne, one of the courtiers, reminds the King that he has an ambassadorial meeting on that very day with the Princess of France. As they prepare to meet the Princess, the King sends his court fool, Costard, to Don Armado to be punished for breaking the rules by flirting with a country girl.

REVIEWS

"There are occasional felicities, some lively speaking by Prunella Scales, Delia Lindsay and Timothy Dalton."

    J.C. Trewin, THE BIRMINGHAM POST, 7 June 1972

"All the lovers are new, and now include a Princess by Prunella Scales who radiates a sense of authority under her playfulness, a tall, lovely Rosaline by Delia Lindsay, a fetching Berowne in flared jeans by Timothy Dalton, and others all most pleasant company."

B.A. Young, FINANCIAL TIMES, 7 June 1972

ROMEO AND JULIET

March 28th,1973

Royal Shakespeare Theatre (Stratford-Upon-Avon)

CAST

Royal Shakespeare Company: Timothy Dalton (Romeo), Estelle Kohler (Juliet), David Suchet (Tybalt), Peter Machin (Benvolio), Jeffery Dench (Capulet), Clement McCallin (Escalus/Chorus), John Abbott (Friar John), Tony Church (Friar Laurence), Brenda Bruce (Lady Capulet), Janet Whiteside (Lady Montague), Bernard Lloyd (Mercutio), Richard Mayes (Montague), Beatrix Lehmann (Nurse), Anthony Pedley (Paris), Janet Chappell (Rosaline), Dennis Holmes (Old Capulet), Brian Glover (Peter), Gavin Campbell (Sampson), Colin Mayes (Gregory), Robert Ashby (Apothecary)

CREDITS

Director: Terry Hands | Author: William Shakespeare | Designer: Farrah | Music: Ian Kellam | Lighting: John Bradley | Fights: B.H. Barry | Dances: John Broome | Assistant to Director: Barry Kyle

THE PLAY

The Prince of Verona announces that the next person who breaks the peace between the Capulet and Montague families will be punished with death. Capulet plans a feast to introduce his daughter, Juliet, who is almost fourteen, to Count Paris who would like to marry her. By a mistake of an illiterate servant, Montague's son, Romeo, and his friends Benvolio and the Prince's cousin Mercutio, hear of the party and decide to go in disguise. Romeo hopes he will see his adored Rosaline but instead he meets and falls in love with Juliet.

DALTON:

"A big, big, company, an extremely good company, but a company that was locked I think at that time in sort of very intellectualised almost passionless productions. Where people would be dressed in, you know, black, grey, light grey, dark grey, back-black, less than black and sets were usually constructed of industrial... shapes and forms made out of pseudo steel, so there wasn't a lot of joy on the stage in those days... some people loved the productions."

Savannah Acting Class

REVIEWS

"Timothy Dalton and Estelle Kohler are called upon to shoulder the title roles. Mr Dalton is a dark, good-looking young actor with an athletic physical presence. But he has not, so far, attained either the concentration of passion or the resonance of voice that will enable him to hold the stage in such a commanding role. He is best as the young love transfixes by sudden infatuation – but the later peaks of grief are somewhat beyond his present capacities. Mr Dalton has been pushed too far too soon."

Herbert Kretzmer, DAILY EXPRESS, 29 March 1973

"Timothy Dalton's Romeo shows a similar imbalance between style and feeling. Making great play with a near falsetto top register, and driving the lines forward with unrelenting application, he gives no evidence of the temperamental resources to back up these outward shows of feeling".

Irving Wardle, THE TIMES, 29 March 1973

"Timothy Dalton's Romeo, however, is no match for her [Estelle Kohler] in weight or authority."

Michael Billington, THE GUARDIAN, 29 March 1973

"Timothy Dalton is an excellent gauche Romeo and it is not his fault that adolescents are monotonous."

Anthony Everitt, THE BIRMINGHAM POST, 29 March 1973

"Timothy Dalton, making his debut with the company, has his moments, too, but there are times when he tends to lose his way and our interest. He is at his best in the balcony scene, in which Farrah's bleak but functional settings allow a mobility for Juliet which Miss Kohler employs to poignantly telling effect."

David Isaacs, COVENTRY EVENING TELEGRAPH, 29 March 1973

"The Romeo of Timothy Dalton is relatively quiet through all this [the Prince's warring]; then is loud in cries for Juliet, and athletic in movement as passion grows, and he is frustrated, endangered, faces a matter of life and death, or, worse, of banishment. (…) One can hardly believe in Romeo as a real, suffering person. Timothy Dalton's performance, though strongly projected and highly articulate, needs blood as well as simulation of passion, heart as well as vocal cries."

> R.B. Marriott, THE STAGE, 5 April 1973

"He [Dalton] grins and flings his arms loosely about a good deal, boyishly dashing hither and thither, before settling into a sort of gangling, flailing angst, all arms and legs like a demented tree in a hurricane."

> Benedict Nightingale, NEW STATESMAN, 6 April 1973

"Timothy Dalton as Romeo has his own troubles. Loyally attempting to fly as high as the interpretation demands he prances ceaselessly around the stage; vocally he never lets up for a moment. One can see why Mr Dalton was brought to Stratford – like Peter Egan he is one of this year's actors, a timely blend of dark good looks and quivering intestines, and such opportunist casting has been known to justify itself. For the moment, though, his reputation has clearly outstripped his capabilities. He, too, is insulated from any humorous contact, since Bernard Lloyd has been set to play a Satanic Mercutio (...). The performance is something of a tour-de-force though when Romeo, fresh in love with Juliet, starts joining in the games one can only reflect that he was really better off when pining for Rosaline."

> Robert Cushman, PLAYS AND PLAYERS, May 1973

LOVE'S LABOUR'S LOST

August 7th, 1973

Royal Shakespeare Theatre (Stratford-Upon-Avon)

CAST

Royal Shakespeare Company: Ian Richardson (Berowne), Sebastian Shaw (Boyet), Timothy Dalton (Costard), Tony Church (Armado), Dennis Holmes (Dull), Michael Ensign (Dumaine), Bernard Lloyd (King of Navarre), Derek Smith (Holofernes), Louise Jameson (Jaquenetta), Janet Chappell (Katharine), Robert Ashby (Longaville), Catherine Kessler (Maria), Susan Fleetwood (Princess of France), Estelle Kohler (Rosaline), Tony Valls/Joseph Murru (Moth), Wilfred Grove (French Lord), Leon Tanner (Marcade), Gavin Campbell (A forester), Jeffery Dench (Sir Nathaniel)

CREDITS

Director: David Jones | Author: William Shakespeare | Designer: Timothy

O'Brien, Tazeena Firth | Music: William Southgate | Lighting: John Bradley | Assistant to the director: Barry Kyle

THE PLAY

King Ferdinand of Navarre decides to have a three-year period of study and contemplation at his court. To avoid distraction, he imposes a ban on women, who will not be allowed within a mile of the court. Berowne, one of the courtiers, reminds the King that he has an ambassadorial meeting on that very day with the Princess of France. As they prepare to meet the Princess, the King sends his court fool, Costard, to Don Armado to be punished for breaking the rules by flirting with a country girl.

REVIEWS

"The comic scenes involving the locals never quite ran free, despite the unruffled stupidity of Denis Holmes as Constable Dull, the energy of Timothy Dalton as Costard the Clown and the glorious conceit of Derek Smith as the schoolmaster."

        N.K. W., COVENTRY EVENING TELEGRAPH, 8 August 1973

"This central scene gains a nice cumulative roll of laughter, which is matched by the love life comedy from Denis Holmes as Dull, and Timothy Dalton as Costard. (...) I liked especially Timothy Dalton's scurrilous inflexion on 'I Pompey am'."

        Garry O'Connor, PLAYS AND PLAYERS, October 1973

HENRY IV, parts I & II

9th & 10th September / October 28th / November, 1974

Round House Theatre (London) / Theatre Royal (Newcastle) / Round House Theatre (London)

CAST

Prospect Theatre Company: George Shannon (Archbishop of York), Colin Prockter (Bardolph), Helen Cotterill (Doll Tearsheet), John Warner (Earl of Northumberland/Shallow), Kenneth Gilbert (Earl of Warwick), Walter Brown (Earl of Westmoreland), Tim Hardy (Hotspur/Fang/Bullcalf), Patrick Murray (Francis), Ken Bones (Gower/Wart), Peter Penry-Jones (Hastings), Edgar Wreford (Henry IV), Timothy Dalton (Henry, Prince of Wales), Andrew

McCulloch (John of Lancaster), Marion Desmond (Lady Northumberland), Pauline Munro (Lady Percy), Christopher Burgess (Lord Chief Justice), Sylvia Coleridge (Mistress Quickly), Michael Graham Cox (Pistol), Seymour Matthews (Poins/Mouldy), William-Huw Thomas (Servant), Robert Edwards (Shadow), Tim Barlow (Silence), Michael Goldie (Sir John Colville), Paul Hardwick (Sir John Falstaff), Russell Dixon (Snare/Feeble), Michael Shannon (Thomas Mowbray/Davy)

CREDITS

Director: Kenny McBain | Author: William Shakespeare | Setting: John Fraser | Lighting: Keith Edmundson

THE PLAYS

Henry Bolingbroke has usurped the throne of England to his cousin, Richard II. News of a rebellion in Wales and the North arrives, where Harry Hotspur, the young son of the Earl of Northumberland, is fighting with the Earl of Douglas. King Henry IV has been victorious at the Battle of Shrewsbury, but the Earl of Northumberland hears rumours that his son has been the victor. Northumberland and the Archbishop of York decide to oppose the king's forces, led by Lord John.

Part II it is focused on Prince Hal's journey toward kingship, and his ultimate rejection of Falstaff.

REVIEWS

"Indeed, anyone who left at the interval last night would have missed the better part, though Mr McBain had already made his principal point – he does not depend on them – in Timothy Dalton's utterance of 'I do, I will' after the Boar's Head charade. Throughout, Mr Dalton is a direct, vibrant Hal: he cannot command the man to us entirely – no Hal has done so – but it is a portrait vocally and physically right."

J.C. Trewin, THE BIRMINGHAM POST, 10 September 1974

"Thus Timothy Dalton has led Hal as consistently as possible from the first gleam of the steel early in *Part I*. We do not forgive the treatment of Falstaff, but Mr Dalton plays the part as it is written, and the way is clear for his *Henry V* in which we may note even more his physical resemblance to Olivier."

J.C. Trewin, THE BIRMINGHAM POST, 11 September 1974

"Timothy Dalton's joylessly sullen Hal comes over as no less thin-blooded and calculating than his brother John; and for some reason the production conceals his reactions at crucial moments. His icy first soliloquy, 'I know you all' is delivered with his face away from the audience, and likewise his response to the King's awakening on the deathbed. When he kills Hotspur the production goes into exhausted slow motion, showing the last thrust as a crude butchery. He then delivers the epitaph heroically, and on top of that he salutes the fallen Falstaff in precisely the same hollow voice."

Irving Wardle, THE TIMES, 11 September 1974

"Timothy Dalton and Tim Hardy as Hal and Hotspur come off the best, as bold, witty, thoroughly fit younger men can hardly help but do in two of the handsomest parts in the repertoire."

Hilary Spurling, THE OBSERVER, 15 September 1974

"Timothy Dalton as Hal conveyed the faintest confusion covered quickly by resolution. But his political manoeuvres did not bite hard enough – he appeared brave rather than a man who, at rock-bottom, knew himself invincible."

Merete Bates, THE GUARDIAN, 15 September 1974

"Timothy Dalton's performance as Prince Hal is a very considerable piece of work, most meticulously planned, and played with great control. Planted throughout his early scenes with Poins and Falstaff are sudden moments of revulsion for the aimless, dissolute life they lead, and he becomes so strange in mood that Sir John's jest, 'Thou art essentially mad without seeming so,' sounds almost true. But these are merely intimations of the majesty Henry is to assure so magnificently at the end, and Mr Dalton really does seem to grow several inches for his triumphal entrance as King."

Philip Glassborow, THE STAGE, 19 September 1974

"Timothy Dalton's performance of Hal in the Prospect Theatre's productions of the two plays at the Roundhouse is a perfectly balanced illustration of growing up. As the boy, he is charmingly impish and devil-may-care, the burden of duty transforms him into a man of increasing dignity; finally, as king, he achieves absolute authority and nobility. His playthings, left behind, are unfortunately human, but Mr Dalton wins everyone's heart, and is forgiven."

E. Victor, THE TABLET, 21 September 1974

"But the fault shrinks when Timothy Dalton, as Hal, finally strikes home. He may have lacked the cold, stony quality to make his early, calculated double-life convince. But he does not lack deep affection when moved by his dying father's condemnation. Through a quiet, very ordinary voice, he conveys bewilderment and distress."

Merete Bates, THE GUARDIAN, 16 October 1974

"Timothy Dalton makes an ideal Prince Hal, a clean-cut schemer moving towards his apotheosis."

Malcolm Grey, EVENING CHRONICLE, 29 October 1974

"There are other and more satisfying memories: a Prince Hal, by Timothy Dalton, that shows the glint of steel and prepares us for Henry V."

J.C. Trewin, ILLUSTRATED LONDON NEWS, 1 November 1974

"There are exceptions to this general mediocrity. Timothy Dalton, for instance, is a potentially fine Prince Hal. He embraces effectively the prince's shrewd calculating nature underlying his carousing with Falstaff and company. Almost alone of the company, he speaks his soliloquies as if they were articulated thoughts, as opposed to mindless rantings grating the ear. The intellectual consistency of his performance gives the production two of its rare moments of gold amid the prevailing dross. In the scene in Eastcheap when he is rehearsing with his father, he does the moment when his ultimate rejection of Falstaff is foreshadowed with a cold, vicious arrogance that had the effect of surprising and galvanising Paul Hardwick as Falstaff momentarily to life. In the final scene of all, where as the new king spurns Falstaff, this time for real, the releases a cruel, ruthless intensity that leaves the correct nasty taste in the audience's mouth, while making one look forward immensely to his interpretation of *Henry V*."

Jonathan Hammond, PLAYS AND PLAYERS, November 1974

"Timothy Dalton misses, I think, a golden opportunity to show us what a wretched man Prince Hal was. (...) Yet we must always believe in Hal's reformation, even though it is followed by his brutal treatment of Falstaff and the imprisonment of Doll and Mistress Quickly. Mr Dalton clearly reformed at the moment when the King caught his trying on the crown; his tears were genuine, and moving, and his behaviour, repellent as it was, clearly motivated by his new standards. I liked him better as a tearaway."

B.A. Young, THE FINANCIAL TIMES, 11 November 1974

HENRY V

November 27th, 1974

Round House Theatre (London)

CAST

Prospect Theatre Company: Timothy Dalton (Henry V), Edgar Wreford (Chorus), Helen Cotterill (Alice), John Warner (Charles of France), Tim Hardy (Dauphin), Christopher Burgess (Exeter), Michael Shannon (Fuellen), Pauline Munro (Katherine), Sylvia Coleridge (Mistress Quickly), Michael Graham Fox (Pistol)

CREDITS

Director: Kenny McBain | Author: William Shakespeare | Setting: John Fraser | Lighting: Keith Edmundson

THE PLAY

King Henry V, after succeeding his father, is determined to prove his right to rule, including over France. An ambassador arrives from the French Dauphin with a provocative gift of tennis balls. Henry responds by preparing to invade France. Three of the king's friends are discovered to be plotting against him, and he condemns them to death. Pistol, Nym, and Bardolph, the companions of Henry's dissolute days in London, join the king's forces and set off for the wars. Also, the news of Sir John Falstaff's death arrives.

REVIEWS

"Timothy Dalton as King Henry V does not develop upon his momentary promise during his father's death scene. He tries, but seems hard pushed to cope. There is valiance, but not the cold ruthlessness that could envisage 'infant spitted upon pikes.' There is a constant boyish eagerness that is at odds with the young king's obvious consciousness of his role and position. Dalton's public face does not alter in private. We believe that Henry V is, possibly, a moral man. Yet his doubt, upon realisation that his pride, ambition, and greed also involve senseless destruction, is conveyed too self-consciously and dismissed too easily to imply a glimpse of an alternative morality."

Merete Bates, THE GUARDIAN, 23 October 1974

"Timothy Dalton, who has taken the character from the taverns to the glory of the battlefield, copes well with the great heroic speeches."

Malcolm Grey, EVENING CHRONICLE, 31 October 1974

"Timothy Dalton is a splendid King Harry; he makes even the most unlikeable speeches, like the shameful bargaining, with God that starts so promisingly 'God of battles, steel my soldier's hearts,' sound richly heroic. His great cadenzas on ceremony and on St. Crispin's Day spring out full of youth and pride; I was only bored with him in his final wooing of Katherine, and that was neither his fault nor Pauline Munro's but Shakespeare's."

B.A. Young, THE FINANCIAL TIMES, 28 November 1974

"A rousing, well spoken, strongly flowing production which has Timothy Dalton has a handsome, vigorous, dominating King."

R.B.M., THE STAGE, 5 December 1974

"Timothy Dalton, master of Hal, is himself mastered by Henry. Mr Dalton takes refuge under the noble speeches and is attacked rather than attacker. This king is diplomat not warrior; his thought and intellect are never coloured by passion. But Agincourt was not won without a glowing conviction, nor sparked off without fury."

E.Victor, THE TABLET, 7 December 1974

"Timothy Dalton, now an exceedingly fine Henry in the Prospect revival, makes neither of these errors [to play Henry as an animated stained-glass Saint George or intellectualise it]. He knows that the piece must excite; he knows that Henry is the 'star of England': but he has also thought himself into the central speeches, found the man beneath the king, and given us, with real vigour of mind and presence, the wartime leader who is Prince Hal with a fresh wisdom and fire. The 'ceremony' speech is most intelligently spoken. Mr Dalton, in looks and style, is of the Olivier school, but it is an influence, not a copy. I came from the Round House with new respect for an actor who will do much."

J.C. Trewin, THE BIRMINGHAM POST, 12 December 1974

"(...) Timothy Dalton as the king, who fulfils all the promise of his Prince Hal in the earlier play. He is Shakespeare's dashing, bold, belligerent, fierce-tempered monarch to the life, adding his own quality of boyish exuberance, which sharply differentiates his Henry from Olivier's more restrained and mature interpretation in the film. Reflecting the production's own greater certainty of what it's about, he is more confident of himself than in his (sometimes) rather tentative stab at Hal. He speaks the verse thoughtfully and the big set-pieces of 'Once more unto the breach' (excitingly and imaginatively staged by McBain) and 'St Crispin's Day' speech come over particularly well, if with no great new slabs of insight."

Jonathan Hammond, PLAYS AND PLAYERS, February 1975

"It can be written off condescendingly, yet Henry is by no means an easy part if the actor resolves to act it and not to slide into glib heroics. Certainly Timothy Dalton refused to take the simple way. It was long since the 'star of

England' had so stirred me as in the Prospect company's production at the Round House: much the best of the three histories staged – almost a reproach to the minor director's theatre – without superfluous parade. The company, in general, was capable – I would not say more – but Mr Dalton, reminding me strongly of the young Olivier, was forcibly enough to have won Agincourt single-handed: he considered the speeches so freshly that all of us that night, I believe, were with the band of brothers on Crispin's Day."

J.C. Trewin, ILLUSTRATED LONDON NEWS, 01 February 1975

A KIND OF BONUS [radio]

January 22nd,1975

BBC Radio 4

CAST

Nerys Hughes (Frances), Timothy Dalton (Tommy), Sion Probert (Mr Marple), Haydn Jones (doctor), Victor Lucas (Charles)

CREDITS

Producer: Harry Catlin | Author: John Whitewood

THE PLAY

Tommy is an aspiring young writer who has sought the seclusion of a Spartan existence in an ill-furnished country cottage and finds his home unexpectedly "invaded" by a beautiful girl, Frances, and a middle-aged man, Charles.

THE HAPPIEST DAYS OF YOUR LIFE?

May 4th, 1975

Shaw Theatre (London)

CAST

Robin Ellis, Martin Jarvis, Helen Mirren, Paula Wilcox, Timothy Dalton, Barrie

Rutter, Neil Stacy, John Stride, Simon Ward

CREDITS

Director: Michael Croft

THE PLAY

Fundraising performance in aid of the National Youth Theatre: An anthology of poetry and prose on the subject of English school life.

THE VORTEX [radio]

June 9th, 1975

BBC Radio 4

CAST

Elizabeth Sellars (Florence), Martin Jarvis (Nicky Lancaster), Timothy Dalton (Tom), Peter Woodthorpe, Gerald Cross, Madi Redd, Sarah Lawson, Gudrun Ure, Peter Williams, Kate Coleridge

CREDITS

Director: Glyn Dearman | Author: Noël Coward

THE PLAY

Nicky Lancaster is a talented but useless young composer and pianist in post-World War I England. Nicky is engaged to Bunty Mainwaring, a journalist; his mother Florence, an ageing socialite beauty, has extramarital affairs with younger men in an attempt to recapture her youth.

REVIEW

"Dearman's revival, performed by a cast led by Sellars, Jarvis and a pre-James Bond Timothy Dalton as a soft-spoken Tom (Florence's young lover) – did the play proud."

Laurence Raw, radiodramareviews.com

THE VORTEX

October 2nd, 1975

Greenwich Theatre (London)

CAST

Vivien Merchant (Florence Lancaster), Timothy Dalton (Nicky Lancaster), Jennifer Hilary (Helen Saville), Gabrielle Drake (Bunty Mainwaring), Alan Judd (David Lancaster), Barry Quinn (Tom Veryan), David William (Pauncefort Quentin), Joyce Grant (Clara Hibbert), Hywel Jones (Bruce Fairlight), Douglas Milvain (Preston)

CREDITS

Director: James Roose-Evans | Author: Noël Coward | Designer: Peter Rice | Lighting: Graham Phoenix | Dances: Karen Rabinowitz | Music: Sandy Wilson | Piano player: Chuck Mallett

THE PLAY

Nicky Lancaster is a talented but useless young composer and pianist in post-World War I England. Nicky is engaged to Bunty Mainwaring, a journalist; his mother Florence, an ageing socialite beauty, has extramarital affairs with younger men in an attempt to recapture her youth.

DALTON:

"I remember doing a part that Sir John Gielgud had once done in a Noel Coward play and went to see him about it. He was delightful and charming and wonderful, and I asked him if he had any tips. He didn't even remember doing the play."

DAILY MAIL

REVIEWS

"Timothy Dalton grades his hysteria more deliberately and achieves moments of really impressive weight at the climax. Until then the performance could do with more volatility: its changes of mood should take you by surprise instead of coming as sluggish delayed reactions. And are there no young actors these days who can play the piano?"

Irving Wardle, THE TIMES, 3 October 1975

"In the Coward role of the son Nicky, Timothy Dalton is less good at the typically Twenties stuff than when he's striving to jerk our tears: it's not his fault the lines won't stand it. A more controlled approach would work better."

      Tom Sutcliffe, THE GUARDIAN, 3 October 1975

"It is shallow, brittle-play about shallow, brittle people, with Timothy Dalton sniffing cocaine, with no obvious ill-effects and getting upset when the bright young thing in his life (Gabrielle Drake) falls for the handsome young thing (Barry Quinn), who is coveted by his mother."

      Ian Christie, DAILY EXPRESS, 3 October 1975

"Timothy Dalton makes a saturnine Nicky, with the disadvantage that he cannot play the piano."

      B.A. Young, FINANCIAL TIMES, 4 October 1975

He [Coward] is fair enough to make his mouthpiece Nicky more than slightly suspect, though little of this emerges in the performance of Timothy Dalton, who seems undernourished but thoroughly healthy."

      Robert Cushman, THE OBSERVER, 5 October 1975

"It is in the bedroom scene that Timothy Dalton, in the part Coward himself created completes a performance that reminds me uncannily of the young Olivier. Physically and vocally, Dalton has the manner; he acts with a sustained, thrusting decision."

      J.C. Trewin, THE BIRMINGHAM POST, 6 October 1975

"Timothy Dalton, an essentially 'modern' actor, may not quite have the measure of Nicky Lancaster, but he makes the role convincing, not least in its sexual ambiguity."

      Peter Hepple, THE STAGE, 9 October 1975

"Timothy Dalton as Nicky, the son, does not have quite the same problem; Nicky is never drawn as a caricature: being an intellectual or an artist – he is, from the start, surrounded by an aura of doom. Timothy Dalton succeeds in conveying this quality of brooding, saturnine unhappiness; but in the bedroom scene with the mother he falls victim to the melodramatic, as against the tragic, element is the text and becomes somewhat shrilly theatrical."

      Martin Esslin, PLAYS AND PLAYERS, December 1975

WHITE LIARS & BLACK COMEDY

June 28th, 1976

Shaw Theatre (London)

CAST

WL: Dolphin Theatre Company: Maggie Fitzgibbon (Sophie, Baroness Lemberg), Peter Machin (Frank), Timothy Dalton (Tom)

BC: Dolphin Theatre Company: Celia Bannerman (Clea), Gemma Craven (Carol Melkett), Timothy Dalton (Harold Gorringe), Maggie Fitzgibbon (Miss Furnival), Max Latimer (Georg Bamberger), Peter Machin (Brindsley Miller), Milo Sperber (Schuppanzigh), Neil McCarthy (Colonel Melkett)

CREDITS

Director: Paul Giovanni | Author: Peter Shaffer | Designer: Dee Greenwood | Lighting: Steve Kemp

THE PLAYS

White Liars tells a fateful encounter between a down and out fortune teller, a rock musician, and his agent. The agent tips Baroness Lemberg to fake some hocus pocus over a crystal ball, to discourage the musician from pursuing his girlfriend. The trickery entangles each of them in a dense web of lies.

In *Black Comedy*, young sculptor Brindsley Miller embellishes his apartment with furniture and luxurious objects "borrowed" from the absent collector next door hoping to impress his fiancée's pompous father and a wealthy art dealer, Schuppanzigh. His fussy neighbour returns when a blown fuse brings the apartment into darkness.

REVIEWS

"Paul Giovanni's production does extract some nice shoulder-shrugging comedy from Maggie Fitzgibbon, and gives Timothy Dalton and Peter Machin the pretext for two pairs of strikingly contrasted performances when we move into the second play. The showiest contrast is Mr Dalton's, who begins the evening in the guise of a surly Yorkshire megalomaniac, and winds up in *Black Comedy* as the mincing antique-fancier, Harold Gorringe. Even with memories of Finney, I had not realised what a good part that is; and Mr Dalton caps it, at the long-delayed moment of Harold's recognition that his furniture has been borrowed with an off-stage howl fit for Oedipus and an entrance as a grey-suited Fury bearing a lighted taper."

Irving Wardle, THE TIMES, 3 October 1975

"Peter Machin and Timothy Dalton play the couple with endearing fanaticism (....). // The furniture belongs to an effete neighbour (Timothy Dalton in ginger wig, puttied nose and pink shirt, so he must be, you know...) who conveniently takes up the theme of *White Liars* by considering himself closer to Brinsley than Brinsley either knows or imagines."

Michael Coveney, FINANCIAL TIMES, 29 June 1976

"The trouble is it [*White Liars*] could just as easily be a short-story as a play; and the then naturalistic convention and having Timothy Dalton's singer address the audience as if they were a public meeting."

Michael Billington, THE GUARDIAN, 29 June 1976

"The piece [*White Liars*] does go on rather too long; but its performance carries it, particularly with Maggie Fitzgibbon as the fortune-teller and Timothy Dalton, looking more than ever like the young Olivier, as the youth who – it seems – is everything he is not. (...) Again [*Black Comedy*], Miss Fitzgibbon and Mr Dalton are first-rate."

J.C. Trewin, THE BIRMINGHAM POST, 30 June 1976

"The play [*White Liars*] suffers, like many of Mr Shaffer's, from its failure to find a believable idiom, especially for its young; Timothy Dalton as the singer is wet, but he is not helped by his author or by Mr Giovanni, who lowers the lights on him and leaves him to soliloquise."

Robert Cushman, THE OBSERVER, 4 July 1976

"There is an ingenious plot to accompany the basic idea, and although Paul Giovanni's direction tends towards untidiness at times, the performances are generally engaging enough to divert attention away from the less than crisp staging. A fun evening."

Clive Hirschhorn, EXPRESS ON SUNDAY, 4 July 1976

"It is to the author's great credit that the hilarious incidents, notably Brinsley's efforts to sneak Harold's effects to his flat, do not detract from the incisive characterisation, so ably conveyed by Peter Machin as Brindsley, Timothy Dalton as Harold, Gemma Craven and Celia Bannerman as the steel-tipped girls, Neil McCarthy as the colonel and Milo Sperber as the charming electricity man."

P.H., The Stage, 8 July 1976

THE LUNATIC, THE LOVER AND THE POET

March 15th / March 18th* / March 26th** / May, 1980

Fortune Theatre (London) / European Tour: Moscow, Helsinki, Teatre Romea* (Barcelona), Teatro Bellas Artes** (Madrid), Portugal, Cyprus, Greece / Cervantine International Festival (Mexico)

CAST

Old Vic Theatre Company: Timothy Dalton (Lord Byron), Robin Davis, Donald Fraser, Charles Kay, Alan Lawrence, Trevor Martin, Adrianne Posta

CREDITS

Director: Toby Robertson | Writer: Jane McCulloch | Music: Robert Fraser

THE PLAY

A performance based on Lord Byron's life (his travels and love life) from his birth in London, in 1788, until his death in Missolonghi, Greece, in 1824. The show, illustrated with music, presents Byron's poems and letters as well as articles and reviews by the poet.

DALTON:

"It [the title] expresses Byron's three characteristics. He was a lover in the passionate sense, but not only in the man-woman sense, but also in the man-man aspect, or in the man-mankind one. He was a great poet, but some people didn't understand him because they thought he was a fool. Byron, also, belonged to the high society; he always fought among the aristocracy and against everything oppressing the people. He died in Greece fighting for their liberty. (...) I sing, but I'm not a singer. (...) It [the music] has been included for two reasons: as a link between the word, the thought and the feelings. In addition, some of Byron's poems have inner music that must be expressed. It is necessary to sing in some passages of his work because the content is best expressed this way."

       La Vanguardia

REVIEWS

"The expressivity, not only from the whole cast but also from the dramatic structure of the play, is here – without a doubt – the fulcrum of the Old Vic."

       Gonzalo Pérez de Olaguer, El Periódico, 20 March 1980

"It's an excellent quartet. Their educated voices are capable of all shades and inflexions. Sober gestures, thin underlining. A perfect mechanism between all of them, and with the small musical group. (...) The work of the actors crosses frontiers and wins the ovations."

Eduardo Haro Teglen, EL PAÍS, 29 March 1980

SHAKESPEARE'S ROME [Julius Caesar + Antony and Cleopatra]

October 13th, 1981

Mermaid Theatre (London)

CAST

Morgan Sheppard (Caesar), Timothy Dalton (Antony), Colin Bennet (Cassius), Andre Winterton (Cinna), Aaron Shirley (Decius/Cicero), Peter Welch (Lepidus), Gilbert Wynne (Brutus), Derek Ware (Casca), Andrew Branch (Octavius), Fred Bryant (Trebonius), Nigel Nobes (Metellus), Michael Roberts (Scarus), Robbie McNab & Christopher Merrick (Flag bearers)

Timothy Dalton (Antony), Carmen Du Sautoy (Cleopatra), Colin Bennett (Agrippa), Andrew Branch (Octavius), Fred Bryant (Pompey), Karen Ford (Charmian), Nigel Nobes (Alexas), Angela Phillips (Octavia), Michael Roberts (Strato), Aaron Shirley (Eros), Derek Ware (Menas), Andre Winterton (Decretas), Gilbert Wynne (Maecenas), Morgan Sheppard, (Enobarbus), Gaynor Sinclair (Iras), Peter Welch (Lepidus), Robbie McNab & Christopher Merrick (Flag bearers)

CREDITS

Director: Bernard Miles, Ron Pember | Author: William Shakespeare | Designer: Robin Don

THE PLAYS

The tribunes Marullus and Flavius break up a gathering of Roman citizens who seek to celebrate Julius Caesar's triumphant return from war. The victory is marked by public games in which Caesar's friend, Mark Antony, takes part. On his way to the arena, Caesar is stopped by a stranger who warns that he should 'Beware the Ides of March.'

After defeating Brutus and Cassius, following the assassination of Julius Caesar, Mark Antony becomes one of the three rulers of the Roman Empire, together with Octavius Caesar and Lepidus, and is responsible for the eastern part of the empire. He falls in love with Cleopatra, the Queen of Egypt, and settles in Alexandria. However, he is compelled to return to Rome when the empire is threatened by the rebellion of Sextus Pompey, the son of Pompey, who had been defeated by Julius Caesar.

REVIEWS

"As we advance into the second play, it becomes clear that the only thing that could hold the programme together would be a heroic scale Antony. This thought is evidently shared by Timothy Dalton, who does everything in his power to enlarge himself in the role – from his space-filling gestures and straddling gait to pushing his delivery to the limit. The result, alas, is still lightweight, and it deprives this sensitive actor of his best equipment. The performance is monotonous and undetailed: a fiery opportunist in the first play, then an unshaven voluptuary who goes through the entire second play in a dressing gown (exactly measuring up to Octavius' most contemptuous descriptions)."

      Irving Wardle, THE TIMES, 14 October 1981

"Timothy Dalton's Antony only demonstrates how totally unrelated are the characters in each play, although he trades heavily in boyish charm throughout."

      Michael Coveney, FINANCIAL TIMES, 14 October 1981

"Timothy Dalton's Antony snarls vigilantly, conceiving Antony as a sharp diplomat."

      Nicholas de Jongh, THE GUARDIAN, 15 October 1981

"The company is full of energy and drive as it ranges through great events during notable periods, outstanding being Timothy Dalton (the two Antonys), Colin Bennett (Cassius), Gilbert Wynne (Brutus), Morgan Sheppard (Caesar and Enobarbus), Carmen du Sautoy (Cleopatra) and Karen Ford (Charmian)."

      R.B. Marriott, THE STAGE, 22 October 1981

"Antony and Cleopatra were the two best performances (...). Timothy Dalton was too slight and young, which was scarcely his fault as he had to be an athletic youth before the interval."

      Mark Armory, THE SPECTATOR, 23 October 1981

HENRY IV, part I

May 7th / June 9th, 1982

Barbican Centre (London) / Aldwych Theatre (London)

CAST

Royal Shakespeare Company: John Rogan (Bardolph), Colin Tarrant (Cutter), Graham Turner (Dick), Brian Poysner (Earl of Warwick/Chamberlain), Bernard Brown (Earl of Westmoreland), Simon Templeman (Edmund Mortimer/Thomas Duke of Clarence), Miles Anderson (Edward Poins), Dexter Fletcher (Francis), Robert Eddison (Henry Percy), Timothy Dalton (Hotspur), Gerard Murphy (Henry Prince of Wales), Philip Walsh (Hotspur's servant/Ralph a drawer), Patrick Stewart (King Henry IV), Gemma Jones (Lady Mortimer), Harriet Walter (Lady Percy), Miriam Karlin (Mistress Quickly), Bernard Lloyd (Owen Glendower/First Carrier), James Fleet (Peto), Philip Franks (Prince Humphrey of Gloucester/Sir Michael), Kevin Wallace (Prince John of Lancaster), John Burgess (Second Carrier/Richard Scroop), Joss Ackland (Sir John Falstaff), Hugh Quarshie (Sir Richard Vernon), Ray Jewers (Sir Walter Blunt), Griffith Jones (The Lord Chief Justice/Sheriff), John Franklyn-Robbins (Thomas Percy), John McAndrew (Tom), Ronan Wilmot (Earl of Douglas), Ken Robertson (Will)

CREDITS

Director: Trevor Nunn | Author: William Shakespeare | Designer: John Napier | Composer: Guy Woolfenden

THE PLAY

Henry Bolingbroke has usurped the throne of England to his cousin, Richard II. News of a rebellion in Wales and the North arrives, where Harry Hotspur, the young son of the Earl of Northumberland, is fighting with the Earl of Douglas. King Henry IV has been victorious at the battle of Shrewsbury but the Earl of Northumberland hears rumours that his son has been the victor. Northumberland and the Archbishop of York decide to oppose the king's forces, led by Lord John.

DALTON:

"With Hotspur and the RSC there's no money, and less of an audience will see it. But if I do it well, the rewards are much greater. Of course I could go away and make a fortune and be famous filming rubbish. But that wouldn't please me."

    PHOTOPLAY

"At least there are backstage signposts for the actors here, which is more than the National ever bothered to provide in their first few months, but it's still a huge, impersonal inhuman space which we have somehow got to fill with life. It's a vast area, probably one of the deepest stages in Europe, with a fly tower five storeys up from the stage; but John Napier has come up with a *Henry IV* set which has a sense of structure and above all of texture, so that you want to get your fingers into it, and that might give us some idea of personality."

    THE TIMES

"We opened the Barbican Theatre in London which is in fact a *horrible* building, and a *horrible* theatre where you virtually have to *shout* to be heard but we did a wonderful production of *Henry IV* in which I played the role of Hotspur, and you know, fortunately it was a great success and I was very happy."

    Savannah Acting Class

"If you're offered Hotspur which is a very famous part which all the famous actors have done, and it's going to be for the opening of the New Barbican Centre. And for the RSC with Trevor Nunn directing it, you know you've got to do it."

    CINEMA

"I subscribed a long time ago to the notion that you can pass on information and it's okay to ask. (...). He [Michael Redgrave] had done a famous Hotspur in *Henry IV* and I was about to play the part, but he didn't remember either. He said, 'I think I played it with a Northern accent'."

    DAILY MAIL

REVIEWS

"In Part 1, Timothy Dalton's tearfully petulant Hotspur forms both a contrast and interesting complement to Hal. Their fight at Shrewsbury is the exhausted combat of blood brothers. As in all the confrontations in these plays, it is characterised by the generous recognition of an opponent's reputation and worth."

    Michael Coveney, FINANCIAL TIMES, 10 June 1982

"About the only thing to recommend Part I is Timothy Dalton's dashing, fast-talking Hotspur - at once ridiculous and heroic in his literally leapfrogging hurtle to self-immolation. The minor scene in which he receives a letter from a lord who backs off from the revolt is surprisingly touching: Mr Dalton keeps refolding the letter aimlessly as he vainly tries to hide his panic from his wife (Harriet Walter). The actor also taps into a rich boyishly sarcastic vein of humor as he irrepressibly mocks the supernatural pretensions of his trying ally Glendower (Bernard Lloyd)."

Frank Rich, THE NEW YORK TIMES, 12 June 1982

"Hal's other main antagonism goes for too little, since Timothy Dalton makes an obstinately lightweight Hotspur with no chest-notes."

Robert Cushman, THE OBSERVER, 13 June 1982

"Timothy Dalton as driving, mettlesome Hotspur."

R.B. Marriott, THE STAGE, 17 June 1982

"We can be grateful for Timothy Dalton's Hotspur, mercifully without the traditional stammer; and less grateful for Gerard Murphy's Prince Hal who – whatever the speculations about a need for a father-figure and so one – seems to be sadly uncouth."

ILLUSTRATED LONDON NEWS, 31 July 1982

"At the other end of that spectrum is Timothy's Dalton youthful, rather starry-eyed, Hotspur, romantically handsome, dashing and impetuous, vibrant with pent-up energy and enthusiastic conviction for his cause. His anger with the 'certain lord, neat and trimly dressed' who came to demand the prisoners is wittily, and infectiously described while his scene with Glendower, excellently played in all his determined Welsh pomposity by Bernard Lloyd, proves a rich source of comedy, with Hotspur's mischievous goading of the tenacious self-esteem and impenetrable smugness of his ally. The battle between Hotspur and Hal begins as a chivalrous confrontation of adversaries but ends in exhaustion as strength ebbs and heavy bodies wrestle and blunder together in a horrible quest for the killer blow, at last achieved, desperately and meanly, with a dagger."

R.L. Smallwood, CRITICAL QUARTERLY, #25 1983

"The duel with Hotspur (Timothy Dalton) was a protracted contest between two exhausted boys that ended in an unchivalrous dagger thrust. (...) Nunn, with his fondness for self-reflexive theatrical artifice, repeatedly staged the choices confronting Hal: Hotspur appeared in a spotlight during Hal's first soliloquy."

David Bevington, HENRY IV, PART I (Oxford University Press), 1987

ANTONY AND CLEOPATRA [TV]

October 1983

Bravo Channel 5

CAST

Lynn Redgrave (Cleopatra), Timothy Dalton (Mark Antony), Nichelle Nichols (Charmian), John Carradine (Soothsayer), Barrie Ingham (Enobarbus), Anthony Geary (Octavius Caesar), Walter Koenig (Pompey), Brian Kerwin (Eros), Jack Gwillim (Rustic), Michael Billington (Ventidius), Claude Woolman (Silius), Kim Miyori (Iras), Anthony Holland (Alexas), James Avery (Mardian), Earl Boen (Lepidus), Joseph R. Sicari (messenger), Ted Sorel (Menas), Earl Robinson (Maecenas), Tom Rosqui (Agrippa), Alvah Stanley (Thidias), Sharon Barr (Octavia), John Devlin (Dolabella), Dan Mason (Euphronius), Henry Sutton (Proculeius), Ralph Drischell (Seleucus), Paul Bowman, Tom Everett, Michael Keyes-Hall, Grey O'Neill, Alex Wright (soldiers)

CREDITS

Director: Lawrence Carra | Author: William Shakespeare | Producer: Ken Campbell | Production Design: Donald L. Harris | Costume Design: Noel Taylor | Lighting: Jeffery Chang | Music: John Serry | *Running Time*: 179 mins.

THE PLAY

After defeating Brutus and Cassius, following the assassination of Julius Caesar, Mark Antony becomes one of the three rulers of the Roman Empire, together with Octavius Caesar and Lepidus, and is responsible for the eastern part of the empire. He falls in love with Cleopatra, the Queen of Egypt, and settles in Alexandria. However, he is compelled to return to Rome when the empire is threatened by the rebellion of Sextus Pompey, the son of Pompey, who had been defeated by Julius Caesar.

REVIEWS

"It [the production] has the virtue, for a novice audience, of being a less complicated reading of the play than Miller's, and it allows Lynn Redgrave (Cleopatra) and Timothy Dalton (Antony) to give full reign to the play's passionate moments."

Samuel Crowl, SHAKESPEARE AND THE MOVING IMAGE (Cambridge University Press), 1994

UNCLE VANYA [radio]

September 15th, 1985

BBC Radio 3

CAST

Robert Stephens (Vanya), Brenda Blethyn (Sonya), Timothy Dalton (Astrov), Cheryl Campbell (Yelena), Michael Gough (Serebryakov), Madoline Thomas (Nanny), David Sinclair (Telyegin), Pauline Letts (Madam Voynitksy), Alan Dudley (Yefim/Labourer)

CREDITS

Director: Jane Morgan | Author: Anton Chekov | Adaptor: Christopher Hampton | Guitar: Anthea Gilford

THE PLAY

Vanya and his daughter Sonya manage the state of Professor Serebryakov. When the Professor arrives for a visit with his much younger wife Yelena, Vanya and his friend Astrov, the local doctor, try to get Yelena's attention.

REVIEWS

"Robert Stephen's voice had just the right dotty quality for Vanya, the ideal contrast to Timothy Dalton's sincere, sensible Astrov and Michael Gough's dry, self-satisfied Serebriakov."

> B.A. Young, FINANCIAL TIMES, 21 September 1985

"As Astrov, an ineffectual would-be conservationist, Timothy Dalton, appeared to know what he was talking about, yet seemed incapable of direct action – for example, continuing his love-affair with Yelena. Yet perhaps this was not his fault: Chekhov, a doctor himself, was aware of the limitations placed on country practitioners."

> Laurence Raw, radiodramareviews.com

THE TAMING OF THE SHREW

April 17th / June 7th, 1986

Theatre Clwyd (Mold) / Haymarket Theatre (London)

CAST

Timothy Dalton (Petruchio), Vanessa Redgrave (Katherina), Gerald James (Baptista), Kika Markham (Bianca), Richard Lees (Biondello), Robert O'Mahoney (Gremio), Bunny May (Grumio), Martin Chamberlain (Hortensio), Margot Leicester, Christopher Bowen (Curtis/tailor), Delaval Astley (Lucentio), Hayward Morse (Peter/pedant), Sylvester McCoy (Tranio), Ken Bones (Vincentio), Madalyn Morgan (servant), Steven Woodcock (Nathaniel), Andrew Lucre (Philip/Haberdasher), Ben Ellison (Nicholas), Andrew Wheaton (Tailor's Model)

CREDITS

Directors: Toby Robertson, Christopher Selbie | Author: William Shakespeare | Designer: Simon Highlett | Lighting: Pat Nelder | Music: Robert Stewart | Choreography: Terry John Bates

THE PLAY

Lucentio, a student arrived in Padua, hears that the merchant Baptista has two daughters, but the younger, prettier daughter, Bianca, cannot be married before her strong-willed sister, Katherina. On seeing Bianca, Lucentio falls in love with her. Meanwhile, Petruchio, a young adventurer from Verona, arrives to visit his friend Hortensio. He learns about Katherina and decides to woo her, with the help of Gremio and Hortensio.

DALTON:

"I loved doing Petruchio in *The Taming of the Shrew*. (...) *Taming of the Shrew* was a great hit, again through luck and judgment, and was a great show. But, of course, its subject matter – I don't think there's anything wrong with its subject matter at all, fundamentally; it's saying that true love exists when two people get to know each other. If they fall in love with each other superficially on surface appearances, it's going to fall apart. We see that story in *Taming of the Shrew*. The two people actually explore each other, get to know each other, struggle with each other, and end up truly loving each other. But, you know, a lot of people see it as a chauvinistic or anti-feminist play. And I remember one of the critics who happened to be hugely enjoying it, laughing all the way through, decided to write for his paper a sort of feminist review. His only comment about me was that I was the best Henry V of my generation!"

007

"And we have had wonderful ones [reviews] for *The Shrew* as well although not everybody's... reviewers seem to find a lot of problem with *The Shrew* because they seem to think that it's, it's... I don't know either a feminist or an anti-feminist play and think that this is a problem. It wasn't a problem to Shakespeare I mean it is a wonderful play and a very funny play. It is a play about love and I think we do it terribly well as some of the reviewers of..., well you have seen the reviews there smashing. (...) *The Shrew* is a comedy which is sort of rigorous in its language, is very bouncy and jaunty in its language."

JCET's Celebrity Spotlight

REVIEWS

"Timothy Dalton, dashing pell-mell through his wooing has neither breath nor energy for pursuit or a snatched dalliance in spontaneous physical contact. Constantly referring to his 'Kat' he plots, plans, and executes his scheme as with the veriest bird of prey."

Stella Flint, PLAYS AND PLAYERS, June 1986

"Shakespeare's heroines are usually the educators; here it is Petruchio who lays down the law's conditions Timothy Dalton follows his splendid Antony with a sympathetic roisterer that is much more than the flamboyant bully of tradition."

Michael Coveney, FINANCIAL TIMES, 11 June 1986

"Both Vanessa Redgrave and Timothy Dalton seem happy to place a winsome, sentimental gloss upon the play's nastier business. (...) The context in which she [Miss Redgrave] and Dalton, who was surely the best Henry V of our times, have to function is one of no more than a desperately jocular but unfunny display of imaginary Elizabethan farcicals."

Nicholas de Jongh, THE GUARDIAN, 11 June 1986

"As Redgrave plays it, Kate's conversion comes in a moment when she is alone and suddenly sees the light, undergoing a radiant transformation rather than having her will broken. It may sound implausible but, given the strength of affection that she and Mr Dalton put into the final scenes, it is irresistible at the time."

Irving Wardle, THE TIMES, 12 June 1986

"That this succeeds as well as it does Toby Robertson and Christopher Selbie's Theatr Clwyd production is almost entirely due to Timothy Dalton's tender, witty, well-spoken and invincible Petruchio, closer to John Cleese in Jonathan Miller's BBC production than to the formidable Alfred Molina who recently played Petruchio as a gang lad thug for the RSC. When the role is played with such heartfelt intelligence and charm as it is at the Haymarket – and Mr Dalton takes care to get us on his side even before he tackles Kate herself (pronounced Kat throughout) – of course Kate is not slow to catch on as to what is at stake. Mr Dalton is superb."

Michael Ratcliffe, THE OBSERVER, 15 June 1986

"Timothy Dalton is as likeable that you can hardly believe in his brutality."

John Peter, SUNDAY TIMES, 15 June 1986

"Timothy Dalton, too, deserves much credit for his Petruchio, a study full of virile attraction but played with a resounding twinkle and a feeling that there is tenderness behind his determination."

Peter Hepple, THE STAGE, 19 June 1986

"You come to see stars playing leading roles and it must be said that both Vanessa Redgrave and Timothy Dalton are well worth watching. (...). But the play really belongs to Timothy Dalton's excellent Petruchio. There is not a trace of the demented sadist we have encountered in recent years. Instead here is Hazlitt's idea of the part. Dalton acts the assumed character of the mad-cap railer with complete presence of mind, with conscious theatricality and without a particle of ill humour. It is an engaging and sympathetic performance."

Christopher Edwards, THE SPECTATOR, 20 June 1986

"Timothy Dalton swaggers bravely with a rough chin and a chillingly charming smile as Petruchio. (...) Timothy Dalton's Petruchio is potentially a good performance, dashing, forceful, attractive, reminiscent of Kevin Kline, one of the few American actors who tackle Shakespeare with confidence. The early jousting with Redgrave's Kate promised an electric partnership. Unfortunately, when Kate had nothing to say, Redgrave failed to command attention by the horror of her silence; and so Dalton was left to swagger with nothing against."

John Elsom, PLAYS AND PLAYERS INTERNATIONAL, 12 July 1986

"There is good acting all around. Timothy Dalton is physically convincing, though it seems mentally reluctant, tamer. His sensitivity creates poignant moments with Kate when the rhythm is almost embarrassingly slowed down as for the reconciliatory kiss in the street for instance. (...) When the actress [Redgrave] makes for putting her hand under his book, Timothy Dalton anxiously reaches out to prevent the humiliating gesture. The audience did not seem to have any trouble with this straightforward if unfashionable rendering of the end. On the whole, the combined effect of Mr Dalton's and Miss Redgrave's interpretations supports the notion that Petruchio, feels genuine love for Kate very early in the play, and the best cure he can find for her diseased humour only shows the measure of his affection and concern."

Jean-Marie Maguin, CAHIERS ÉLISABÉTHIANS, 1 October 1986

ANTONY AND CLEOPATRA

May 8th / May 28th, 1986

Theatre Clwyd (Mold) / Haymarket Theatre (London)

CAST

Vanessa Redgrave (Cleopatra), Timothy Dalton (Mark Antony), Hayward Morse (Candidius/soldier/Dolabella/Menecrates), Margot Leicester (Charmian), Robert O'Mahone (Enobarbus), Richard Rees (Eros), Madalyn Morgan (Iras), Gerald James (Lepidus/Clown), Christopher Bowen (Maecenas), Steven Woodcock (Mardian), Martin Chamberlain (Menas/Seleucus), Ken Bones (Octavius Caesar), Delaval Astley (Proculeius/Varrius), Taylor McAuley (Scarus/Alexas), Ben Ellison (schoolmaster/messenger), Sylvester McCoy (Sextus Pompey), Andrew Wheaton (Agrippa), Bunny May (Gallus/soothsayer)

CREDITS

Directors: Toby Robertson, Christopher Selbie | Author: William Shakespeare | Designer: Simon Highlett | Lighting: Pat Nelder | Music: Robert Stewart | Choreography: Terry John Bates

THE PLAY

After defeating Brutus and Cassius, following the assassination of Julius Caesar, Mark Antony becomes one of the three rulers of the Roman Empire, together with Octavius Caesar and Lepidus, and is responsible for the eastern part of the empire. He falls in love with Cleopatra, the Queen of Egypt, and settles in Alexandria. However, he is compelled to return to Rome when the empire is threatened by the rebellion of Sextus Pompey, the son of Pompey, who had been defeated by Julius Caesar.

DALTON:

"Antony in Antony and Cleopatra that we are doing here is always assumed that Antony must be god knows 55 and grey hair and all the rest of it which of course is not true, Antony was in his 30's when he was having his affair with Cleopatra and died at the age of 43... which I think is important that is not to say that he can't be a bit grey because he has to be as there is reference to a little bit of greyness, but it is important because if you are playing a man who is already beyond his prime politically as a soldier you're really saying there is no future other than a downward, a downhill future. When you are talking about Antony and Cleopatra you're talking about... the possibility of a wonderful future both politically and passionately, which he has thrown away, which he has lost because of this, this mad compulsion he has for this woman, I mean, he is besotted, he is a fool in love as they all say of him, but normally of course, to come back to your point, he is played by again someone 50 or 55 or whatever. (...) I would say Antony is his [Shakespeare] greatest play, wonderful, wonderful play deeply felt, deeply emotional, deeply serious."

CELEBRITY SPOTLIGHT

REVIEWS

"The pairing of Redgrave with Timothy Dalton provides the best sexual chemistry since Janet Suzman and Richard Johnson, with an extra dollop of lissom carnality. (...) This welcoming of death is ecstatically undertaken by Dalton, who disrobes joyfully to his loincloth and is winched up to Cleopatra's tomb on a right-angled pulley arrangement that would seem less ludicrous if unaccompanied by some wheezy harmonium chords. The suicidal impulse is strongly played, the abandonment of Antony by Hercules underlined with doomy music and Dalton sliding inexorably to his fate."

Michael Coveney, FINANCIAL TIMES, 27 May 1986

"Dalton's Antony is a Roman gone so native he resembles some fantasy prince from a Valentino movie."

Jack Tinker, DAILY MAIL, 27 May 1986

"Timothy Dalton is too young to be an ideal Antony (no sign of the 'grizzled head') but he suggests well enough a decent Roman soldier going madly native in silk scarves and bandanas; and one of the productions' few touches of real invention comes when he is hauled up to the monument like a bleeding, El Greco Christ."

Michael Billington, THE GUARDIAN, 28 May 1986

"What the opening establishes is that Timothy Dalton's hypnotized Antony is in thrall to a creature who will certainly bring about his downfall: and that nothing exists for Cleopatra beyond the desires of the moment."

Irving Wardle, THE TIMES, 28 May 1986

"As for Timothy Dalton's Antony, he is both impressive and moving in his growing self-disgust, but far too young and vigorous and alert for the part. Far from decadence, he positively radiates discipline: as soon as the first summons comes from Rome, he is on his feet, eyes shining, as if he can't wait to get back to some hard work. And that is the production's gravest weakness. At no point you sense that this pleasant, rational couple lives through their senses. It is hard to imagine an Antony and Cleopatra with less sexual spark, and, for all the romping, there is come chilliness in their caresses that makes them uncomfortable to watch."

Mary Harron, THE OBSERVER, 1 June 1986

"Not surprisingly, Timothy Dalton seems unsure what sort of Antony to play: he opts for vacuous good nature and a puzzled expression, like a male model from Mill Hill, or one of those young men ravaged by a domineering woman and not knowing whether to be smug or terrified. 'The old ruffian'? 'The demi-Atlas of this world'? No, no. But he is good where the production itself is good: in the scenes of political confrontation. Here Dalton acquires weight and stature."

John Peter, THE SUNDAY TIMES, 1 June 1986

"Shakespeare's Antony is also full of 'infinite variety', and though Timothy Dalton plods through the first half, in the second the turns in a magnetic, mood-shifting, charismatic performance of dignity and despair."

Paul Chand, The Stand, 5 June 1986

"Dalton and Redgrave are escapist lovers, prisoners of their own fading fantasies."

Carole Woddis, CITY LIMITS, 12 June 1986

"Vanessa Redgrave, whose Cleopatra has developed during the last dozen years, and Timothy Dalton are amply in control."

ILLUSTRATED LONDON NEWS, 26 July 1986

"Antony is Timothy Dalton, all grizzled boyishness. He actually rings true as one of those gifted charismatic military commanders at home in the field or even the bedroom but at sea (fatally and literally in this case) in politics. By the lights of the straightforward and linear production he is a powerful and, when necessary, impassioned figure — a good contrast to Ken Bones' consummately political Octavius."

Martin Hoyle, PLAYS AND PLAYERS, September 1986

"Timothy Dalton's Antony goes from swashbuckling self-confidence, wearing a splendid multi-coloured cloak, rather abruptly to a self-pitying end and is final winched up into the Monument as bleeding body, clad in nothing but a loin cloth. (...) Uneasy titter from some sections of the audience suggested that the spectacle of the wounded Antony dangling from a single arm did not quite achieve the desired impact, and the link with Christ crucified suggested by his appearance was tenuous. It was a pity if Antony's end evoked this response: Timothy Dalton had projected throughout a noble figure led astray by his infatuation, but still dynamic politically and worthy of the eulogy accorded to him by Cleopatra after his death."

Jill Pearce, CAHIERS ÉLISABÉTHIANS, 1 October 1986

A TOUCH OF A POET

January 28th / March 10th*, 1988

Young Vic (London) / Theatre Royal (Brighton) / Comedy Theatre* (London)

CAST

Timothy Dalton (Cornelius Melody), Vanessa Redgrave (Nora Melody), William Armstrong (Mickey Maloney), John McEnery (Jamie Cregan), Rudi Davies (Sara Melody), James Berwick (Dan Roche), Simon Coady (Paddy O'Dowd), Shay Gorman (Patch Riley), Amanda Boxer (Deborah), Malcolm Tierney (Nicholas Gadsby), John Murphy (Piper)

CREDITS

Director: David Thacker | Author: Eugene O'Neill | Designer: Saul Radomsky | Lighting: Paul Denby

THE PLAY

In a village near Boston, 1828, Con Melody, a proud and an ill-tempered tempestuous Irishman, owns a tavern. He has been born with wealth in a castle, and he has been a major with the Duke of Wellington at the Battle of

Talavera. He is determined to show his pride and importance to the Yankee townsmen; repressing, at the same time, his wife and daughter.

DALTON:

"As soon as Vanessa gave me the script I knew that we had to do it. This is just so funny and touching and moving and true a play that it has to be done, and the miracle for us was that no one in London had ever tried it before. The passion and the contradictions and the humour all ring so true. Although it's a commercial production, Vanessa and I were very keen to restart it at the Young Vic because seat prices are still so low that you really do get a young student audience. As soon as we started rehearsing, all the problems of the play, its focus on the Irish immigrants to America in the last century, its length and its detailed references to American politics of the period, seemed to get ironed out by sheer strength of O'Neill's poetry: it's a play that grows all the time you do it."

THE TIMES

"Certainly I loved doing the O'Neill play *A Touch of the Poet*. I'm very proud of that production. (...) He [O'Neill] is one of the 20th century's greatest writers. It was forgotten play and the way we did it, was I think right. And several of the critics said that this much now be regarded as one of his masterpieces. Well, if you can do that to a 'forgotten play' then that, of course, gives one tremendous satisfaction."

007

REVIEWS

"Timothy Dalton presents the kind of 'big-chested, chiselled-mug, romantic old boy' that O'Neill demanded. He is also very moving in those endlessly recurring passages where Con, having launched a tirade of unforgivably brutal insults against his womenfolk, instantly caves in with tender, heartfelt pleas for forgiveness. Beyond that, he shows the character an arm's length, posturing in front of the shebeen mirror and quoting Byron. Con may be tragic (as where he finally reverts to his bog-Irish identity); he is certainly funny."

Irving Wardle, THE TIMES, 3 February 1988

"Mr Dalton registers these ludicrous transformations with a crackling wit and some gusto. He is marvellous in the role, a dissipated Don Juan, a fading braggart in heroic outline."

Michael Coveney, FINANCIAL TIMES, 4 February 1988

"Released from Bondage, Timothy Dalton brings to Con Melody exactly 'the look of wrecked distinction' O'Neill demanded. There is a wonderful comic vanity about the way he crooks his left knee to gaze admiringly at himself in the mirror while quoting Childe Harold. But Mr Dalton also shows us the lacerating self-disgust that lies behind the Byronic posturing and when he cries. 'I'm but a ghost haunting a ruin,' it is with the ferocity of recognition. As his Antony recently proved, Mr Dalton is an actor who has steadily matured with the years."

  Michael Billington, THE GUARDIAN, 4 February 1988

"Dalton is a very good actor – elegant, devilish, witty – but Con is a huge part for a resourceful monster-performer, and that he is not."

  Michael Ratcliffe, THE OBSERVER, 7 February 1988

"Dalton's swaggering seedy charmer reminded me strongly of Olivier in his prime, in his achievement in letting us see all sides of the man. Cornelius is disastrously out of place in America — "You can't fight duels in America," his daughter screeches at him, "they use lawyers here!"— but the New World is poorer for the destruction of that 'touch of the poet'."

  Della Couling, THE TABLET, 13 February 1988

"Mr Dalton is galvanizing – full of blarney without forsaking the wit visible in his James Bond, but also plausibly a poetic Byronic hero. He may yet push 'Poet' into the tragic, if he can make Con's final-act descent into hopelessness more than the hysterical symbolic gesture it now appears."

  Frank Rich, THE NEW YORK TIMES, 16 February 1988

"The émigre Irishman, desperately clinging to English accent and pretensions to gentility in his new American home, is played by Timothy Dalton with a broken virile charm that encompasses his drunken generation and his power both to deceive himself and others. It is a fine performance, but coloured by Dalton's age, which lets the voice of a young man leak through infrequently and which does not allow him a certain tremulous quality."

  Gerard Werson, THE STAGE, 18 February 1988

"Timothy Dalton's Melody is fatuously upper-crust in company, frighteningly venomous when spitting out hatred for his 'thick-wristed peasant' daughter (and believably repentant a few seconds later), and superbly conveys the streak of bitterness underlying his final conversion into an unaffected broth of a boy. This is a remarkable performance, notwithstanding the smudged streaks of brown make-up furrows with which Mr Dalton attempts to age."

  Martin Hoyle, PLAYS AND PLAYERS, March 1988

"Lies, truth and booze in O'Neill's quart-sized masterpiece with superb performances from Vanessa Redgrave and Timothy Dalton as the Irish Melodys."

Michael Billington, THE GUARDIAN, 11 March 1988

"Timothy Dalton's strong physical presence gives the character its seedy charm and poseur's smile, the explosions of fury and whimpering pleas for forgiveness, but until he finds, and movingly responds to, his come-uppance in the last act is a curiously un-involving performance."

Jeremy Kingston, THE TIMES, 11 March 1988

"I'm convinced by his [Dalton's] fierce changes of mood."

Susan Jameson, LONDON BROADCASTING, 11 March 1988

"Dalton's performance goes right to its heart, illuminating the underlying integrity with which he imbued Con. At the end of the play Melody's reversion to his 'real' [i.e. peasant Irish] self sounds and looks much more gratingly phoney than did his assumed airs, and there is an edge of calculated mockery in this performance. The true tragic self-knowledge - as Dalton reveals when he screams at Sara as she is about to call his bluff - is that Cornelius knows that his is just as much an escapist fantasy as the old, exploded persona. There is no solution - and his daughter, who was the scathing satirist of the 'Major Melody' act, becomes, thought-provokingly at the end, its sobbing elegist."

Paul Taylor, THE INDEPENDENT, 12 March 1988

"The contrasting absurdity and pathos of a life of constant falsehood was brought superbly by Dalton."

Francis King, SUNDAY TELEGRAPH, 13 March 1988

"Timothy Dalton's Melody is fatuously upper-crust in company, frighteningly venomous when spitting out hatred for his 'thick-wristed peasant' daughter (and believable repentant a few seconds later), and superbly conveys the streak of bitterness underlying his final conversion into an unaffected broth of a boy. This is remarkable performance, notwithstanding the smudged streaks of Brown make-up furrows with which Mr Dalton attempts to age."

Martin Hoyle, FINANCIAL TIMES, 14 March 1988

"But the play's great strength is Timothy Dalton's Cornelius, whose every speech is a collage of needs replacing each other: 'Leave me alone... I'm sorry... forgive me... now get out.' Each is felt to be the 'real' him, making for a tearing at the very core of identity."

Dominic Gray, WHAT'S ON, 16 March 1988

"Con Melody (superbly played by Timothy Dalton) lives in an alcohol-fuelled dream-world made up of two main elements. His crippling exposure [was] often farcically funny as well as painful."

Christopher Edwards, THE SPECTATOR, 19 March 1988

"Dalton's acting is massively dignified but self-conscious, almost wooden."

John Peter, SUNDAY TIMES, 20 March 1988

"Timothy Dalton proves that, although he may not be in the Olivier class as a portrayer of battered heroes, he is nevertheless among the best large-scale heroic actors we have at present, rising to the occasion in this epic role even against the competition of Vanessa Redgrave, in the self-effacing but often profoundly moving role of his downtrodden wife, treated as a bog-ignorant equal of the noisy drinkers in the adjacent bar."

Peter Hepple, THE STAGE, 24 March 1988

"One who does not have youth as his shield is Timothy Dalton, who bellows and bawls his way through *A Touch of the Poet* showing every effort of being an *Actor*. Somewhere in the long day's journey to the Comedy Theatre from the intimacy and bare stage of the Young Vic, where his performance was excellent, he appears to have been given a Beginner's Guide to Oratory – and to have read it."

Laura Cotton, ILLUSTRATED LONDON NEWS, 1 May 1988

"Thacker's production owed much of its success to Dalton's carefully-nuanced portrayal of Con, together with Vanessa Redgrave's universally admired performance as Nora. Dalton's thoughtful and sympathetic performance also illuminates the strength and subtlety of the play itself."

Christine Dymkowsy, A TOUCH OF THE POET: Introduction to the Play (Nick Hern Books), March 1992

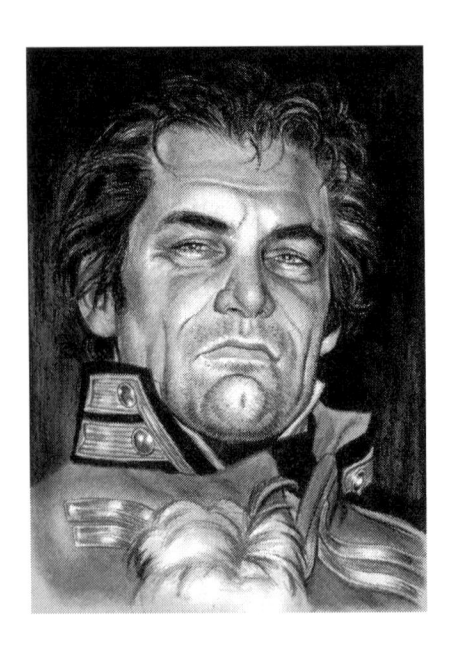

SAVE THE ROSE

June 4th & 12th, 1989

The Rose (London)

CAST

Vanessa Redgrave, Timothy Dalton (Hamlet), Leslie Grantham, Ian McKellen, Dame Peggy Ashcroft, James Fox, Anthony Quayle, Susan Tully, June Brown

CREDITS

Author: William Shakespeare

THE PLAY

A campaign to save the 16th century Rose Theatre remains that included 'Hamlet – The Paperback', a potter version of the original.

DALTON:

"This site which has attracted enormous international response would become a focus for tourism all we would have would be a monument to philistinism, an office block with huge piles going down to this precious site?

No, it's nonsense."

    TV interview (1)

"I am ashamed to say that it never occurred to me for a second that this site was precious would be threatened and when I did discover so I was shocked and that is why I am here now. I mean it is part of learning, it is part of education, it is part of our history. The English language is one of the greatest languages in the world, it is what the kids are about, it is what we are about, it is what everybody's about. Who would want an office block on that? You know it is precious."

    TV interview (2)

LOVE LETTERS

August 3rd, 1991

Canon Theatre (Beverly Hills)

CAST

Timothy Dalton (Andrew Makepeace Ladd III), Whoopi Goldberg (Melissa Gardner)

CREDITS

Director: Ted Weiant | Author: A. R. Gurney

THE PLAY

Andrew Makepeace Ladd III and Melissa Gardner, both born to wealth and position, are childhood friends whose lifelong correspondence begins with birthday party thank-you notes and summer camp postcards. Romantically attached, they continue to exchange letters through the boarding school and college years – where Andy goes on to excel at Yale and law school, while Melissa abandons a series of good schools.

DALTON:

[About the play breaking the colour barrier]

"That's rather surprising, isn't it? It doesn't seem to me to be at all odd, and I'm very happy to be working with Whoopi."

    Press Conference

"We wanted to work together. Just as simple as that. (...) We would *love* to do a film together. (...) They [producers] wanted us to do it, though they kept suggesting different partners. (...) We wanted to do it with each other. (...) It's a series of letters between a man and a woman, it starts when they both little children, 5, 6 years old, just pals, really, and it follows them through their lives, they're brought in a difficulty WASPy sort of environment and, really, their lives are destroyed, both their lives, really, by the kind of world they were brought up. So it's the love that should be... *is* really between them, it's kind of lost. It's sad sometimes, you know, it's gloomy."

    Arsenio Hall TV interview

REVIEWS

"Mr Gurney's well-known two-character play, which began its professional life at the Long Wharf in New Haven, has been crisscrossing the country for 13 years, with innumerable dream pairings (Elaine Stritch and Jason Robards) as well as seemingly unlikely ones (Whoopi Goldberg and Timothy Dalton)."

    Alvin Klein, THE NEW YORK TIMES, 9 July 2000

PETER AND THE WOLF

September 1994

Hollywood Bowl (Los Angeles)

CAST

Timothy Dalton (Narrator) & the Hallé Orchestra of Manchester

CREDITS

Director: Kent Nagano | Author: Sergei Prokofiev

THE PLAY

Peter, a young pioneer, lives at his grandfather's home in a forest clearing. One day, Peter goes out into the clearing, leaving the garden gate open, and the duck that lives in the yard takes the opportunity to go swimming in a pond nearby. The duck starts arguing with a little bird. Peter's pet cat stalks them quietly, and the bird flies into a tall tree.

DALTON:

"I did two concerts, reading *Peter and the Wolf*, at the Hollywood Bowl. About 18.000 seats. It scared the bleep out of me. The truth is, it's hard work while you do it, and you have fun after if you've done it well. You've got to ensure that the audience is having fun."

PARADE

REVIEWS

"Another British actor, Timothy Dalton, brought welcome wit, reserve and verbal point to the spoken lines accompanying Prokofiev's 'Peter and the Wolf,' but the unmotivated conducting of Nagano and the characterless playing of his Halle band fell short of true effectiveness."

Daniel Cariaga, LA TIMES, 12 September 1994

STAR CROSSED LOVERS

January 26th,1998

Symphony Center (Chicago) / PBS

CAST

Lynn Redgrave (Narrator), Timothy Dalton (Narrator), Rennée Fleming (Singer), Plácido Domingo (Singer), Daniel Barenboim (Conductor) & the Chicago Symphony Orchestra

CREDITS

Director: Daniel Barenboim | Authors: William Shakespeare, J.W. von Goethe, Leonard Bernstein, Stephen Sondheim, Charles Gounod, Duke Ellington, Irving Mills, Manny Kurtz, Carlos Gardel, Giuseppe Verdi, Pyotr Ilych Tchaikovsky, Franz Lehár

THE PLAY

A show that mixes music and poetry including musical selections (amongst them Bernstein/Sondheim's *West Side Story*, Gounod's *Faust*, Ellington/Mills/Kurtz, Gardel, Verdi's *Othello*, Tchaikovsky's *Romeo and Juliet* and Lehár's *The Land of Smiles* and *The Merry Widow*) sang by tenor Plácido Domingo and soprano Renée Fleming. The dramatic readings (from works by Shakespeare or Goethe) are done by actors Timothy Dalton and Lynn Redgrave.

HIS DARK MATERIALS

December 20th, 2003

NT: Olivier Theatre (London)

CAST

Anna Maxwell Martin (Lyra Belacqua), Samuel Barnett (Pantalaimon), John Carlisle (Lord Boreal), Dominic Cooper (Will Parry), Niamh Cusack (Serafina Pekkala), Timothy Dalton (Lord Asriel), Patrick Godfrey (Farder Coram), Stephen Grief (John Faa), Jamie Harding (Billy Costa), Patricia Hodge (Patricia Hodge), Akbar Kurtha (Dr Cade), Chris Larkin (Jopari/Iofur Raknison), Inika Leigh Wright (Tortured Witch/Harpy), Helena Lymbery (Salcilia), Tim McMullan (Fra Pavel/Lee Scoresby), Iain Mitchell (Professor Hopcraft), Helen Murton (Macaw-Lady), Emily Mytton (Stelmaria), Cecilia Noble (Ruta Skadi), Katy Odey (Mrs Lonsdale), Nick Sampson (Thorold), Danny Sapani (Iorek Byrnison), Jason Thorpe (Ben), Russell Tovey (Roger Parslow), Daniel Tuite (Perkins), Andrew Westfield (Professor of Astronomy/Dr West), Ben Whishaw (Brother Jasper), Katie Wimpenny (Angelica), Ben Wright (Golden Monkey), Richard Youman (Tony Costa)

CREDITS

Director: Nicholas Hytner | Author: Philip Pullman | Designer: Giles Cadle | Costumes: Jon Morrell | Puppets: Michael Curry | Lighting: Paule Constable | Music: Jonathan Dove | Sound: Paul Groothuis

THE PLAY

Pullman's epic trilogy of fantasy novels (*Northern Lights*, *The Subtle Knife* and *The Amber Spyglass*) tells the coming of age of two children, Lyra Belacqua and Will Parry, as they wander through a series of parallel universes fighting against epic events. During their quest, the pair encounters various fantasy creatures such as witches and armoured polar bears in a journey which they hope will take them to The Republic of Heaven.

DALTON:

"I've found myself rehearsing with, as my two co-stars, a daemon made out of pipe cleaners and curtain rods, and a wooden doll nine inches high".

    THE TELEGRAPH

"It struck me right at the beginning of rehearsals, that here you are, looking at a bit of bent wire and curtain material, and you invest it with personality, you feel for it, because it has a story."

THE ART OF DARKNESS

"I was at the Royal National Theatre of Great Britain and you've heard of Philip Pullman, the writer of 'The Golden Compass' and all those wonderful books? We turned them into a six hour stage show, split into two performances, three-hours a piece. And one of the most fundamental things in understanding the story is this concept of what the word 'dust' means — it was a magical substance — and we accomplished this by having a lecture scene. I was playing Lord Asriel, the explorer, and there was a lecture scene with all the professors and leading men of science and I was explaining this new discovery to them and explaining the importance through a slide show. And I remember asking in rehearsal, 'Can we get ahold of the slide machine? I want to thoroughly understand how it works and do everything in my own timing.' And I was told, 'No, you can't. It's all going to be done digitally (and remotely) by the stage manager. We'll have a slide machine as a prop on stage, but it won't be functional — the actual projection is going to be handled by the stage manager.' And I thought: Oh dear, oh dear — oh, never mind. And I was on stage one night and it didn't work. I pulled the lever and nothing worked. I did it again and nothing. I did it a third time and absolutely nothing. And the play couldn't really proceed without this information, it was vital. And I thought, 'What the hell am I going to do? I've got to do something here. So I took the bull by the horns, took a few steps down stage to the audience, opened my arms to encompass all the professors and scientists on stage and said, 'Obviously we're having trouble with this slide projector. So I want you all to imagine an icy arctic landscape. Glaciers!' *(Laughs)* You know, the whole thing: 'And in the distance is a man ...' and what I did was I described every single slide that I was going to show them, I think it was about seven slides. I was just improvising the whole thing. And when I came off stage I saw most of the company had gathered around. They had been listening to this and realized that something was afoot because that's *not* how the play was supposed to go! Dalton is doing something different — he's improvising! *(Laughs)* And when I came off everyone was very excited and complimentary. I talked to members of the audience after the show and I said, 'But what about when it went wrong, though? How did you react to that?' And they said, 'What do you mean? When did it go wrong?' And I said, 'You know, when the slides didn't work.' And they said, 'Oh! We thought that was just an excuse so that we as an audience could be included in that moment! It was fabulous!' That could have been a terrible moment and it wasn't terrible at all. It was an opportunity for something new and exciting. It worked. And everyone was happy."

What was going through Dalton's mind when he realized there would be no slides?

"I would think the words 'Oh f---' were very powerfully going through my brain. And then you do get a little wave of panic because you think, I am in charge of this scene. *Me*. And there are 900 people out there wondering what I'm going to do next and I don't know what I'm going to do. So let's have a think *(laughs)*. But that's what you have to do. The emotion I felt after the scene itself was a kind of exhilaration because it worked. But there was also a little bit of, 'I told you (flipping) so' — because I wanted a machine that I could control myself. But it's nobody's fault, really. And it might have gone wrong even if I was the one controlling it. It's hard to imagine a simple slide projector going wrong, but you never know."

      CHICAGO TRIBUNE

REVIEWS

"As her former lover, the ever-impelled Lord Asriel, Timothy Dalton draws as much inspiration from Sir Ranulph Fiennes as he does from his earlier incarnation as James Bond. No rock is too high, no world too distant as Mr Dalton leaps the giant stage in a leggy one-two-three."

      THE ECONOMIST, 20 December 2003

"Patricia Hodge is better at expressing that character's yen for power than her growing maternal instincts, but she gives a strong performance, and Timothy Dalton an ever stronger, more charismatic one as the soaring Asriel."

      Benedict Nightingale, THE TIMES, 5 January 2004

"Timothy Dalton is an ardent, swaggering Lord Asriel."

      Nicholas Jongh, EVENING STANDARD, 5 January 2004

"John Carlisle is splendidly dastardly as the villainous Lord Boreal and there is fine work too from Timothy Dalton as Lyra's charismatic father, Lord Asriel, Niamh Cusack as a sensual Queen of the Lapland witches, and Tim Mcmullan, Stephen Greif and Ben Whishaw as variously odious men of God."

      Charles Spencer, DAILY TELEGRAPH, 5 January 2004

"Timothy Dalton's Lord Asriel, an aristocratic Satan challenging a crumbling divine authority, mixes Miltonic pride with boyish adventurism."

 Michael Billington, THE GUARDIAN, 5 January 2004

"Timothy Dalton, however, brings a thrilling surge of noble energy to Lord Asriel's every episode; Niamh Cusack makes Serafina Pekkala inspiringly lyrical."

 Alistair Macaulay, FINANCIAL TIMES, 5 January 2004

"Patricia Hodge as Mrs Coulter and Timothy Dalton as Lord Asriel are, respectively, a conniving villain and a bombastic anti-hero."

 Mike Parker, MORNING STAR, 5 January 2004

"Patricia Hodge is terrific as Lyra's devious glamour puss of a mother. A shame, then, that Timothy Dalton plays her super-intelligent but emotionally narrow father, Lord Asriel, as the hearty games teacher from hell."

 Paul Taylor, THE INDEPENDENT, 5 January 2004

"I especially warmed to the agitated snow leopard who perseveres at the side of Timothy Dalton's dashing Lord Asriel, the tale's boldest antagonist of the church, or God, here described as the Authority."

 Matt Wolf, VARIETY, 6 January 2004

"Timothy Dalton, however, inclines to woodenness and is sometimes guilty of garbling his words as Lord Asriel, especially in Part One."

 Susan Elkin, THE STAGE, 8 January 2004

"As Lyra's sinister mother Patricia Hodge isn't very scary and Timothy Dalton, as her father, shouts a lot."

 Robert Gore-Langton, DAILY EXPRESS, 9 January 2004

"Hodge, whose role is steeped in treachery, does not project the magnetism required, but Dalton is well cast, giving us a touch of Henry V as he rallies his army of men, witches, angels and bears against the church."

 Robert Hewison, SUNDAY TIMES, 11 January 2004

"Patricia Hodge is a glamorous Mrs Coulter, a Cruella de Vil swathed in mink; best is Timothy Dalton as Lord Asriel, a seriously satanic baddie. He is of course, part James Bond, never out of his depth. But he is a much purer adventurer, covering the ground in bounding energetic strides, a fearless, rugged Ranulph Fiennes type. Until he kills, and his heartless ruthlessness is revealed."

 Georgina Brown, MAIL ON SUNDAY, 11 January 2004

"Patricia Hodge perfectly captures Mrs Coulter's malevolent love (but doesn't quite convey her hypnotic charisma), while Timothy Dalton's gruff, no-nonsense Lord Asriel is a rugged breath of fresh air as he sweeps arrogantly into the midst of the stuffy scholars. He's less convincing tackling some overblown 'Once more unto the breach'-style speeches, but the fevered urgency with which he pursues his quest to build 'the republic of heaven' is infectious."

Madeleine North, THE INDEPENDENT ON SUNDAY, 11 January 2004

"There are sturdy performances from, among other, Timothy Dalton, Niamh Cusack, and John Carlisle, while Patricia Hodge makes a suave and disturbing Mrs Coulter."

SUNDAY TELEGRAPH, 11 January 2004

"In Nicholas Hytner's epic production – on a set by Giles Cadle that is constantly evolving – there's also strong human support from former 007 actor Timothy Dalton as a swashbuckling adventurer, Patricia Hodge as a sinister mother figure and Niamh Cusack as the Queen of the Lapland Witches."

Mark Shenton, EXPRESS ON SUNDAY, 11 January 2004

"The performances, too, are uniformly good, with Timothy Dalton, Anna Maxwell Martin, Dominic Cooper, John Carlisle, Danny Sapani, Patrick Godfrey and Tim McMullan all doing outstanding work."

Toby Young, THE SPECTATOR, 17 January 2004

"The cast, by the way, includes such stalwarts of the British stage as Ms Hodge and Timothy Dalton (the former James Bond, who is here indeed rather Bond-like as a God-defying explorer)."

Ben Brantley, THE NEW YORK TIMES, 25 January 2004

"Timothy Dalton and Patricia Hodge turn in what the director calls 'high-definition' performances, which I felt made them less interesting, less mysterious."

Rowan Williams, THE GUARDIAN, 10 March 2004

THE LION IN WINTER CONCERT

May 23rd, 2004

Carnegie Hall (New York)

CAST

Timothy Dalton (Interviewer & Presenter), John Barry, Orchestra of St. Luke's, Collegiate Chorale

CREDITS

Director: Robert Bass | Author: John Barry

THE PLAY

Q & A session with John Barry and Timothy Dalton followed by a concert performance of *The Lion in Winter* score (accompanied by relevant clips from the film) in homage to composer John Barry on his 70th birthday.

REVIEWS

"Actor Timothy Dalton, who made his film debut in *The Lion in Winter*, was on hand to introduce the evening, conducted by Robert Bass."

    Michael Storck, johnbarry.org.uk, 2004

JOHN BARRY: THE MEMORIAL CONCERT

June 20th, 2011

Royal Albert Hall (London)

CAST

Shirley Bassey, David Arnold, Derek Watkins, Don Black, Nicholas Dodd, George Martin, Michael Parkinson, Timothy Dalton, Wynne Evans, Michael Caine

CREDITS

Director: Laurie Barry & David Arnold | Author: John Barry

THE PLAY

Concert homage to composer John Barry. Dalton read the passage "Blessing" by priest and poet John O'Donohue.

DALTON:

"John Barry was a kind and generous man warm and funny."

>John Barry Site

REVIEWS

"Former Bond star Dalton was on hand to speak at the event, while Beatles producer Sir George Martin also delivered a speech."

>WORLD ENTERTAINMENT NEWS NETWORK, 22 June 2011

THE STORY OF OUR YOUTH

September 18th, 2016

Shaftesbury Theatre (London)

CAST

NYT Rep Company (Michael Crean, Ellie Henderson, Will Alder, Oliver Byng, Gabrielle Leadbeater, Amy Yeates, Mo Hocken, Tom Royall, Tom Royall, Natalie-Disney Brown-Streep, Georgia Scott, Alex Bradley, Dani Wilson, Gabrielle Leadbeater, Nicola Stimpson, Alice Wooding, etc.) + Gina McKee, Timothy Dalton, Barry Rutter, Krishnan Guru-Murthy, Matt Smith, Nichola McAuliffe, Chris Bryant, Jessica Hynes, Cerrie Burnell, Daisy Lewis, Paula Wilcox, Sair Khan, Karla Crome

CREDITS

Creator & Director: Paul Roseby, Bea Holland, Tristan Parkes | Lighting: Oli Matthews | Video: Simon Eves | Sound: Owen Visser | Choreography: Alastair Postlethwaite

THE PLAY

The Diamond Anniversary Gala celebrated the 60 years of the National Youth Theatre. The Gala was structured by decades, with songs and dances from each era, bits of plays from the NYT repertory performed by the youngest generation and appearances – on stage or screen – of famous alumni. Dalton talked about the NYT; then he recited a bit of Shakespeare's

Antony and Cleopatra, and he introduced the video of Helen Mirren.

DALTON:

"I'm here to celebrate the National Youth Theatre 60th anniversary. (…) How many organisations do you know in the world take kids, teenagers, right through, young men and women in university, and offers them wonderful challenges (…)?"

> Heart Radio

"The courage of youth is a very empowering thing."

> [at the Gala]

REVIEWS

"Equally passionate was Timothy Dalton, articulately sharing his moment of youthful revelation: of course, Shakespeare's Antony would be completely beguiled by Cleopatra when the great Helen Mirren was in the role – and a majestic reprisal from Mirren, who said the NYT launched her career, proved his point."

> Marianka Swain, broadwayworld.com, 19 September 2016

"Slid between all this are appearances from ex-NYT actors such as Timothy Dalton (riveting), Barry Rutter (hilarious) and Nicola McAuliffe (gloriously outrageous)."

> Susan Elkin, sardinesmagazine.com, 19 September 2016

VOICE ACTING

BRAIN'S FAGGOTS COMMERCIAL [TV] 233
FAIRIE TALE THEATRE [TV] 233
THE SURVIVAL FACTOR [TV] 234
STORIES FROM MY CHILDHOOD [TV] 234
ESU Emergency Services Unit [TV] 236
CZARS: 400 Years of Imperial Grandeur Exhibition [audio tour] 236
DUNKIRK [TV] 237
TALES FROM EARTHSEA [cinema] 238
QUIRKE trilogy [audiobook] 239
TOY STORY 3 [cinema] 240
TOY STORY short films [cinema] 243
SECRET OF THE WINGS [cinema] 245
TOY STORY OF TERROR [TV] 247
TOY STORY THAT TIME FORGOT [TV] 249
TOY STORY 4 [cinema] 250

BRAIN'S FAGGOTS COMMERCIAL [TV]

1984

TV

Timothy Dalton (Narrator)

CREDITS

Running Time: 40 secs.

THE COMMERCIAL

Dalton narrates the story of Herbert Hill Brain, a butcher from Bristol who in 1925 created the meat of pork, liver and onions, served with the traditional West Country sauce. The add ends with the slogan: "So tasty; you'll wish you'd tried them years ago".

FAIRIE TALE THEATRE [TV]

1985

Showtime

Dick Shawn (Emperor), Art Carney (Morty), Alan Arkin (Bo), Clive Revill (Prime Minister), Barrie Ingham (Finance Minister), Georgia Brown (Maggie), Taylor Negron (Soldier), Harry Frazier, John Achorn, Lyman Ward, Patrick DeSantis (Pub Men), Ty Crowley, Lise Lang, Mimi Seaton, Tim Maier (Courtiers), Timothy Dalton (Narrator), Shelley Duvall (Host)

CREDITS

Director: Peter Medak | Producers: Shelley Duvall, Fred Fuchs, Sandra Pearson, Bridget Terry | Writer: Mark Curtiss, Rod Ash | Based on the tale *The Emperor's New Clothes* by Hans Christian Andersen | Editing: Marco Zappia | Production Design: Michael Erler | Art Direction: Richard Charles Greenbaum, Jane Osmann | Costume Design: Terrence Tam Soon | Music: Stephen Barber | *Running Time*: 49 mins.

THE EPISODE

Episode 4x07: "The Emperor's New Clothes".

Bo and Morty show up to a new kingdom just in time for the Emperor's weekly fashion show and convince him they can create the finest, most beautiful outfit in the world – which just happens to be invisible to anyone who is stupid and unfit for the position.

THE SURVIVAL FACTOR [TV]

1987

Anglia Television

CAST

Timothy Dalton (Narrator)

CREDITS

Director: John Mills | Producers: Jeremy Bradshaw, Mike Linley | Writers: Mike Linley | Cinematography: Cindy Buxton, Annie Price | Editing: Leslie Parrie | *Running Time*: 30 mins.

THE SERIES

TV miniseries documentary renamed *Wildlife Chronicles* in the US. The Episodes narrated by Dalton are: "Spadefoot", "They Walk on Water", "White Water, Blue Duck", "Water Voles, "Mr Ratty the Real Story", "Technical Animals", "Life on the Edge".

STORIES FROM MY CHILDHOOD [TV]

1998

PBS

CAST

Jessica Lange (The Swan Princess), Timothy Dalton (Prince Gvidon), Allan Rich (Czar Saltan), Donald Bishop, Graham Haley, David Huband, Caroly Larson, Kathleen Laskey, Mary Long, Debra McGrath, Colin Mochrie, Ron Rubin, John Stocker

CREDITS

Directors: Ivan Ivanov-Vano, Lev Milchin | Producers: Mikhail Baryshnikov, Joan Borsten, Ricky Magder, Larry Swerdlove, Oleg Vidov | Writers: Ivan Ivanov-Vano, Lev Milchin | Based on the poem *The Tale of Tsar Saltan, of His Son the Renowned and Mighty Bogatyr Prince Gvidon Saltanovich, and of the Beautiful Princess-Swan* by Alexander Pushkin | English adaptation: Sarah Woodside Gallagher, Judith Feldman, Stephanie Mathison | Art Direction: Ivan Ivanov-Vano, Lev Milchin | Music: Thomas Chase, Steve Rucker | *Running Time*: 41 mins.

THE FILM

Episode 12: "The Prince and the Swan.

Tsar Saltan chooses the youngest of three sisters to be his wife. When the tsar goes off to war, the tsarina gives birth to a son, Prince Gvidon. The older sisters, jealous of her, arrange to have the Tsarina and the child sealed in a barrel and thrown into the sea. Luckily, they arrive at Buyan, a remote island. The son, having grown quickly while in the barrel, goes hunting but he ends up saving an enchanted swan. The swan creates a city for Prince Gvidon to rule, but he is homesick.

REVIEWS:

"These handsome shorts and featurettes (the longest films last only 60 minutes) offer new takes on familiar fairy tales, as well as an introduction to some lesser-known Russian stories. (...) The Studio City-based company Films by Jove has spent more than $1.5 million digitally restoring the often badly damaged prints, adding new music and re-dubbing the films with major stars, including Amy Irving, Tim Curry, Sarah Jessica Parker, Kathleen Turner, Jessica Lange, Rob Lowe, Timothy Dalton and Gregory Hines. Baryshnikov served as an executive producer and helped round up the new voice talent. Although the Disney influence is often clear, these films present a very different vision of what animated fairy tales should be: The storytelling is simple and straightforward, the animation fairly limited. (...) The enchanted city in Ivan Ivanov-Vano's 'The Prince, the Swan and the Czar Saltan' is a glittering fantasy of onion domes, flamboyant murals and rich tapestries. (...) The result is an often enchanting sequence of visuals that delights the eye, even when the stories grow repetitious or the rhyming narratives begin to cloy."

Charles Solomon, LA TIMES, 5 June 1998

ESU Emergency Services Unit [TV]

1998

The Learning Channel

CAST

Timothy Dalton (Narrator)

CREDITS

Director: Producer: Image Group Entertainment | Cinematography: Scott Hillier | Assistant: Ali Grossman | *Running Time*: 60 mins.

THE SERIES

A three-episode series which offers an insider's look at an elite law-enforcement team. The ESU embraces five areas: The Tactical Team, Dive Team, Bomb Squad, K-9 Patrol and Aviation Unit.

- Nerves of Steel (1): K-9 units sniff out drugs, track fugitives; joint DEA/ESU mission.

- In Harm's Way (2): Bomb squad; dive team.

- 24/7 (3): The team hunts drug dealers who previously had a shootout with local police.

CZARS: 400 Years of Imperial Grandeur Exhibition [audio tour]

2002

Wonders: The Memphis International Cultural Series

CAST

Timothy Dalton (Narrator)

CREDITS

Curator: Carol Emert |Production: Antenna Audio Inc.

THE AUDIO

Dalton narrates the audio tour of this exhibition of over 250 objects from the Kremlin State Museum that illustrate the glory, majesty and intrigue of the Romanov dynasty.

The exhibition was shown in Memphis and – with different audio guides – in Topeka and five other US cities.

DUNKIRK [TV]

2004

BBC

CAST

Timothy Dalton (Narrator), Simon Russell Beale (Winston Churchill), Clive Brunt (Pte Alf Tombs), Phil Cornwell (Harry Noakes), Benedict Cumberbatch (Lt Jimmy Langley), Ricci Harnett (Guardsman Desmond Thorogood), Nicholas Jones (Maj Angus McCorquodale), Michael Legge (LCpl Wilf Saunders), James Loye (Sub Lt David Mellis RN), Kevin McNally (Maj Gen Harold Alexander), Roland Manookian (Frankie Osborne), Alex Noodle (Lukie Osborne), Adrian Rawlins (Capt Bill Tennant RN), Rick Warden (Maj Philip Newman RAMC), Ben Abell (Cpl Gill), Nicholas Asbury (Capt Michael Denny RN), Richard Attlee (Clement Attlee MP), Alex Avery (Capt J Hendry), Mark Bagnall (Pte Robert Garside), Nick Bagnall (Leading Seaman Harold Porter), Richard Bremmer (Vice Adm Sir Bertram Ramsay RN)

CREDITS

Director: Alex Holmes | Producers: Mike Dormer, Peter Lovering, Laura Mackie, Robert Warr | Writer: Alex Holmes, Neil McKay, Lisa Osborne | Cinematography: Graham Smith | Editing: Oliver Huddleston, Julian Rodd | Production Design: Maurice Cain | Art Direction: Michael Fleischer, Karl Probert | Set Decoration: Stefaan Lejon | Costume Design: Jo Rainforth | Music: Samuel Sim | *Running Time*: 60 mins.

THE SERIES

A dramatised documentary of three episodes about the evacuation of the British Expeditionary Force from Dunkirk in May 1940 during World War II.

REVIEWS

"The lack of visual cohesion is at least partly compensated for by the urgent narrative that keeps a strong sense of time as we zap between Whitehall, Vice Admiral Bertram Ramsey's HQ in Dover, ships in the Channel, Dunkirk itself and rural Flanders."

Paul Hoggart, THE TIMES, 19 February 2004

"Timothy Dalton's sonorous narration searched for gravitas but found, instead, the faintest echo of Tom Baker's voiceover in *Little Britain*."

LEICESTER MERCURY, 19 February 2004

"With reassuring narration by Timothy Dalton and strong performances by Simon Russell Beale as Churchill and Christopher Good as Neville Chamberlain, the reconstructions are well done."

WESTERN MORNING NEWS, 19 February 2004

TALES FROM EARTHSEA [cinema]

2006

Toho (Japan) / Walt Disney Pictures (International)

CAST

Matt Levin (Prince Arren), Timothy Dalton (Ged / Sparrowhawk), Blaire Restaneo (Therru), Mariska Hargitay (Tenar), Brian George (King of England), Susan Blakesee (Queen of England), Willem Dafoe (Cob), Cheech Marin (Hare), Kat Cressida (Vendor), Jess Harnell (dealer)

CREDITS

Director: Gorô Miyazaki | Producers: Steve Alpert, Javier Ponton, Toshio Suzuki | Writers: Gorô Miyazaki, Keiko Niwa, Hayao Miyazaki | Based on the book series *Earthsea* by Ursula K. Le Guin | Art Direction: Yôji Takeshige | Music: Tamiya Terashima | *Running Time*: 115 mins.

THE FILM

The kingdom is deteriorating, and people are beginning to act strangely. Also, the dragons start to enter the world of humans. Ged, a wandering wizard, begins to investigate these strange events. During his journey, he meets Prince Arren, a young distraught teenage boy. Arren looks shy, but he has a severe dark side, which grants him strength and anger, and has no mercy, especially when it comes to protecting his friend Teru.

REVIEWS

"He [Arren] finds an Obi-Wan Kenobi-style mentor in the powerful wizard Sparrowhawk (voiced by Timothy Dalton)."

    Allan Hunter, DAILY EXPRESS, 3 August 2007

"Former James Bond Timothy Dalton is good value as the voice of the heroic magician while Willem Dafoe and Cheech Marin ham it up and are in rampant form."

    Alan Frank, DAILY STAR, 3 August 2007

"Dominating the 'toon from start to finish, Dalton booms away as a Gandalf type in a mystical realm. (...) I did enjoy Dalton, though."

    Marshall Julius, EXPRESS ON SUNDAY, 5 August 2007

"He [Arren] flees into the countryside, where he is rescued from wolves by the movie's hero, Lord Sparrowhawk (Timothy Dalton), an enlightened sorcerer searching for a way to restore the kingdom's balance."

    Stephen Holden, THE NEW YORK TIMES, 13 August 2010

QUIRKE trilogy [audiobook]

2007–2008–2010

Audio Renaissance / Macmillan Audio

CAST

Timothy Dalton (Narrator)

CREDITS

Director: | Producers: | Writer: Benjamin Black | Music: | *Running Time*: 9 hours 30 mins. / 10 hours / 9 hours

THE AUDIOBOOKS

"Christine Falls" (2007): One night, after a few drinks at an office party, Quirke shuffles down into the morgue where he works and finds his brother-in-law, Malachy, altering a file he has no business even reading.

"The Silver Swan" (2008): When an almost forgotten acquaintance comes to Quirke about his beautiful young wife's apparent suicide, his 'old itch to cut into the quick of things, to delve into the dark of what was hidden' is roused again.

"Elegy for April" (2010): April Latimer, a junior doctor at a local hospital, is something of a scandal in the conservative and highly patriarchal society of 1950s Dublin. Now April has vanished, and her friend Phoebe, Quirke's daughter, suspects the worst.

REVIEWS

"Timothy Dalton reads this intriguing mystery about an Irish woman's apparent suicide. It [*The Silver Swan*] will keep you awake at the wheel."

    Caroline Leavitt, PEOPLE, 17 March 2008

"Their [Black and Dalton] collaboration on this mystery novel, the second in Black's Quirke series, offers an excellent opportunity for Dalton to flash his acting chops. Dalton's reading is hushed, intense and dramatic, read as if being performed onstage. This risky approach ends up melding perfectly with Black's atmospheric whodunit, with Dalton underscoring the literary quality of the prose. Dalton drops to a whisper nearly every other sentence, but it is the kind of whisper that penetrates the eardrums of even the duffers in the back row of the theater. The acted approach — Dalton playing every role, embodying every voice — is not always perfect, but the partnership between author and narrator is a definite success."

    publishersweekly.com, 28 April 2008

TOY STORY 3 [cinema]

2010

Walt Disney Studios Motion Pictures

CAST

Tom Hanks (Woody), Tim Allen (Buzz Lightyear), Joan Cusack (Jessie), Don Rickles (Mr. Potato Head), Wallace Shawn (Rex), John Ratzenberger (Hamm), Estelle Harris, (Mrs. Potato Head), Ned Beatty (Lotso), Michael Keaton (Ken), Jodi Benson (Barbie), John Morris (Andy), Emily Hahn (Bonnie), Laurie Metcalf (Andy's Mom), Blake Clark (Slinky dog), Teddy

Newton (Chatter telephone), Bud Luckey (Chuckles), Beatrice Miller (Molly), Javier Fernandez-Peña (Spanish Buzz), Timothy Dalton (Mr. Pricklepants), Lori Alan (Bonnie's Mom), Charlie Bright (Young Andy), Kristen Schaal (Trixie), Jeff Garlin (Buttercup), Bonnie Hunt (Dolly), John Cygan (Twitch), Jeff Pidgeon (Aliens), Whoopi Goldberg (Stretch), Jack Angel (Chunk), R. Lee Ermey (Sarge), Jan Rabson (Sparks), Richard Kind (Bookworm), Erik von Detten (Sid), Charlie Bright / Amber Kroner / Brianna Maiwand (Peas-in-a-Pod), Jack Willis (Frog)

CREDITS

Director: Lee Unkrich | Producers: Darla K. Anderson, John Lasseter | Writers: Michael Arndt, John Lasseter, Andrew Stanton, Lee Unkrich | Editing: Ken Schretzmann | Production Design: Bob Pauley | Art Direction: Daisuke 'Dice' Tsutsumi | Music: Randy Newman | *Running Time*: 103 mins.

THE FILM

Andy is about to leave for college, and he intends to take only Woody with him. He puts Buzz Lightyear, Jessie, Mr Potato Head and the other toys in a box to be stored in the attic but his mother mistakenly takes the box on the street for garbage pickup. The toys escape and, believing Andy intended to throw them away, decide to climb into a donation box bound for Sunnyside Daycare. Woody follows them, but he is unable to convince them of the mistake.

DALTON:

"I loved the idea of being in Toy Story. I didn't know who I was gonna play, initially. I just love the idea of being in it, you know. I remembered it's a terrific story, I liked the idea of being in a good family animated movie. And then they told I was going to play a little hedgehog who wears leather pants, leather shorts suspended in what we would say in Britain, braces. A bit weird, isn't it? (...) Kids go to see a lot of movies, but there's not a lot great kids' movies out there, and the great thing with this, it is a great kids' movie and it's also actually a movie, as you said, you were in tears at the end, so most parents, and most adults are because it's so available to us, it's so human."

  EMPIRE MAGAZINE

"He [Mr P.] is a sort of an actor-manager who takes himself too seriously. (...) The little character, the little hedgehog, probably loves Shakespeare. [*Mr P.'s favourite Shakespeare play?*] If it's still in the movie, obviously, it has to be *Romeo and Juliet*, because he belongs to Bonnie. (...) I think one of the great things is that, in regular movies, obviously, there are really talented people who really cares, deep passion, we all care but then they are limited by time and budget, all sorts of things, but this company seems to be able to create committed excellence with the ability to really ensure that people get what they want, with time and money, I suppose."

Omelette

"I know it's a terrific film that, as a film in itself has a story and the way it has been realised, I love it. I thought it was great. [*Favourite thing working on TS3*] People. Welcome, warm, freedom. Terrific quality. Just people who are talented and committed to excellence. [*Favourite childhood toy*] Is it possible to have a favourite? I suppose it is possible, but I have to say there wasn't one because when I grew up, which it is a long time before you're growing up, we didn't... get toys. You might get some toys at Christmas but maybe a little train set... or a ball... for the most part we played with our imagination, we played with each other, games with each other, we made up characters... and we played on the street or in the field. We just... played. [*Who would win in a duel between Mr Pricklepants and James Bond?*] Oh, my God, I don't know, I have to begin to think about it... let's take the other, Mr Pricklepants, 'cause he'll make James laugh".

Gamer Live

"Remember those headlines: 'Grown men weep watching Toy Story 3?' [*laughs*]. I must admit, at the time I thought, 'Oh, this is for kids,' but then I watched it and I wept with the rest of them. But this is what Disney and Pixar do so well – they take real human problems and make stories that children and adults alike can understand. Who doesn't want to feel moved?"

DAILY EXPRESS

"It's a shockingly good film. I had no idea how moving the film was really going to be, with such great characters, including some wonderful new characters. If anyone liked what I did, I truly give credit to them. I came in and spent a couple of hours with Lee [Unkrich] having a lot of fun with a microphone in between us. Then he sorts of figured out the character. I'm just thrilled to have been in it."

ENTERTAINMENT WEEKLY

"What's great about animation is that everything has such a strong emotional base, in a way that you could never have with people in a live action film."

THE SUNDAY TELEGRAPH

REVIEWS

"Humans are notably improved, especially young Bonnie (Emily Hahn), who takes Woody home at one point and introduces him to the film's most appealing new characters, including Shakespearean hedgehog Mr. Pricklepants (Timothy Dalton, whose performance amusingly suggests another level of split-personality delusion among toys) and scatterbrained triceratops Trixie (Kristen Schaal)."

    Peter Debruge, VARIETY, 8 June 2010

"But for every tear, a laugh: a new group of toys Woody meets includes a *veddy* serious hedgehog named Mr Pricklepants (Timothy Dalton), who approaches pretend tea parties with the thespian seriousness of Daniel Day-Lewis."

    Ann Hornaday, THE WASHINGTON POST, 18 June 2010

"Timothy Dalton as Mr Pricklepants, the over-the-top thespian hedgehog? Golly!"

    THE TIMES, 10 July 2010

"Ned Beatty is enlisted as the elderly and enigmatic Lotso Bear, Michael Keaton gives us a twirl as fashion-conscious Ken (of Ken and Barbie fame), and a hilarious Timothy Dalton voices thespian hedgehog Mr Pricklepants. You'll really believe a hedgehog can do Shakespeare."

    THE SUNDAY HERALD, 15 July 2010

"Best of all, it is given added freshness thanks to the introduction of the new toy characters, including Lotso, pompous hedgehog Mr Pricklepants (Timothy Dalton), the disturbing Big Baby and the hilariously camp Ken."

    David Edwards, DAILY MIRROR, 16 July 2010

"Another great addition is a lederhosen-wearing luvvie hedgehog called Mr Pricklepants (voiced by Timothy Dalton) who treats playtime like a performance at the Old Vic."

    Andy Lea, DAILY STAR ON SUNDAY, 18 July 2010

TOY STORY short films [cinema]

2011–2012

Walt Disney Studios Motion Pictures

CAST

Tom Hanks (Woody), Tim Allen (Buzz Lightyear), Joan Cusack (Jessie), Kristen Schaal (Trixie), Wallace Shawn (Rex), Axel Geddes (Rexing Ball), Jeff Garlin (Buttercup), Estelle Harris (Mrs. Potato Head), Don Rickles (Mr. Potato Head), Timothy Dalton (Mr. Pricklepants), Jeff Pidgeon (Aliens), Zoe Levin (Peas-in-a-Pod), Emily Hahn (Bonnie), Lori Alan (Bonnie's Mom / Tae-Kwon Doe), Blake Clark (Slinky Dog), John Ratzenberger (Hamm), Michael Keaton (Ken), Jodi Benson (Barbie), Bonnie Hunt (Dolly), Angus MacLane (Captain Zip), Bud Luckey (Chuckles), Javier Fernández-Peña (Spanish Buzz), Carlos Alazraqui (Koala Kopter), Bob Bergen (Condorman), Josh Cooley (Cashier / Lizard Wizard), Emily Forbes (Roxy Boxy), Jess Harnell (Fun Meal Zurg / Vlad The Engineer), Kitt Hirasaki (Nervous Sys-Tim), Jane Lynch (Queen Neptuna), Angus MacLane (T-Bone / Super Pirate / Gary Grappling Hook / Funky Monk), Teddy Newton (Mini Buzz), Bret 'Brook' Parker (DJ Blu-Jay), Peter Sohn (Recycle Ben), Jason Topolski (Ghost Burger / Pizza Bot), Jim Ward (Franklin), Corey Burton (Captain Suds), Tony Cox / Donald Fullilove (Chuck E. Duck), Mark A. Walsh (Drips), Sherry Lynn (Cuddles), Lori Richardson (Babs), Jessica Evans (Dolphina)

CREDITS

Directors: Gary Rydstrom, Angus MacLane, Mark A. Walsh | Producers: John Lasseter, Galyn Susman, Kimberly Adams | Writers: Gary Rydstrom, Jason Katz, Erik Benson, Erik Benson, Christian Roman, Angus MacLane, John Lasseter, Josh Cooley, Mark A. Walsh | Editing: Axel Geddes, Torbin Xan Bullock | Music: Mark Mothersbaugh, Henry Jackman, BT | *Running Time*: 7 mins.

THE SHORT FILMS

Hawaiian Vacation: The toys throw Ken and Barbie a Hawaiian vacation in Bonnie's room. [Shown before *Cars 2*]

Small Fry: A fast food restaurant mini version of Buzz switches places with the real Buzz, and his friends have to deal with the annoying impostor. [Shown before *The Muppets*]

Partysaurus Rex: When Rex finds himself left behind in the bathroom, he puts his limbs to use by getting a bath going for a bunch of new toy friends. [Shown before *Finding Nemo 3D*]

DALTON

"The little ones! They started in 5 minutes, 10 minutes and now half an hour, just to keep the characters alive. I've just finished a little one, yeah, but I was only a little bit in it, and they're great, they're wonderful. I love, love, love that show and see those people, those brilliantly creative people who make that *Toy Story*. They're wonderful. I love it."

Flicks And The City

REVIEWS:

"As Pixar has demonstrated through abbreviated efforts like the laugh-a-second theatrical short 'Small Fry' (featuring the debut of Internet sensation DJ Blu-Jay), good *Toy Story*s can come in small packages, too."

Erik Adams, avclub.com, 2 December 2014

SECRET OF THE WINGS [cinema]

2012

Walt Disney Studios Motion Pictures

CAST

Mae Whitman (Tinker Bell), Lucy Hale (Periwinkle), Timothy Dalton (Lord Milori), Jeff Bennett (Dewey / Clank), Lucy Liu (Silvermist), Raven-Symoné (Iridessa), Megan Hilty (Rosetta), Pamela Adlon (Vidia), Angela Bartys (Fawn), Matt Lanter (Sled), Debby Ryan (Spike), Grey Griffin (Gliss), Rob Paulsen (Bobble), Jane Horrocks (Fairy Mary), Anjelica Huston (Queen Clarion)

CREDITS

Director: Roberts Gannaway, Peggy Holmes | Producers: John Lasseter, Makul Wigert | Writers: Roberts Gannaway, Peggy Holmes, Ryan Rowe, Tom Rogers | Art Direction: Barry Atkinson | Music: Joel McNeely | *Running Time*: 75 mins.

THE FILM

Curious Tinker Bell crosses the border of the Winter Woods, and her wings start to glow. Seeing this, Tink is convinced that she is meant to explore the Woods. She crosses the border again, and she arrives at the Winter Library where she spots the Keeper, Dewey. But before she can talk to him, another winter fairy rushes into the room and proclaims that her wings sparkled the day before. Tink meets the fairy, whose name is Periwinkle.

DALTON:

"He is the ruler; he is a father figure. He probably could seem perhaps a little aloof, a little stern, but that conceals a deep love for all the fairies that are his subjects, I suppose you would call, or family, might be a better way of expressing it. And he also conceals a secret that he's carrying, or let's say a pain or something inside him. (...) It's a struggle for love and their [*the two fairies*] triumph ultimately because they overcome every obstacle with tenacity, with care, with adventure, and with love they succeed. And the fabulous thing it is because their triumph, that triumph reflects among others. My character was once in love. The Queen's character was once in love. And they rediscover their love too, because instead of quashing the surge and the journey for love, it's allowed, and everyone benefits, and everyone is happy. (...) What amazes me and excites me very much about the idea of an animation [is] you can have what you want. A director, actually, can make whatever choices, can continually change those choices, can imagine in a way and make things happen in a way they never could in a non-animated movie."

  Electronic Press Kit [DVD]

"And *Secret of the Wings*, too, is [a great movie] – you're not going to think 'I've got to run out see Tinker Bell, the story about fairies,' but when you see it, all those reservations are swept away. It's a joyous experience. It's a joyous movie. It's an adventurous film. It's a funny film. It's a very moving film about young women and families and sisters trying to come together. Essentially they're for kids, of course, but what better than introducing our children to wonderful movies and sharing that with them?"

  NBC CHICAGO

"I certainly wouldn't have been interested in *Tinker Bell* as a child. As a young boy it was all about crocodiles, Peter Pan, Captain Hook and pirates. Every Christmas I would go to those Disney events and I loved the pantomimes. It felt very innocent back then."

  DAILY EXPRESS

"The clash of two different worlds and cultures is a great theme and it is made with such purity and emotional and dramatic simplicity. (...) You go into a studio for an hour or so and you are completely on your own. You never meet the other actors but you do talk with the directors who created it and you have fun. You have more freedom than in a live action movie. You can just play around and experiment."

  EXPRESS ON SUNDAY

REVIEWS:

"Anjelica Huston's Queen Clarion and Timothy Dalton's Lord Milori add some class to this wholesome animated adventure."

Allan Hunter, DAILY EXPRESS, 14 December 2012

"Voice acting by Timothy Dalton and Anjelica Huston add a bit of gravitas."

Henry Fitzherbert, EXPRESS ON SUNDAY, 16 December 2012

"Angelica Huston, Timothy Dalton and Lucy Liu speak splendidly."

Alan Frank, DAILY STAR, 5 April 2013

TOY STORY OF TERROR [TV]

2013

Disney – ABC

CAST

Tom Hanks (Woody), Tim Allen (Buzz Lightyear), Joan Cusack (Jessie), Carl Weathers (Combat Carl / Combat Carl Jr.), Stephen Tobolowsky (Ron the Manager), Timothy Dalton (Mr. Pricklepants), Wallace Shawn (Rex), Don Rickles (Mr. Potato Head), Kristen Schaal (Trixie), Kate McKinnon (PEZ Cat), Lori Alan (Bonnie's Mom), Peter Sohn (Transitron), Emily Hahn (Bonnie), Dawnn Lewis (Delivery Lady), Jason Topolski (Vampire / Tow Truck Guy)

CREDITS

Director: Angus MacLane | Producers: John Lasseter, Andrew Stanton, Galyn Susman | Writers: Angus MacLane, Andrew Stanton, John Lasseter | Editing: Axel Geddes | Production Design: Bob Pauley | Music: Michael Giacchino | *Running Time*: 22 mins.

THE SHORT FILM

TV Special. The toys are on a road trip with Bonnie and her mother when a flat tire leads them to spend the night in a roadside motel. After Mr Potato Head goes missing, the others begin to search for him, but they find themselves caught up in a mysterious, monstrous, and terrifying sequence of events that lead them to a big conspiracy.

DALTON:

"They're wonderful, those specials, aren't they? They keep the whole series alive. You're working with really special people. I don't mean the actors. I mean the creative people who make them, people that you and I, and our audience, don't often really get to hear and know about. I can't take credit for Mr Pricklepants. It's the people who conceived him and who drew him and who gave him this storyline. You're working with people who will settle for nothing less than the best, which is all of our dreams. You just go into a room and play. You don't meet anybody else. You don't meet the cast. You just play with the director, and we have fun and try lots of different approaches and see if we can make something funny or serious or whatever. It's a lovely thing to do."

 Yahoo! TV

REVIEWS

"Yet when one of their number disappears, they're treated to a *Mwa-ha-ha* lesson in the tropes of horror movies from Mr Pricklepants (Timothy Dalton, again riotous), before they begin to realize toys are going missing for a nefarious reason."

 Brian Lowry, VARIETY, 13 October 2013

"Mr Pricklepants (Timothy Dalton), the stuffed hedgehog, takes the opportunity to show off his knowledge of horror movie tropes."

 Neil Genzlinger, THE NEW YORK TIMES, 16 October 2013

"Pricklepants gets to make an impression here since he's the one who knows how things are supposed to work. Timothy Dalton has never met a plate full of ham that he has not gleefully devoured, and I love him for it. He seems to relish the absurdity of playing a character named Pricklepants who speaks in such positively Shakespearean diction."

 Drew Mcweeny, hitfix.com, 17 October 2013

"I particularly enjoyed how 'Toy Story of Terror!' turned Timothy Dalton's theatrical Mr Pricklepants into the Abed of this fictional universe, commenting on the tropes of the special before they happened."

 Alan Sepinwall, hitfix.com, 2 December 2014

TOY STORY THAT TIME FORGOT [TV]

2014

Disney – ABC

CAST

Tom Hanks (Woody), Tim Allen (Buzz Lightyear), Kristen Schaal (Trixie), Kevin McKidd (Reptillus Maximus), Emily Hahn (Bonnie), Wallace Shawn (Rex), Steve Purcell (The Cleric), Jonathan Kydd (Ray-Gon), R.C. Cope (Mason), Don Rickles (Mr. Potato Head), Timothy Dalton (Mr. Pricklepants), Lori Alan (Bonnie's Mom), Joan Cusack (Jessie), Emma Hudak (Angel Kitty), Ron Bottitta (Mason's Dad)

CREDITS

Director: Steve Purcell | Producers: John Lasseter, Galyn Susman | Writer: Steve Purcell | Cinematography: Robert Anderson, Erik Smitt | Editing: David Suther | Production Design: Anthony Christov | Art Direction: Belinda van Valkenburg | Music: Michael Giacchino | *Running Time*: 22 mins.

THE SHORT FILM

TV Special. Bonnie brings Trixie, Woody, Buzz Lightyear, Rex and Angel Kitty to his friend Mason party. There, the toys discover that Mason has a huge toy line of dinosaur-themed action figures called The Battlesaurs, led by Reptillus Maximus and The Cleric. Rex and Trixie are armed as warriors by Reptillus, and he and Trixie grow close.

REVIEWS:

"The big names might have limited roles in this film, but you'll be happy to know that it's Tom Hanks voicing Woody and Tim Allen voicing Buzz Lightyear once again. There are also very brief returns of Don Rickles, Joan Cusack, Wallace Shawn, and even Timothy Dalton."

Gino Sassani, upcomingdiscs.com, 5 November 2015

TOY STORY 4 [cinema]

2019

Walt Disney Studios Motion Pictures

CAST

Tom Hanks (Woody), Tim Allen (Buzz Lightyear), Annie Potts (Bo Beep), Tony Hale (Forky), Keegan-Michael Key (Ducky), Madeleine McGraw (Bonnie), Christina Hendricks (Gabby Gabby), Jordan Peele (Bunny), Keanu Reeves (Duke Caboom), Ally Maki (Giggle McDimples), Jay Hernandez (Bonnie's Dad), Lori Alan (Bonnie's Mom), Joan Cusack (Jessie), Bonnie Hunt (Dolly), Kristen Schaal (Trixie), Wallace Shawn (Rex), John Ratzenberger (Hamm), Blake Clark (Slinky dog), Don Rickles (Mr. Potato Head), Estelle Harris, (Mrs. Potato Head), Jack McGraw (Young Andy), Laurie Metcalf (Andy's Mom), Mel Brooks (Melephant Books), Carol Burnett (Chairol Burnett), Betty White (Bitey White), Carl Reiner (Carl Reineroceros), Patricia Arquette (Harmony's Mom), Timothy Dalton (Mr. Pricklepants)

CREDITS

Director: Josh Cooley | Producers: Peter Docter, Mark Nielsen, Denise Ream, Jonas Rivera | Writers: John Lasseter, Andrew Stanton, Josh Cooley, Valerie LaPointe, Martin Hynes, Stephany Folsom, Rashida Jones, Will McCormack | Editing: Axel Geddes | Production Design: Bob Pauley | Art Direction: Craig Foster, John Lee, Laura Phillips | Music: Randy Newman | *Running Time*: 100 mins.

THE FILM

While Woody starts worrying he is not the favourite toy anymore, Bonnie take some toys for a family trip. She adds Forky to her toy's collection, but Forky doesn't know what is to be a toy. In the Amusement Park, Woody meets Bo Peep again and discovers her new life and friends and new foes.

DALTON:

"We're doing another Toy Story as we speak, I did expect it to come by again. But when I learned in Toy Story 3 that it took 'em six years to get that one going, I mean... I might be dead by the time 4 comes out!"

    SFX

BIBLIOGRAPHY

"The real spies are in a library somewhere, pouring over newspapers."

Timothy Dalton

The author would like to acknowledge her gratitude to the many critics whose work has been consulted and quoted in the reviews. The following is a list of all the other sources used.

AFI. Catalogue of Feature Films (2015). *Timothy Dalton.* [online] [visited in 2016]. Available at http://www.afi.com/members/catalog/SearchResult.aspx?s=&Type=CA&Tbl=PN&CatlD=&ID=147060&searchedFor=Timothy%20Dalton%20&SortType=ASC&SortCol=RELEASE_YEAR

AHDS. (2008). *Arts and Humanities Data Service.* [online] Katrin Tiedau. [visited in 2015]. Available at http://www.ahds.ac.uk/

Alcock, N. (2014). Victorian Horror Story. *Empire.* (300)

Ansorge, P. (1972). In and out of disguise. Timothy Dalton. *Plays and Players.* (19/12)

AP. (1989). The new and improved, modern 007. *Associated Press.* (14 July)

Arar, Y. (1991). A touch of evil for Timothy Dalton. *Los Angeles Daily News.* (16 July)

Araya, M. (2016). Timothy Dalton's interview at the NYT Red Carpet partially recorded. *Heart Radio.* (18 Sept.)

Armstrong, D. (1990). Unbound by Bond. *The Milwaukee Journal.* (12 Aug.)

Baxter, B. (1970). Timothy Dalton: "I couldn't waste my time". *Woman.* (7 Nov.)

BBC (2010). Lord Rassilon. *Doctor Who Figurine Collection.* (1 January)

BBC Genome (2016) *BBC Genome Project.* [online] [visited in 2016]. Available at http://genome.ch.bbc.co.uk/

Bennet, T. (2019). The former 007 talks playing Dr Niles "The Chief" Caulder in Doom Patrol. *SFX.* (27 March)

Benson, R. (1989). Poetic licence. *007.* (#21)

Bernstein, A. (2015). *Timothy Dalton on Season 2 – Exclusive Interview.* [online] Assignment X (I). [visited in 2016]. Available at http://test.assignmentx.com/2015/penny-dreadful-timothy-dalton-on-season-2-exclusive-interview/#respond

———. (2019). *Timothy Dalton chats about playing The Chief – Exclusive Interview*. [online] Assignment X (II). [visited in 2019]. Available at https://www.assignmentx.com/2019/doom-patrol-timothy-dalton-chats-about-playing-the-chief-exclusive-interview/

BFI (2016). *British Film Institute*. [online] [visited in 2016]. Available at http://www.bfi.org.uk/

Blair, I. (1987). Timothy Dalton's Top Secrets. *Playgirl*. (July)

Blanco y Negro. (1975). 'El hombre que supo amar'. *ABC*. (27 Dec.)

Blauvelt, C. (2010). Timothy Dalton talks 'Chuck', 'The Tourist' and, of course, Bond. [online] *Entertainment Weekly*. [visited in 2016]. Available at http://www.ew.com/article/2010/11/01/timothy-dalton-chuck-the-tourist-bond

Boland, R. (2015). *Blood, sweat and fears on the set of Penny Dreadful*. [online] The Irish Times [visited in 2016]. Available at http://www.irishtimes.com/life-and-style/people/blood-sweat-and-fears-on-the-set-of-penny-dreadful-1.2177093

Brady, J. (1994). In step with: Timothy Dalton. *Parade*

Brown, H. (2020). *Timothy Dalton: 'Why do we need to offer people gratuitous sex in film? There's plenty of porn online'*. [online]. The Independent [visited in 2020]. Available at https://www.independent.co.uk/arts-entertainment/tv/features/timothy-dalton-james-bond-sex-scenes-films-doom-patrol-a9659356.html

Butler, R. (2003). *The Art of Darkness*. London: The National Theatre.

Byrne, B. (2005). It took a while for Tim to bond with his 'Hercules' role. *Associated Press*. (16 May)

Byrne, C. (2019). *Hail to the Chief: Timothy Dalton Talks Doom Patrol* [online] KSiteTV [visited in 2019]. Available at http://www.ksitetv.com/doom-patrol/hail-to-the-chief-timothy-dalton-talks-doom-patrol/189168/

Celebrity Magazine. (1987). *Interview with Timothy Dalton*. (March)

NBC (2010). *Timothy Dalton Chuck 4x07 Interview*. [online] Chuck Italia. [visited in 2016]. Available at https://www.youtube.com/watch?v=6KtxeROUxtw

Cook, B. (2010). Who on Earth is... Timothy Dalton. *Doctor Who Magazine* (417)

Cooney, J. (1997). Timothy Dalton goes... from Bond to Beast. *TV Week*.

Cosford, B. (1988). On location with 007. *KNT News Service*. (2 Sep.)

Crawley, T. (1981). Royal Dalton. *Films Illustrated*. (10/115)

Critics' Choice Movies. (2010). *Interview with Timothy Dalton for The Tourist*. [online] [visited in 2016]. Available at https://www.youtube.com/watch?v=BUscZiWDCpA

Daily Mirror. (1994). Shaken but not stirred. *Daily Mirror*. (1 Dec.)

Disney. (2012). *Tinkerbell Secret of The Wings Timothy Dalton*. [online] apartededisney [visited in 2016]. Available at https://www.youtube.com/watch?v=Pa28wiJ5tks

E! Entertainment Television (1991). Love Letters snippet. *NBC Universal*.

Ebert R. (2015). *Roger Ebert Reviews*. [online] [visited in 2016]. Available at http://www.rogerebert.com/

Empire Magazine (2010). *Toy Story 3 - Timothy Dalton (Mr Pricklepants) & Joan Cusack (Jessie)* [online] [visited in 2016]. Available at https://www.youtube.com/watch?v=OG7zZQX2GcE

Evening Chronicle (1993). Wild Things. *Evening Chronicle*. (3 July)

Evening Chronicle (1994). A Damn Long Running Sage. *Evening Chronicle*. (10 Dec)

Fine, M. (1989). Licence to Act. *Lifestyles*. (11 July)

Ferguson, K. (1989). Timothy Dalton as Bond in Licence to Kill. *Film Monthly*. (June)

Fitzherbert, H. (2012). Give 007 Oscar, says Licence-To-Bleed Bond. *Express on Sunday*. (30 Dec.).

Flicks and the City. (2014). *Penny Dreadful Premiere Interview - Timothy Dalton & Toy Story Shorts*. [online] [visited in 2016]. Available at https://www.youtube.com/watch?v=6mpy3vcfW7g

Fuller, G. (1987). Introducing Timothy Dalton. *Prevue*. (2/27).

GamerLiveTV (2010). *Toy Story 3 Joan Cusack (Jessie) and Timothy Dalton (Mr Pricklepants) Interview*. [online] [visited in 2016]. Available at https://www.youtube.com/watch?v=rIvIofnuq2U

Gates, C. (2020). *Timothy Dalton opens up about Doom Patrol season two - Exclusive interview*. [online] Looper [visited in 2020]. Available at https://www.looper.com/234281/timothy-dalton-opens-up-about-doom-patrol-season-two-exclusive-interview/

Goldberg, L. (1987). Timothy Dalton. The knight of 'The Living Daylights'. *Starlog*. (123)

Goslin, S. (2015). *The Art and Making of Penny Dreadful*. London: Titan Books.

Green, J. (2000). Forces of Good and Evil do battle in *Possessed*. *TV Data Features Syndicate*. (22 Oct.)

Gross, E. (2016). *Penny Dreadful Exclusive: Timothy Dalton on season three*. [online] Empire. [visited in 2016]. Available at http://www.empireonline.com/movies/features/penny-dreadful-exclusive-timothy-dalton-season-three/

Hardy, R. (2007). Daniel Craig doesn't know what he's in for. *Daily Mail*. (24 Feb.)

Harris, W. (2014). *Timothy Dalton on Penny Dreadful, serenading Mae West, and being James Bond.* [online] A.V. Club. [visited in 2016]. Available at http://www.avclub.com/article/timothy-dalton-penny-dreadful-serenading-mae-west--204395

Havers, N. (1994). The making of Lie Down with Lions. *Lifetime Television.*

Helfenstein, C. (2012). *The Making of The Living Daylights.* USA: Spies LLC.

Hibbin, S. (1989). *The Making of Licence to Kill.* London: Hamlyn.

Hirshey, G. (1987). Meet the New Bond: In 'The Living Daylights', Timothy Dalton does it better. *Rolling Stone.* (Aug.)

Hobson, L. B. (1997). Dalton's Bond is broken. *Calgary Sun.* (Feb.)

Howland, K. (2015). *Penny Dreadful's Cast and EP Talk Season 1 and Tease Season 2.* [online] TV Goodness. [visited in 2016]. Available at http://www.tvgoodness.com/2015/01/17/hiatus-helper-penny-dreadfuls-cast-and-ep-talk-season-1-and-tease-season-2/

Hutchinson, C. (1988). Timothy Dalton. Out of Bondage. *Film Review.* (Aug.)

Huver, S. (2012). Timothy Dalton: from 007 to Tinker Bell. *NBC Chicago.* (25 Oct.)

IMDB. *Timothy Dalton.* [online] [visited in 2016]. Available at http://www.imdb.com/name/nm0001096/?ref_=rvi_nm

Inflightfight (2002). *TD in 2002 BAFTA Tribute.* [online]. [visited in 2016]. Available at https://www.youtube.com/watch?v=6C98C2y_6tA

Interviews. (2008). *Hot Fuzz.* DVD. Rogue Pictures.

Interviews. (2001). *Time Share.* DVD. Constantin Films.

Interview with Timothy Dalton. (1997). Live *with Regis and Kathie Lee.* [online] ABC. [visited in 2016]. Available at https://www.youtube.com/watch?v=62HZPNAbMvg

John Barry (2016). *John Barry. The Man With The Midas Touch.* [online] Geoff Leonard. [visited in 2016]. Available at http://www.johnbarry.org.uk/

Kirklands, B. (1997). Not slumming. *Toronto Star.* (9 Sep.)

Late Night. (1999). *Timothy Dalton interview on Conan O' Brien.* [online] OfficialMi6007. [visited in 2016]. Available at https://www.youtube.com/watch?v=BRpB-cezKrY

Logan, M. (2011). Favorite Actress, Villain & Couple Who Have. *TV Guide.* (12 April)

Lord, A. (1993). A reluctant superstar. *Plays and Players.* (Aug.)

Lynn, F. (1982). Passing through. *Cinema.* (9)

Making of 'American Outlaws', The & Creating the Old West. (2001). *American Outlaws.* DVD. Morgan Creek Productions, Inc.

Making of 'Cleopatra', The. (1999). *Cleopatra.* DVD. Hallmark Entertainment.

Malcolm McDowell Net. (2008). *Sat'day While Sunday*. [online] Alex D. Thrawn. [visited in 2016]. Available at http://www.malcolmtribute.freeiz.com/satday.html

Malins, S. (1993). Wild Time for Dalton. *Daily Mirror*. (3 July)

Masó, A. (1980). Timothy Dalton: Our fight is to keep on maintaining the protection of the theatre. *La Vanguardia*. (19th March).

Mawson, T. (2007). *Hot Fuzz*. [online] BBC. [visited in 2016]. Available at http://www.bbc.co.uk/films/2007/02/12/timothy_dalton_hot_fuzz_2007_interview.shtml

McAsh, I.F. (1970). A demon in a man's shape. *ABC Film Review*. (Oct.)

McCullen M. (2003). Leigh at the top of his art; Former Coventry school kid who began his career in rep at the Belgrade returns in worldwide comedy success. *Coventry Evening Telegraph.*

McGough, R. (2006). *Said and done*. London: Arrow.

McMurtry, A. (2020). *Former James Bond Timothy Dalton on the superhero genre and the 'imaginative absurdity' of Doom Patrol* [online] News.com.au [visited in 2020]. Available at https://www.news.com.au/entertainment/tv/streaming/former-james-bond-timothy-dalton-on-the-superhero-genre-and-the-imaginative-absurdity-of-doom-patrol/news-story/0ea33c9ac96ee120e23a78d8651acf02

Meslow, S. (2014) *Timothy Dalton opens up about Penny Dreadful, leaving James Bond, and the demon in all of us*. [online] The Week. [visited in 2016]. Available at http://theweek.com/articles/447045/timothy-dalton-opens-about-penny-dreadful-leaving-james-bond-demon-all

Metz, N. (2020). *My worst moment: Timothy Dalton and the time he had to improvise live on stage when a prop malfunctioned*. [online] Chicago Tribune. [visited in 2020]. Available at https://www.chicagotribune.com/entertainment/tv/ct-ent-my-worst-moment-timothy-dalton-0701-20200630-pu6fmwdqljhdjmd357szikx6wy-story.html

MI6 (2016). *Time Tunnel: Review Rewind* [online] MI6. The Home of James Bond 007. [visited in 2016]. Available at https://www.mi6-hq.com/sections/articles/history_press_tld_critics.php3

Moe, J. (2015). Timothy Dalton wrestles with love among monsters. *Famous Monsters*. (279)

Morley, S. (1982). Into battle at the Barbican. *The Times*. (5 June)

———. (1988). Back where he belongs. *The Times*. (10 March)

MRQE. (2010). *Movie Review Query Engine*. [online] Stewart M. Clamen [visited in 2016]. Available at http://www.mrqe.com/

Myth Comes Alive, The. (2005). *Hercules*. DVD. Hallmark Entertainment.

Nagna_Gella's Home Page (2009). *Timothy Dalton*. [online] [visited in 2014]. No longer available.

Nightingale, B. (1987). Timothy Dalton fins a Hamlet in the hero. *The New York Times*. (26 July)

No Sweat Shakespeare (2016). *Shakespeare Play Summaries*. [online] [visited in 2016]. Available at http://www.nosweatshakespeare.com/play-summary/

O'Connor, J.J. (1979). A Barbara Cartland romance. *The New York Times*. (15 Oct.)

Omeleteve. (2010). *Toy Story 3: Omelete Entrevista Timothy Dalton e Joan Cusack*. [online] Collider [visited in 2016]. Available at https://www.youtube.com/watch?v=9H6YZ_clOew

Parks, L.B. (2000). The Wild West comes back to life. *Houston Chronicle*.

Paton, M. (2006). Shaking off the bonds of 007. *The Telegraph*.

Pearce, G. (1988). Bond is back and tougher than ever. *Daily Express*. (11 Oct.)

———. (1989). Licenced never to thrill. *Today*. (27 May)

Penfold, P. (1989). It's that Bond again! *Evening Chronicle*. (4 July)

Potts, K. (2014). *'Penny Dreadful' Star Timothy Dalton Talks About His 'Weak, Foul, Lustful, and Vainglorious' Sir Malcolm*. [online] Yahoo! TV. [visited in 2016]. Available at https://www.yahoo.com/tv/penny-dreadful-star-timothy-dalton-talks-about-his-96731118690.html

Ramos, A. (1976). Timothy Dalton es San Juan de Dios. *Ideal*. (25 Jan.)

Rampton, J. (2006). Bond Star glad to be back. *Express on Sunday*. (30 April)

Raw, L. (2015). *Radio Drama Reviews Online*. [online] [visited in 2016]. Available at http://www.radiodramareviews.com/index.html

Reinhold, T. (1994). *Gone With The Wind II: Rhett*. Reuter News Service. (10 Dec.)

Richards, D. (1970). For courage see Guinness. *Daily Mirror*. (16 July)

Rose, T. (2012). Bond has more fun / Why Timothy Dalton still has a licence to thrill. *Daily Express*. Available at http://www.express.co.uk/celebrity-news/362573/Why-Timothy-Dalton-still-has-a-licence-to-thrill

Samuel French (2016). *Samuel French*. [online] [visited in 2016]. Available at http://www.samuelfrench.com/

Sanello, F. (1989). Talking with Timothy Dalton. *NEA*. (20 July)

Semlyen, N. de. (2012). "One critic complained it was no longer a film six-year-olds could go..." *Empire*. (276)

Schenkman, R. (1989). Timothy Dalton revisited. *Bondage*. (16)

SciFi Now (2015). Set visit. Penny Dreadful. *SciFi Now*. (105)

Simons, J. (1992). A supergrass puts Timothy in the frame. *Daily Express*. (21 Nov.)

Smith, D. (1982). Dalton, the man in the driving seat. *Photoplay*. (33/5)

Solochek, B. (1970). How handsome the hero - Timothy Dalton wanders the English moors swearing eternal passion in Wuthering Heights. *Seventeen*. (17 Dec.)

———. (1971). A talk with Timothy Dalton. *New York Post Saturday*. (13 Feb.)

Soraver, H. (1988). Timothy Dalton: "Why should Bond change my lifestyle? I was living as I liked before". Hello! (12)

Spark Notes (2016). *Shakespeare Study Guides*. [online] [visited in 2016]. Available at http://www.sparknotes.com/shakespeare/

Stamos, A. (2007). *New Beverly 2007: Timothy Dalton 'Flash Gordon'* [online] [visited in 2016] Available at https://www.youtube.com/watch?v=1yPbTigGJTo

Strike TV (2008). *Strike.TV behind the scenes 'Unknown Sender'*. [online] [visited in 2016] Available at https://vimeo.com/1324216

Swertlow, F. (1993). Actor Timothy Dalton Recounts His Adventure In Wolf Country. *Los Angeles Daily News*.

Teodorczuk, T. (2010). Toying with our emotions. *The Sunday Telegraph*. (27 June)

The Free Library. (2016). *The Free Library by Farlex* [online] Farlex, Inc. [visited in 2016] Available at http://www.thefreelibrary.com/

The James Bond Car Collection (2007). *Dalton's Bond*. (67)

The Lion in Winter film programme (1968). London: Avco Embassy Pictures Corp.

The Living Daylights: The Official Poster Magazine. (1987). *Timothy Dalton (James Bond / Agent 007)*. Jacobs Publications.

Timothy Dalton Chat Group. (1986) *Timothy's Celebrity Spotlight Interview*. [online] Deb Best [visited in 2016]. Available at http://www.pelicanpromotions.com.au/dalton/celebint.html

———. (2001). *Timothy's Savannah Acting Class*. [online] Deb Best [visited in 2016]. Available at http://pelicanpromotions.com.au/dalton/savactclass.html

Timothy Dalton Fishers (2014). *Arsenio Hall interview (1990) part 1*. [online]. Margarida Araya [visited in 2016]. Available at https://www.facebook.com/timdaltonator/videos/1635444523343747/

Timothy Dalton Info (2014). *Timothy Dalton Plays*. [online]. Tigerlily [visited in 2016]. Available at http://obr.lh.pl/timothydalton/plays1.html

Timothy Dalton Russian Traceries (2003). *My roles* [online]. E&T [visited in 2016]. Available at http://www.geocities.ws/tdrus2000/indexe.htm

Thomas, B. (1998). Timothy Dalton plays cop, bad cop. *Associated Press*. (14 March).

Thomas, J. (1972). The bloody battle of the Queens. *Daily Mirror*. (28 March)

Trove (2016). *National Library of Australia*. [online] [visited in 2016]. Available at http://trove.nla.gov.au/

Truit, B. (2010). Chuck. *USA Today*. (24 Nov.)

Villacastín, R. (1994). Timothy Dalton. El galán maldito. *El Semanal*. (20 Nov.)

Wigg, D. (1989). Unlicensed to thrill. *Daily Express*. (10 June)

———. (1990). Bonds have more fun. *Daily Express*. (7 June)

Wikipedia (2016). *Timothy Dalton on stage and screen*. [online] [visited in 2016]. Available at https://en.wikipedia.org/wiki/Timothy_Dalton_on_stage_and_screen

Williams, A. (2007). *60 Seconds: Timothy Dalton*. [online] Metro. [visited in 2016] Available at http://metro.co.uk/2007/02/15/60-seconds-timothy-dalton-86308/

Williams, R. (1969). When 'stardom' means a drop in pay. *Coventry Evening Telegraph*. (11 Nov.).

Woodward, C. (1994). Just Rhett for this role. *Evening Chronicle*. (29 Oct.)

———. (2014). Drama has a licence to thrill. *Express on Sunday*. (11 May)

Woodward, I. (1984). About Town. *Woman's Weekly*. (18 Aug.)

Yakir, D. (1989). Timothy Dalton. The Private Bond. *Starlog*. (145)

ABOUT THE AUTHOR

Margarida Araya (Barcelona, 1973) has a Bachelor Degree in Translation and Interpreting and a Master's in Theatrical Studies. Amongst her published works are *Sir Laurence Olivier in Spain* (in English and Spanish versions), *Laurence Olivier Stage Work* and the translation of the play *Frost/Nixon* by Peter Morgan. She is the administrator of the "Timothy Dalton Fishers" Facebook page, and Twitter and Instagram accounts.

She decided to create this guide when she realised that it didn't exist any properly published book about Timothy Dalton.

A special thanks to the Coventry History Centre for their help and to Pat Carbajal for his generosity.

Printed in Germany
by Amazon Distribution
GmbH, Leipzig